A RESTATEMENT OF RABBINIC CIVIL LAW

A RESTATEMENT OF RABBINIC CIVIL LAW

VOLUME I

LAWS OF JUDGES
LAWS OF EVIDENCE

Emanuel Quint

Jerusalem Institute of Jewish Law

Jason Aronson Inc.
Northvale, New Jersey
London

Library of Congress Cataloging-in-Publication Data

Quint, Emanuel B.
    A restatement of Rabbinic Civil Law / Emanuel Quint.
      p.   cm.
    Includes bibilographical references.
    Contents: v. 1. Laws of judges and laws of evidence
    ISBN 0-87668-765-6 (set)
    ISBN 0-87668-799-0
    1. Justice, Administration of (Jewish law) 2. Karo, Joseph ben
Ephraim, 1488–1575. Hoshen mishpat.   I. Title.
LAW <GENERAL Quit 1990>
349.5694--dc20
[345.694]   89-18546
                                                              CIP

Manufactured in the United States of America. Jason Aronson Inc. offers books and cassettes. For information and catalog write to Jason Aronson Inc., 230 Livingston Street, Northvale, New Jersey 07647.

To my wife Rena

The voice of Rena (rejoicing) and salvation
is in the tents of the righteous;
the right hand of the Lord doeth valiantly.

CONTENTS

Chapter 3

THE NUMBER OF JUDGES
REQUIRED FOR A BETH DIN
29

Chapter 4

SELF-HELP
34

Chapter 5

THE DAYS ON WHICH A TRIAL
MAY NOT BE HELD, AND THE DAYS
ON WHICH A SUMMONS MAY NOT BE SERVED
37

Chapter 6

THE MINIMUM MONETARY
JURISDICTION OF THE BETH DIN
44

Chapter 7

WHO IS ELIGIBLE TO JUDGE
AND WHO IS NOT ELIGIBLE TO JUDGE
47

Chapter 8

THE APPOINTMENT OF JUDGES
64

Chapter 9

THE PROHIBITION AGAINST TAKING BRIBES:
HOW JUDGES MAY BE COMPENSATED
70

Chapter 14

TRIAL VENUE AND MOTION PRACTICE
107

Chapter 15

BETH DIN CALENDARS
AND SUSPECTED FRAUDULENT CLAIMS
119

Chapter 16

EXTENSION OF TIME TO PLEAD
OR TO PRESENT EVIDENCE

PRIORITIZATION OF CASES

SUBPOENA FOR EVIDENCE
125

Chapter 17

EQUALITY OF TREATMENT IN THE BETH DIN AND OTHER CONDUCT OF THE BETH DIN
132

Chapter 18

DELIBERATIONS OF THE BETH DIN
138

Chapter 19

THE DECISION
142

Chapter 20

VACATING A JUDGMENT
146

Chapter 21

STIPULATIONS REGARDING THE TRIAL
150

Chapter 22

STIPULATIONS REGARDING INELIGIBLE JUDGES, INELIGIBLE WITNESSES, AND OATHS
153

Chapter 23

LOST DECISION OF THE BETH DIN
158

Chapter 24

PLAINTIFF TO OPEN THE CASE
162

Chapter 25

FINALITY OF JUDGMENTS, BETH DIN ERRORS, AND APPEALS
163

Chapter 26

THE PROHIBITION AGAINST SETTLING DISPUTES IN GENTILE COURTS
174

Chapter 27

NOT TO CURSE A JUDGE OR ANY JEW
183

PART II

LAWS OF EVIDENCE

Chapter 28

TESTIFYING IN BETH DIN
189

Chapter 29

A WITNESS MAY NOT RECANT HIS TESTIMONY
207

Chapter 30

INTERROGATION OF WITNESSES
212

Chapter 31

THE ACCEPTABILITY OF TESTIMONY OF A WITNESS WHO MAY HAVE PERJURED HIMSELF IN A PRIOR TRIAL
223

Chapter 36

IF SOME OF THE WITNESSES WERE KINSMEN OR INELIGIBLE TO TESTIFY
258

Chapter 37

WITNESSES INELIGIBLE ON ACCOUNT OF INTEREST IN THE LAWSUIT
263

Chapter 38

A FEW LAWS OF REFUTED WITNESSES
271

Appendix

THE ROLE OF WOMEN IN THE
BETH DIN SYSTEM
275

PUBLISHER'S NOTE

The series of volumes entitled *A Restatement of Rabbinic Civil Law*, by Rabbi Emanuel Quint, of which this book is the first, is a restatement of the fourth part of R. Joseph Karo's *Shulhan Aruch*. This fourth part, called *Hoshen haMishpat* ("Breastplate of Judgment"), codifies such laws as court procedure, torts, contract law, agency, inheritance, theft, destruction of property, and labor. Volume I covers Laws of Judges and Laws of Evidence and contains the first 38 chapters of *Hoshen haMishpat*. Subsequent volumes in this series go chapter by chapter through *Hoshen haMishpat*, and the series includes all 427 chapters of Part Four of R. Karo's work.

The Jewish code of civil law is at once one of the most difficult fields of study for the expert and one of the most compelling for the lay person. Based on biblical injunction, reinforced by Rabbinic enactments and by thousands of Rabbinic court rulings, Jewish civil law is a sophisticated legal system, built upon meticulous moral standards.

The Jerusalem Institute of Jewish Law, founded by Rabbis Adin Steinsaltz and Emanuel Quint, is dedicated to the study of Jewish civil law through two of Judaism's seminal legal texts, the Talmud and the *Shulhan Aruch*. While other portions of the *Shulhan Aruch* have been greatly explicated and popularized, *Hoshen haMishpat*, the section dealing with civil law, has been regarded as a closed book to all but the most scholarly. Yet, especially in today's complex commercial environment, the study of Jewish business ethics should be an urgent reminder that Jewish law governs all areas of life.

In order to clarify and simplify the law and render it more certain, the first step must be the preparation of an orderly restatement of the common law, including in that term not only the law developed solely by judicial decision but also the law that has grown from the application by the courts of generally and long adopted statutes.

The function of the courts is to decide the controversies brought before them. The function of the Jewish Institute of Law is to state, clearly and precisely in the light of the decisions, the principles and rules of the common law. The sections of the Restatement express the result of a careful analysis of the subject and a thorough examination and discussion of pertinent cases.

ACKNOWLEDGMENT

O give thanks unto the Lord, for He is good,
For His mercy endureth forever.

Psalm 136:1

It is with great pleasure that I express my thanks:

To my dear friend Marvin Klitsner for the help he has given me. His repeated and painstaking readings of my manuscript produced a considerable number of suggestions for the clarification of the text and the notes, which proved useful and profitable.

To Arthur Kurzweil, Gloria Jordan, and the staff of Jason Aronson Inc. who produced a book from a mere manuscript.

To my children and grandchildren who helped make *aliyah* so easy:
Menucha, Ezra, Odeliyah, Moriyan, Eliyana, Chamutal, and Carmi Chwat
Naomi, Ruven, Eliyana, and Shoshana Silverman
Jodi and Daniel Patt
Rachel and David Quint.

Our age has been especially faithful to the enterprise of making Jewish sources available to nonexperts. It has proven to be a boon not only for non-Jews who are curious about Judaism, but also for Jews who lack the language skills, scholarly background, and general training to study the sources of their tradition in the original Hebrew.

The latest and most welcome of these efforts is Emanuel Quint's new *A Restatement of Rabbinic Civil Law*, Vol. 1. The author, an ordained rabbi and a member of the bar who has distinguished himself both in talmudic scholarship and in the law, is eminently qualified to undertake this exposition of *Hoshen haMishpat*, the Standard Code of the Halachah's civil law.

What we have here is not a translation, but something better—in the sense of more comprehensible as well as more comprehensive—a "restatement" of the first part of *Hoshen haMishpat*, dealing with the laws relating to judges and witnesses. The language is clear and, despite the complexity of the issues involved, unencumbered by unnecessarily technical jargon. The work is at once lucid and authoritative.

The general reader will find this introduction to rabbinic law enlightening. And lawyers, especially those interested in comparative law, will find this a mine of relevant information.

Dr. Norman Lamm

The magnificent world of Torah is closed for so many people, not only due to linguistic and external difficulties, but largely because it contains means of expression and ways of thinking that are very different from those prevailing in the Western world today.

Rabbi Quint's work is paving a way; it is a means of orientation with which a contemporary person can find his way in the great sea of Jewish Law, thus training and inspiring the thought of the student and the reader.

Rabbi Adin Steinsaltz

Part I

LAWS OF JUDGES

Chapter 1

BETH DIN AND ITS SUBJECT MATTER JURISDICTION

INTRODUCTION

This opening chapter provides and describes a simple judicial system that recognizes the fact that at the present time there are no ordained judges in the Land of Israel. The title of this chapter therefore has been changed from its title in the *Shulhan Aruch* to more accurately reflect its subject matter.[1] It cannot deal with the appointment of judges to the beth din, but instead deals with the jurisdiction of the beth din. The proposed system lends some structure to a system that actually seems to exist without a formal structure.

The ordained judges had broad jurisdiction over all controversies. When ordination ceased, the subject matter jurisdiction was curtailed (see notes 2 and 3). Thus there are now certain limitations to the jurisdiction of the beth din. However, most of these limitations pertain to matters that would have little present-day practical application. Recognizing that the halachah was always able to compensate for its limitations by adopting new methods to ensure a system of justice, the

---

1. In *Shulhan Aruch*, this chapter is called "The Appointment of Judges in the Land [of Israel] and Outside the Land [of Israel]."

jurisdiction of the beth din has been extended here to almost every conceivable commercial matter that might be brought to a beth din today. Therefore, while most of the matters that have traditionally been excluded from the jurisdiction of the nonordained judges have been retained here as nonjurisdictional matters, this text moves from nonjurisdictional to jurisdictional matters concerned with assault damages that have heretofore not been enforced by nonordained judges.

The laws dealing with the subject matter jurisdiction of the beth din are based on *Sanhedrin*, Chapter 1; *Baba Kamma*, beginning Chapter 8; *Gittin* 88b; and Rambam, *Laws of Sanhedrin*, Chapter 5.

There is in the State of Israel a state-sponsored Beth Din, which was organized by Chief Rabbi Avraham Isaac Kook in 1921 in what was then the mandate Palestine. The Beth Din system was incorporated into the State of Israel court system and was granted autonomy over certain jurisdictional matters. As is clear from the following excerpts from the enabling legislation, the Beth Din has exclusive jurisdiction over marriage and divorce, the two main matters dealing with personal relationships. They also have jurisdiction over ancillary matters arising from the exclusive jurisdiction.

The Law of the Jurisdiction of the Rabbinic Beth Dins (Marriage and Divorce), passed in 1953

1. The Rabbinic beth dins shall have exclusive jurisdiction over matters of marriage and divorce regarding Jews in Israel, whether citizens of the State or residents thereof.
2. Marriage and divorce of Jews in Israel shall follow the laws of the Torah.
3. When a claim is brought to the Rabbinic beth din regarding a divorce between Jews, the Rabbinic beth din shall have exclusive jurisdiction in all ancillary matters to the divorce claim, including support for the wife and offspring of the union.
4. After the Rabbinic beth din has issued a final judgment to compel the husband to give a writ of divorce to his wife, or to compel the wife to accept a writ of divorce from her husband, the district court may, after six months from the date of the issuance of the judgment, at the request of the state attorney, compel imprisonment to enforce the decree.

TEXT

The beth din

At the present time[2] there are no ordained judges,[3] ordination having

---

2. The judicial system as set up in the Torah was three-tiered.

A. There is the Great Sanhedrin, which consists of seventy-one judges and has exclusive jurisdiction over the following:

a. Cases in which a majority of a city (*ir hanadachas*) or tribe is accused of being guilty of idolatry. (If a majority of the people are found to be guilty, then those who are guilty are put to death and the city is destroyed. [See *Sanhedrin* 110b, and Rambam, *Laws of Idolatry*, Chapter 4.] The Talmud, *Sanhedrin* 71a, has an opinion that the law of *ir hanadachas* never was and never will be applied.)

b. Cases in which a person is accused of being a false prophet. (See Rambam, *Laws of Idolatry*, Chapter 5.)

c. Cases in which the high priest is accused of a crime for which he faces the death penalty. (If it is a civil suit, or if the penalty involved is not the death penalty, the high priest is tried in the same beth din as anyone else. [See Rambam, *Laws of Sanhedrin*, Chapter 5.])

d. To declare nonobligatory wars. All wars are nonobligatory except three. 1. When the Jews entered Canaan to conquer the land (obligatory); 2. A war to eradicate Amalek (obligatory); [see Exodus 17:14]; 3. Defensive wars (obligatory). All other wars are nonobligatory. (See Rambam, *Laws of Kings and Their Wars*, Chapter 5.)

e. In conjunction with the king, the prophet, and the Urim and Tummim cases in which it is to be determined whether an area of geographic holiness is to be enlarged. (As described in a Mishnah in *Kelim*, Chapter 1, there are ten ascending degrees of geographic holiness. Jerusalem has more sanctity than other cities in the Land of Israel. And even within the city of Jerusalem, certain areas have higher degrees of sanctity, one of these areas being the Temple courtyard. [See Rambam, *Laws of the Holy Temple*, Chapter 7, para. 13. Regarding the Urim and Tummim, see Exodus 28:30 and the commentaries thereon.])

f. Setting up a Lesser Sanhedrin and appointing all of its judges. (See Rambam, *Laws of Sanhedrin*, Chapter 5, para. 1.)

g. Cases to determine whether a person is a rebellious elder. (The Torah describes a person who has become known in Rabbinic literature as a rebellious elder. "And the man that doeth presumptuously, in not hearkening unto the priest that standeth to minister there before the Lord thy God, or unto the judge, even that man shall die; and thou shalt exterminate the evil from Israel" [Deuteronomy 17:12]). An elder is not to be considered a rebellious elder unless he has ruled contrary to a decision of the Great Sanhedrin. (The entire procedure in convicting a rebellious elder is described in Rambam, *Laws of Rebels*, Chapter 3.

h. The matter of warning a woman suspected of adultery regarding the ritual of the drinking of the bitter waters. (The Torah describes a ritual that a woman suspected of adultery was compelled to undergo if she asserted her innocence. Before the suspected adultress underwent the ritual of the drinking of the bitter waters, she was brought before the Great Sanhedrin to instill fear into her heart to confess and not to undergo the ceremony. [See Numbers, chapter 5; Rambam, *Laws of the Wayward Woman*, Chapter 3.])

i. To judge a tribal president accused of a capital crime. (See *Sanhedrin* 16a and the comments of Rashi thereon.)

j. To settle boundary disputes between tribes. (See *Sanhedrin* 16a.)

k. To designate five of its members to measure the closest city to a person found slain, so that the elders of that city may perform the ritual of breaking the heifer's neck. (See Rambam, *Laws of Murder*, Chapter 9.) (The Torah describes a ritual to be followed if a murdered corpse was found in a field. Part of the ritual is to have the elders of the closest city slaughter a heifer in a rough valley.)

l. To determine the ascendancy to the throne in the event of a dispute among the dead king's heirs. This determination was made together with the prophet. (See Rambam, *Laws of Kings and Their Wars*, Chapter 1, para. 3.)

m. To appoint a high priest. (See Rambam, *Laws of Vessels of the Sanctuary*, Chapter 4, para. 15.)

n. To designate three of its members to lay their hands on a special sin offering, which was occasioned by an erroneous legal decision made by this court, where a majority of the people had sinned in reliance on this ruling. (See Rambam, *Laws of Offerings for Transgressions Committed Through Error*, Chapter 12.)

o. To supervise the burning of the red cow. (See Numbers, chapter 19; Rambam, *Laws Concerning the Red Cow*.)

p. To examine the priests and levites as to pedigree. (The priests were examined to see whether they were bona fide priests and whether they were truly qualified to perform the duties in the Holy Temple.) (See Rambam, *Laws Concerning Entrance into the Sanctuary*, Chapter 6.)

q. To correct the Torah, which the king must write for himself. (The Torah requires the king of Israel to write a Torah for himself in addition to any he might have inherited.) (Deuteronomy 17:18; see Rambam, *Laws of Kings and Their Wars*, Chapter 3.)

r. To supervise the procedure for intercalating the month or the year. (The months of the Jewish calendar are fixed according to the new moon, which may vary from month to month, although the year is solar-based. To compensate for the differences between the lunar months and the solar year, an additional month is occasionally added to the calendar. [See Rambam, *Laws of the Sanctification of the New Moon*.])

s. To count the years toward the jubilee year and to proclaim the jubilee year. (See Rambam, *Laws of Shemita and Jubilee*, Chapter 10.)

t. To be the final arbiter of the law in each generation. (See Rambam, *Laws Concerning Rebels*, Chapter 1.)

B. In addition to the Great Sanhedrin, which sat in the Chamber of Hewn Stone at the side of the Temple Court, there was also a series of courts known as the Lesser Sanhedrin, each consisting of twenty-three members. There was generally one such court for each city and also two special Lesser Sanhedrin on the Temple Mount. According to Ramban, there was also a Lesser Sanhedrin that acted as a sort of supreme court for each tribe. The jurisdiction of the Lesser Sanhedrin is listed in the Mishnayoth in the opening chapter of *Sanhedrin*. This court, because of the subject matter with which it dealt, was restricted in its scope of jurisdiction. It dealt solely with the death penalty for persons or animals. Rambam, in Chapter 15 of *Laws of Sanhedrin*, lists the following thirty-six cases in which the death penalty is inflicted on humans:

> Those condemned to death by stoning are: a male who has inter-course with (1) his mother, (2) or his father's wife, (3) or his daughter-in-law, (4) or a betrothed maiden, (5) or a male, (6) or a beast; (7) a woman who has intercourse with a beast; (8) a blasphemer; (9) an idolater; (10) he who offers of his seed to Molech; (11) a necromancer; (12) a wizard; (13) one who entices another person to idolatry; (14) one who seduces an entire city to idolatry; (15) a sorcerer; (16) one who desecrates the Sabbath; (17) one who curses his father or his mother; (18) a "stubborn and rebellious son."
>
> Those condemned to death by burning are: (19) the married daughter of a priest who commits adultery; the person who has intercourse with: (20) his daughter, (21) or his daughter's daughter, (22) or his son's daughter, (23) or his wife's daughter, (24) or his wife's daughter's daughter, (25) or his wife's son's daughter, (26) or his mother-in-law, (27) or his mother-in-law's mother, (28) or his father-in-law's mother.
>
> Those condemned to death by decapitation are: (29) a murderer; (30) an inhabitant of a city guilty of idolatry if the majority of the city is equally guilty.
>
> Those condemned to death by strangulation are: (31) one who has intercourse with a married woman; (32) one who strikes his father or mother, causing a wound; (33) one who kidnaps a Jew; (34) a rebellious elder; (35) a false prophet; (36) one who prophesied in the name of an idol.

In addition, there are cases in which an animal is sentenced to death for killing a person (for example), or an animal with which sodomy had been committed.

C. The third tier was the court with which most people had contact in their everyday lives—the court of three, or the beth din. The Talmud relates that there were 394 courts in Jerusalem alone.

The members of the Great Sanhedrin and the Lesser Sanhedrin had to be ordained. As a rule, the judges serving on the beth din also had to be ordained, although there is a difference of opinion in the Talmud on whether Torah law would allow a beth din of nonordained judges to judge commercial cases. However, in order "not to shut the door to borrowers" (which would stifle commerce) and in order to ensure that wrongdoers would not escape the law, the requirement for ordained judges on the beth din was increasingly relaxed. Consequently, the beth din consisting of nonordained judges soon acquired jurisdiction over matters formerly considered only by a beth din of ordained judges. This transfer of jurisdiction gained added significance with the lapse of the practice of ordination. The beth din of nonordained judges was called upon to fill the gap and adjudicate matters previously requiring ordained judges. The criterion used by the Rabbis to determine which areas were to be handed over to nonordained judges was that the matter had to be of frequent occurrence and involve a loss of money.

This is the basis for the opening words of R. Karo, in *Shulhan Aruch*, "At the present time [when there are no ordained judges]." The beth din of nonordained judges had jurisdiction over the following matters:

a. *Admissions.* These were cases in which the plaintiff brought to the beth din witnesses who were not actually present when the indebtedness was incurred. Rather, the defendant, in the witnesses' presence and in the presence of the plaintiff, admitted that he was indebted to the plaintiff. The admission was made in the witnesses' presence with the knowledge that they might later testify in a beth din to the defendant's admission in order to prove the plaintiff's claim. The witnesses did not allege that they were present when the indebtedness was incurred. (See Chapters 32 and 81.)

b. *Loans.* These are cases in which the plaintiff brings witnesses to the beth din who were present when the indebtedness was incurred. These might be the witnesses who had signed the document of indebtedness. (See Chapter 45.)

c. *Marriage contracts.* At the time of marriage, the husband, in a document called a *kethubah,* had to obligate himself, his real property, and his estate so that should he eventually divorce his wife, she would then receive a stipulated sum. In the event of his death while he was still married to her, she would receive such sums from his estate. Disputes arising out of this contract were adjudicated by the beth din of nonordained judges. This was instituted to prevent the wife from being at the mercy of her husband or his children. (See *Shulhan Aruch, Eben haEzer,* Chapter 66.) Similarly, the beth din of nonordained judges also had jurisdiction to compel a husband to divorce his wife in an appropriate case, since without the divorce she could never remarry. (See *Shulhan Aruch, Eben haEzer,* Chapter 154.) In the latter cases, the test of both frequency and loss of money does not exist. Nevertheless, the nonordained judges had jurisdiction in these matters, for it is only in monetary matters that the test of loss of money is also required.

d. *The following frequently occurring matters involve loss of money:*
    i. *Inheritances.* (See Chapters 276–289.)
    ii. *Gifts.* (See Chapters 241–249.)
    iii. *Partnerships.* (See Chapters 176–181.)
    iv. *Agency.* (See Chapters 182–188.)

v. *Wage claims.* (See Chapters 333–335.)

vi. *Sales and purchases.* (See Chapters 189–226.)

e. *Damage caused by fire.* Six main types of torts are enumerated in the first chapter in *Baba Kamma:* Damages caused by one's animal (1) "with its horn" (see Chapter 389), or (2) "with its foot" (see Chapter 390), or (3) "with its tooth" (see Chapter 391); damage caused by a person (4) directly (see Chapters 420–427), or (5) "with his pit" (see Chapters 410–412), or (6) "with his fire" (see Chapter 418). (There are, of course, many subcategories of these types enumerated in that chapter of the Talmud.) The reason that the nonordained judges are given jurisdiction in these matters is obvious: If there were no judges to hold the wrongdoer responsible, he could do wrong with impunity.

f. *Damage caused "by pit."* (See note e, above; see also Chapters 410–412.)

g. *Loss of earnings and medical expenses.* It is taught in the first Mishnah of the eighth chapter of *Baba Kamma* that if one wounds another person, he must pay compensation for any of the following five effects caused by the injury: (1) Any *permanent injury* caused, such as the amputation of the victim's hand or foot. (The measure of the damages is the difference between the value of the injured person as a slave about to be sold in the market place before the injury and his value after the injury. (2) Any *pain* caused. (The measure of damages depends upon the person who was wounded; for example, a delicate, pampered, rich person might not submit to pain for even a large sum of money, while a hardened, robust, poor person might voluntarily submit to great pain for even a small amount of money. In the case in which the injured person has been deprived of a limb, the measure of damages is the difference between what this particular person would pay to have the limb cut off with the benefit of an analgesic as opposed to having it cut off without benefit of an analgesic had the king ordered this limb cut off.) (3) *Loss of earnings.* (This is measured by estimating how much the victim looses by being unable to work because of the injury. If the injury is permanent, the measure of damages is the loss of his future earnings, taking into account the loss of the limb.) (4) *Medical treatment.* (This is paid at the outset as estimated for the entire treatment required.) (5) *Embarrassment.* (This is assessed by taking into account the status of the one who causes the embarrassment and the status of the one who is embarrassed. Embarrassment caused by a lesser individual is more injurious than that caused by a prominent individual.) Loss-of-earnings cases as well as medical-expense cases are adjudicated by nonordained judges, since they involve a loss of money and occur frequently. (These matters are discussed in Chapters 420 and 421.) The nonordained judges have jurisdiction over cases involving medical expenses and loss of earnings because these matters entail a loss of money, occur frequently, and do not involve appraisal of the injured person as a slave. However, there are those who hold that the nonordained judges do not have jurisdiction over cases involving medical expenses or loss of earnings.

h. *Indirectly caused damages.* One may cause damage in three ways. One may be the direct cause of the damage; that is, one, or one's instrument, commits a damaging act, such as an assault. Or, one may indirectly cause damage, as when one burns someone's promissory note. Or, one may be the remote cause of damage, such as when one hires a false witness (for it is the false witness who actually causes the damage). It is the second type of damage which is meant here. The person who is the indirect cause of the damage may be judged by nonordained judges. (The laws of indirect and remote cause are discussed in Chapter 386.)

i. *Property damage.* If a person damages another's property, he must pay full compensation. This rule holds regardless of whether the person inflicting the damage acted inadvertently or accidentally, since humans are always regarded as acting deliberately. Since property damage is not unusual and since it entails a loss of money, the nonordained judges have jurisdiction.

j. *Damages caused by an animal with its foot or with its tooth.* As was stated in note e, an animal may cause damage in one of three ways: with its horn, with its tooth, or with its foot. In Chapter 1, para. 1 R. Karo taught that when an animal causes damage with its horn, the nonordained judges do not have jurisdiction, but when an animal causes damage with its tooth or with its foot, the beth din of nonordained judges does have jurisdiction. The reason is that the animal in these two cases does not go through a transitional stage from being an innocent animal, and thereafter if it caused this type of damage a certain number of times, it would achieve the legal consequences of being a forewarned animal. It is always a forewarned animal regarding damage caused with its tooth and with its foot, since it is usual to cause damage in these two ways once the animal enters upon another's property. Since such cases are usual and entail a loss of money, they may be adjudicated by the nonordained judges.

k. *Penalties that are of Rabbinic origin.* R. Ramo, in his emandations to R. Karo, adds that the origin of the penalties is important in determining the scope of jurisdiction. Nonordained judges did not have jurisdiction over cases of Torah penalties or matters that the Sages declared to be in the nature of penalties. However, in those situations in which there was no Torah requirement for ordained judges, the nonordained judges have jurisdiction.

l. *Cases of theft or robbery.* There is a difference between theft and robbery. Robbery entails the use of force, whereas in the case of theft, the victim does not know that the theft is taking place. Thus the legal consequences of the two acts are also different. In cases of robbery, the robber must make restitution, either of the stolen article in money, depending upon the circumstances (see Chapters 345–387). In cases of theft, the thief must return the stolen article or money, but he must also pay the double penalty—that is, another 100 percent of what he stole. The thief is penalized while the robber is not because the robber, in using force against his victim, shows that he is no more fearful of his victim than he is of God, who has commanded him not to steal. The thief, on the other hand, shows that he is not fearful of violating God's commandment not to steal, but is fearful of man and thus steals surreptitiously. Since cases of theft or robbery are not unusual and since they entail a loss of money, the nonordained judges have jurisdiction over cases in which the victim sues the thief or robber to recover the article or its value.

There are situations in which the item that was stolen appreciates in value while in the hands of the thief or robber. It may appreciate through inflation or because of increment; an example of the latter is a stolen sheep which then bears wool. In those cases in which the victim is entitled under the law to obtain the increment, the nonordained judges may not adjudicate the part of the suit for the increment. (There is also an opinion that they may adjudicate that part of the suit.)

Several types of robbery fall within the jurisdiction of the nonordained judges. Such cases include those in which the robber takes something from another by threatening physical force, or in which the robber actually uses physical force and struggles with the victim. In addition to these obvious cases of robbery, there is also the case in which a bailee denies the bailment. At the moment of denial he becomes a robber, because in the presence of the owner he deprives the owner of his article.

There are many views among the codes and commentaries regarding these three types of robbery as they relate to jurisdiction of the nonordained judges. It seems to this author that the better views are those that hold that the nonordained judges may not adjudicate cases involving physical struggle. The reason is that such a type of robbery is not a usual occurrence. Cases of robbery that do not involve physical struggle may be adjudicated by the nonordained judges because such cases are not unusual. Thus both elements are present— frequency and loss of money. The nonordained judges also have jurisdiction over the type of robbery resulting from the denial of the bailment by the bailee.

m. *Informers.* In Chapter 388, R. Karo and R. Ramo discuss the laws of informers, stipulating the circumstances under which they are liable for informing about another's possessions so that the possessions are wrongfully taken from the owner by robbers or others. If the owner now wants to sue the informer, the beth din of nonordained judges may adjudicate the case. The payment obtained from the informer is indemnification and not a penalty.

n. *Refuted witnesses.* Witnesses who have testified may be contradicted in two ways. (1) A second pair of witnesses may state that they saw the occurrence differently. The question then becomes one of credibility between the two pairs of witnesses. Both pairs testify as to the occurrence. These are designated as "contradictory witnesses." (2) After the first pair of witnesses has testified, two more witnesses appear and do not actually contradict the first pair but state that the first pair of witnesses could not have possibly witnessed the event since the first pair of witnesses was with the second pair at a time and place where they could not possibly have witnessed the event. It is the credibility of the first pair of witnesses that is being impugned: they are being accused of testifying to an event that they did not see. In the first case, that of the contradicted witnesses, their integrity is not necessarily impugned, and they may testify at subsequent trials. They also do not have to make restitution to the losing party if the verdict in the case was based on their contradicted testimony. Not so in the second type of case, that of refuted witnesses. As soon as the second pair of witnesses states that the first pair could not possibly have witnessed the event, the first pair becomes known as refuted witnesses. It is a Divine command that the second pair is believed and the first pair is refuted. This designation impugns the witnesses' credibility and disqualifies them from testifying at future trials. It also makes the refuted witnesses liable to the wronged party if he lost money as a result of their testimony; that is when the person who wrongfully recovered a money judgment, based on the testimony of the refuted witnesses, does not have the money to make restitution to the wronged party, or has left the jurisdiction of the beth din. Since the refuted witnesses are the indirect cause of the fraudulent verdict, the beth din of nonordained judges has jurisdiction over the matter.

o. *Liability of admitted false witnesses.* In the second paragraph of Chapter 29, R. Karo states, "Witnesses who stated that they had testified falsely are believed insofar as it concerns themselves and must make restitution for the damage caused by their false testimony." Thus in this case, if the admitted false witnesses fail to make restitution, then the beth din of nonordained judges has jurisdiction over the matter.

p. *Compel a divorce.* See *Shulhan Aruch, Eben haEzer,* Chapter 154, which enumerates those cases in which the beth din may compel a husband to grant his wife a divorce.

q. *Converts.* See *Shulhan Aruch, Yoreh De'ah,* Chapter 268, for the procedures to be followed in accepting converts. The acceptance of converts does not pass the aforementioned test, since no money is involved. This limitation is overcome by stating that just as the jurisdiction of the nonordained judges was expanded so as "not to shut the door to borrowers," so is the jurisdiction of the nonordained judges permitted in cases of accepting converts in order "not to shut the door to converts."

r. *Damages caused by pebbles.* If an animal, while walking in the street, kicks up some pebbles, and the flying pebbles cause damage, the owner of the animal need pay only one-half of the damage caused. When a wrongdoer pays only one-half of the damage that he has caused, it is usually considered a penalty; in the case of kicking pebbles, however, it is not a penalty, but a compensation. The reason for paying only one-half of the damage is that it was so taught to Moses at Sinai.

s. *Halizah.* The ceremony of *halizah* is described in Deuteronomy 25. This ceremony allows a widow whose husband died leaving no surviving issue the freedom to marry again. This ceremony may be performed before the nonordained judges. Although the codes do not specify a reason, it seems to this author that the tests of frequency and loss of money are not relevant here. Rather, the test seems to be "not to close the door to widows who wish to remarry."

t. *Mi'un.* According to Torah law, the father of a minor daughter had the right to betroth her to her husband. The Sages added certain situations in which the

lapsed in the middle of the fourth century c. e.

As a result of various Rabbinic decrees, the nonordained judges have jurisdiction only over those matters that both occur frequently and entail a loss of money.[4] All matters over which nonordained

---

mother or brothers of a minor girl whose father had died might betroth her to her husband. In the cases enacted by the Sages, the enactment provided that the girl, upon reaching the age of majority, could nullify the marriage contracted on her behalf by her mother or brothers. This nullification of the marriage is known as *mi'un*. Mi'un does not require a beth din. In the first instance it should be performed before three persons, but it is valid even if performed before two persons or even one person. The persons before whom mi'un is performed need not be ordained.

3. *Ordained judges*. Ordination, or *semichah* (the laying on of the hands) is the title given to a person who is authorized to adjudicate cases. The Talmud, in *Sanhedrin*, p. 13b, describes the procedure of ordination and traces its origins from the ordination of Joshua by his teacher Moses. The Divine instruction found in Numbers 27:18, "Take thee Joshua the son of Nun, a man in whom is spirit, and lay thy hand upon him" was carried out, "And he laid his hands upon him, and gave him a charge" (Numbers 27:23). This was the only time that the ordination process actually involved the laying on of hands. Thereafter, the procedure was for an ordained person to designate the designee by the title of "Rabbi," and the person so designated was considered ordained.

Ordination may be conferred only in the Land of Israel, but its authorization is then universal. Many persons may be ordained at one time. Thus it is reported in the Jerusalem Talmud in the last chapter of *Sanhedrin* that King David ordained 90,000 men in one day. (It appears from Rambam that the correct reading is 30,000 in one day.) Even for the beth din, there were three standards of ordination. Some judges were given authority to adjudicate only monetary cases. Others were given authority to adjudicate only matters of ritual, while others were given authority to declare first-born animals to be blemished and thus acceptable for nonsacrificial slaughter. Some judges were authorized to act in two of these areas, and some were even given authority to act in all three areas. The entire Torah command of ordaining judges lapsed in the middle of the fourth century c.e. An unsuccessful attempt was made in the middle of the sixteenth century c.e. to reinstitute this command, based on a statement of Rambam both in his Commentary to the Mishnah and in his code. Thus, since the middle of the fourth century, there has not been any ordination. (This is not to be confused with the current practice of ordaining Rabbis, which is not the type of ordination referred to in the *halachah*.)

4. The Talmud (*Baba Kamma* 84b), in discussing the transition from a beth din system composed primarily of ordained judges, states that the nonordained judges were limited in their jurisdiction to those matters that both occurred frequently and entailed a loss of money for the injured party, who could not sue if there had been no beth din available.

judges do not exercise jurisdiction are arbitrarily designated as penalties, whether or not they are actually penalties.

For the efficient functioning of the beth din system, each city must appoint at least one beth din.[5] Large cities should appoint as many beth dins as are necessary to handle the litigation of their citizens.

Rural areas where the towns and villages cannot support a beth din or where there is not sufficient litigation to require a full-time beth din should be reorganized into districts.[6] Each district should have at least one beth din.

Each city or district that has a beth din should also have a review Beth Din to scrutinize the decisions made within that area.[7]

A chief administrative judge should be appointed for each city and for each district.[8] Chief judges should also be appointed for each review Beth Din and for the entire judicial system. One of the functions of the administrative judge will be to appoint beth din officers,[9] clerks, secretaries, and any other personnel required for the orderly operations of the judicial system. The chief judge should also oversee the orderly functioning of the judicial system. Each beth din has jurisdiction only within its own geographic area over anyone who is served with a summons.[10]

---

5. The leaders of the city determine how many beth dins are required in that city. A smaller city would of necessity have fewer beth dins than a larger city. The Talmud (*Kethuboth* 105a) relates that in Jerusalem there were 394 major law courts. It is the obligation of each city and of each district, as well as of the central government, to provide funds for the orderly administration of justice. The Torah requires that there be a judicial system to handle all controversies.

6. The dividing of the land into districts is in keeping with the Torah command that each tribe should have its own courts and that there should be an overseeing court within that tribe. (See commentary by Ramban on Deuteronomy 16:18.)

7. Each city or district that had only one beth din might be merged with other cities or districts for review Beth Din purposes. (Review procedure is discussed in Chapter 25.)

8. The idea of a chief judge is not new in halachah. The concept of chief judge, albeit of the Great Sanhedrin, always played a role in the judicial system. Without an authoritative chief judge, the beth dins would often flounder.

9. In addition to any other duties that may be assigned to the officers by the administrative judge, they also have the duty to serve summonses (see Chapter 11).

10. The summons issued by a beth din should be effective only against defendants served within its geographic jurisdiction. As will be seen in Chapter 14, the question of venue may be determined by the jurisdiction in which the summons is served. (See Chapter 11 regarding the service of the summons and Chapter 14 regarding venue of the various beth dins.)

Appointment of the judges

The seven-member council[11] in each city and in each district should appoint judges for the beth dins. Where such councils do not exist, the heads of the governmental subdivisions should name the judges. In making the appointments, the requirements set forth in Chapter 8 must be observed.

Subject matter jurisdiction of the beth din

A. The beth din has subject matter jurisdiction over every civil controversy except those herein excluded as stated in item B, which follows.[12] (It does not have jurisdiction over criminal matters.)

B. The following civil matters are excluded from the beth din's jurisdiction (except for the limited jurisdiction described in item C:[13]

    a. cases in which an animal injures or kills another animal, or injures a person[14] or causes property damage "with its horn"[15]

---

11. See R. Ramo in Chapter 2, where he states "And this is the practice in all communities that the selectmen of the city stand in the place of the Great Sanhedrin."

12. The jurisdiction of the beth din was intentionally made as broad as possible. It covers every civil matter except the few specifically excluded. To hold otherwise would be to have an impotent beth din. The beth din must adjudicate all matters that concern the citizens of the community. As has been stated several times, to deny jurisdiction to the beth din in any matter would compel a Torah-abiding person to seek relief elsewhere. Such conduct would, of course, create a desecration of the Torah and of the name of Heaven, since it would imply that the Torah could not cope with the modern-day business of man.

13. These matters have been retained here as exclusions from the jurisdiction of the beth din because they have traditionally been excluded.

14. See note 2(C) (j).

15. In Chapters 389–409, the various kinds of damages that one's property may cause are discussed. In the case of one, an animal causing damage, the damage (as was explained in note 2 [C]) may be caused in one of three ways. "With its horn" indicates an intent, as it were, to cause the damage by goring or in a related manner. This category is subdivided into two categories: an animal that does not have a history of goring, and an animal that has shown a propensity to gore. In the former case the payment is assessed at one-half of the damages caused, and the levy may be made only out of the body of the goring animal. This one-half payment is designated as a penalty to encourage people to watch their animals. According to the strict law, the owner should not have to pay for the damage caused by an animal that does not have a propensity to gore. In the case of the animal that has a history of goring, the owner

b. penalties such as[16]
    i. one-half penalty when one animal injures another animal "with its horn";[17]
    ii. the double penalty in cases of theft;[18]
    iii. the fourfold or fivefold penalties in cases of theft;[19]
    iv. penalties arising out of cases of rape or seduction;[20]
    v. penalty paid by the husband who slanders his wife;[21]

---

must make full restitution. The beth din of nonordained judges does not have jurisdiction over either of these two situations, since in the case of the innocuous animal with no history of goring, the one-half payment is a penalty. The nonordained judges were not given jurisdiction over cases involving penalties because such cases did not meet the two-fold standard of both occurring frequently and involving a loss of money. As for the case of the forewarned animal (the one with a history of goring), the Sages also treated this as a case of penalty because it did not occur frequently.

16. When a person pays more than the damage that he or his property caused, the amount exceeding the real compensation is a penalty. Similarly, if the amount of payment is less than the amount of damage caused, the payment is a penalty. The Torah also prescribes specific amounts to be paid in certain cases regardless of the amount of the actual damages. These payments are also penalties. In all such cases, the nonordained judges do not have jurisdiction.

17. See notes 2(C) (j) and 14.

18. The Torah states that one who steals an article must return the article or, in appropriate cases, pay the value of the stolen article. In addition, if the stolen article is discovered in the hands of the thief, the thief must pay a 100 percent penalty; thus the repayment is double the amount of the stolen article. The first part of the payment is compensation equal to the amount of the stolen article, and the second part, or the double penalty which is equal to the compensation, is a penalty. Nonordained judges may not adjudicate penalties.

19. According to Torah law, if a person steals a sheep or a cow and then either sells it or slaughters it, he must pay an additional 300 or 400 percent penalty, respectively. The thief ends up paying 400 percent in the case of the sheep and 500 percent in the case of the cow. Nonordained judges do not have jurisdiction over these penalties.

20. The Torah prescribes certain penalties to be paid in the case of rape or seduction. In the case of rape the Torah states: "If a man find a damsel that is a virgin, that is not betrothed, and lay hold on her, and lie with her, and they be found: then the man that lay with her shall give unto the damsel's father fifty shekels of silver" (Deuteronomy 22:28–29). Regarding seduction the Torah states: "And if a man entice a virgin who is not betrothed, and lie with her, he shall surely pay a dowery for her to be his wife" (Exodus 22:15). In the case of seduction, the fine is also fifty shekels of silver. (See Rambam, *Laws Concerning a Virgin Maiden*, Chapters 1 and 2.) Since these are specified penalties, the nonordained judges have no jurisdiction over cases in which the plaintiff seeks to recover these penalties.

21. The Torah describes a situation in which, on the morning after a marriage, the husband slanders his new wife and declares that she was not a virgin. The Torah

      vi. one-fifth penalty of the robber who swore falsely;[22]

     vii. cases that the Sages have made comparable to Torah penalties, such as the case of an individual slapping another or shouting in another's ear;[23]

  c. blemish of a virgin who has been raped or seduced;[24]

  d. ransom.[25]

C. In those matters over which the nonordained judges do not have jurisdiction to render a money judgment,[26] the beth din may

---

states: "And lay wanton charges against her, saying: 'I have not found in thy daughter the tokens of virginity.'" If the charges are false, "they shall fine him a hundred shekels of silver" (Deuteronomy 22:19). (See Rambam, *Laws Concerning a Virgin Maiden*, Chapter 3.) Since this is a penalty, the nonordained judges do not have jurisdiction over it.

22. The Torah states that if a person commits robbery and then swears falsely to a beth din that he did not commit the robbery but thereafter confesses, the robber, in addition to making restitution, must also pay an additional one-fifth as a penalty. (See Rambam, *Laws of Robbery*, Chapter 7.) Since this one-fifth payment is a penalty, the nonordained judges do not have jurisdiction to enforce its payment.

23. This law is discussed in Chapter 420, where it is shown that the payment made in these cases is a penalty. Therefore, the nonordained judges do not have jurisdiction to collect it.

24. Both a seducer and a rapist must compensate the victim for blemish. Rambam, in *Laws Concerning a Virgin Maiden*, Chapter 2, para. 6, states: "The beth din must consider her physical beauty, and consider her as if she were a slave girl being sold in the marketplace. They must assess the difference in price between that which a master would pay to purchase a virgin slave girl to give [as a consort] to his male slave, and that which he would pay for a nonvirgin slave girl to give his male slave whom he desires to please and satisfy." The nonordained judges do not have jurisdiction over these cases because they do not occur frequently. In addition, the procedure for assessment is not followed, since only ordained judges could carry out this type of assessment. The case of blemish is technically not an item of damages in an assault case, as are the other five cases enumerated in note 2. In fact, blemish is applicable in a rape or seduction case only if there is no permanent injury.

25. If an animal kills a person outside the premises of the animal's owner, the animal is put to death. If the animal had a prior history of killing and is thus a forewarned animal, the animal's owner must also pay a ransom to the heirs of the deceased in an amount that the judges consider to be the value of the deceased. The nonordained judges do not have jurisdiction over the enforcement of the ransom, since it is not a frequent occurrence. Also, the nonordained judges do not have jurisdiction to declare an animal forewarned.

26. As a result of the lapse of ordained judges, there were a great many matters that the nonordained judges could not adjudicate. Such a state of affairs would leave people without recourse in many matters and might often permit the lawbreaker to

excommunicate[27] the liable party until he appeases the injured

---

escape punishment for his illegal or antisocial deeds. In order to fill this gap, it became the practice during the Geonic period to permit the beth din to place a wrongdoer under a ban until he fulfilled his obligations to the injured party. Thus the lack of jurisdiction could not be used as a shield by the wrongdoer. Another method used to compensate the injured party was to permit him to seize and retain something from the injurer. The injured party would thus be in the same position he would have been in had there been a judicial system in place.

27. There are two types of excommunication. The less severe type, *niddui*, is in the nature of a ban, and the more severe type, *herem*, is really excommunication. A ban is generally in force for thirty days, but if the person under ban has not repented, the ban may be extended for another thirty days. Thereafter, if the banned person still had not mended his ways, he was excommunicated. A person under a ban could have social intercourse with others for purposes of study and business. The excommunicated person had to study alone and could manage only a small shop. Both had to conduct themselves as do mourners. No outsiders could visit them, eat with them, or greet them. They could not be counted as part of a *minyan*, nor as one of the three persons to say public grace. After his death a stone was placed on his coffin as a symbolic stoning. Rambam enumerates twenty-four offenses for which the ban was imposed. The ban was placed on anyone who: (1) reviles a Torah scholar, even after his death; (2) reviles a court officer; (3) calls another person a slave; (4) fails to respond to a summons to attend a beth din session; (5) makes light of an enactment instituted by the Sages, and so much more so a Torah law; (6) refuses to accept the decision of a beth din until the judgment is adhered to; (7) keeps on his premises a dangerous item, such as a vicious dog or an unsafe ladder, until the dangerous item is removed; (8) sells his real property to a heathen, until he assumes liability for all injuries that the heathen may cause to his Jewish neighbors; (9) testifies in a heathen court, with the result that a Jew would have to make some payment, and for which there would not have been payment under Jewish law; (10) is a butcher who is also a priest and who does not separate the priestly portion from the animals that he slaughters and give them to another priest, and until he does so; (11) violates the second days of the festivals celebrated outside the Land of Israel, although it is only a custom; (12) performs manual labor on the eve of Passover after midday; (13) takes God's name in vain or takes it in an oath in matters of no importance; (14) causes the public to profane God's name; (15) causes the public to eat sacrificial meat outside of the prescribed area for eating; (16) calculates the annual calendar and the months outside the Land of Israel; (17) causes the blind to stumble; (18) keeps the public from fulfilling a commandment; (19) is a slaughterer who permits forbidden meat to leave his premises; (20) is a slaughterer who did not examine his slaughtering knife in the presence of a Sage; (21) deliberately practices priapism; (22) divorces his wife and enters into a partnership with her or engages in business with her which brings them into close relations; (23) is a Sage who has a bad reputation; (24) places a person undeservedly under a ban.

R. Karo, in *Shulhan Aruch, Yoreh De'ah,* Chapter 334, adds several other matters for

party.[28] As soon as the liable party gives the injured party an amount approximating the measure of the damages,[29] the liable party is released from excommunication, whether or not the injured party is appeased.[30] [31] This remedy also applies to the situation in which the liable party embarrasses[32] the injured party but has not actually

which a person is placed under a ban: (1) breaking a vow; (2) doing work while a corpse lies unburied in the town; (3) disobeying Torah commandments on the strength of spurious analogies or arguments; (4) demanding the performance of the impossible; (5) insisting on minority views overruled by the majority; (6) usurping by a disciple of his teacher's functions; (7) applying to the king or the leader with a vew toward evading or circumventing the authority of the competent court. Placing the wrongdoer under a ban until he appeases the injured person exerts pressure on him to comply with what should have been done had the beth din of nonordained judges had jurisdiction over the matter.

28. There are differences of opinion on the cases to which the method of excommunication applies. It seems to this author that it should apply to any case for which the beth din thinks that it will be effective.

29. One of the ways to have a ban released is to make compensation to the injured party. The amount to be paid need not be the precise amount of the damages, but rather an amount that approximates the damages thought proper by the beth din. The beth din does not reveal their estimate of the amount, however. If the amount paid by the wrongdoer approximates the amount thought proper by the beth din, the judges will release him from the ban. There is a difference of opinion on whether the amount to be approximated also includes the double penalty in cases of theft. Since the intent of the payment made by the wrongdoer is that he should mend his ways and that he should not benefit from his wrongdoing, the heirs of a wrongdoer who dies do not have to make restitution in cases in which the beth din of nonordained judges do not have jurisdiction. Although this is the view of most authorities, it seems to this author that if the stolen article or money is now in the hands of the heirs, they too should not benefit from their father's wrongdoings, and should make restitution. Of course, this is not the case if the father escaped adjudication because the beth din did not have jurisdiction, such as in a case of assault. In such a case, the heirs are obviously not liable for the payment, whether or not the victim is appeased. There need be appeasement or payment, but there is no necessity for both. Otherwise, if the wronged party knew that he could continue to be unforgiving he would be unlikely to ever forgive the wrongdoer. The purpose of the procedure, it seems to this author, is to enable wrongdoers to right their wrongs.

30. The statement in note 29 that there need be either appeasement or payment, but not necessarily both, is also seen in Ramo's emandation when he adds the words "whether or not he is appeased."

31. The ban remains in effect unless the other party is either appeased or paid. It seems to this author that if the wrongdoer appeases the injured party with words or with money, or both, or with some other consideration, the ban would be lifted.

32. See note 2, which states that embarrassment is one of the five things for which

touched him. The injured party, if he is able, may seize the liable party's possessions in an amount that he estimates will compensate him for the injuries.[33] (The author believes that it is preferable for the

---

an assaulter is liable. However, this liability presupposes physical contact with the victim. A mere insult or exchange of embarrassing words does not constitute commitment of a tort (with certain exceptions, such as slandering one's bride). This is not because the judges are not ordained, for even ordained judges did not have jurisdiction over cases of embarrassment if there was no physical contact. Thus, by permitting the nonordained judges to place the slanderer under a ban until he appeased the victim with an amount of money deemed appropriate by the beth din, the law devised a method of dealing with situations over which the nonordained judges did not have jurisdiction. This shows that the judicial system was not frustrated by the lapse of ordination. If the jurisdiction of the nonordained judges could be expanded in this area, there is no reason that the jurisdiction to place a wrongdoer under a ban could not be expanded as deemed proper by the selectmen of the community. The logical aftermath is for the selectmen to grant the beth din jurisdiction over the case itself instead of forcing them to resort to merely imposing a ban.

33. In the first volume of *Jewish Jurisprudence*, Professor Neil Hecht and this author discuss various types of seizure that may affect the rights of the wronged person and the wrongdoer (pp. 104–114). In the second volume, the entire concept of self-help is discussed. In those areas in which the beth din of nonordained judges does not have jurisdiction, it was stated by R. Karo that there are two remedies nevertheless available to the wronged party: (1) excommunication, which was discussed previously, and (2) seizure or self-help. Excommunication is often illusory, since the wrongdoer may not be swayed by being excommunicated, or he may have moved to a faraway place where the excommunication will have little, if any, effect on him. In response to the need for an alternative method of protecting rights, a sort of self-help justice developed, permitting the injured party to remedy his position by seizing something belonging to the injurer. While there are many views regarding this method, the prevailing one seems to be that seizure may be accomplished at any time, and need not be limited to the item that was the basis of the dispute between the parties. There are differing views as to whether the injured party may seize only the amount to make him whole, or also additional amounts, such as the double penalty. The latter seems to be the better view.

The role of the beth din is somewhat different in this case than it is in the case of excommunication. In the latter case, the beth din does not specify the amount to be paid; rather, only after the injured party has seized property will the beth din say whether the amount was sufficient or more than sufficient. In the case of seizure, however, the wronged party may ask the beth din to assess his damages prior to making the seizure. The seizure is subject to review by the beth din to ensure that a surplus was not seized. Once the seizure has been accomplished, the burden of proof rests on the person from whom the property was seized to show a wrongful or surplus seizure. The seizure has the same result as a decision of the beth din, in that the seizing party has valid title to the seized property, and it may not be reseized by

beth din to address such a matter than to permit the injured party self-help.) Where the procedure is followed, the beth din will not provide a prior opinion of the measure of damage. Once the injured party has seized an article belonging to the liable party, however, the beth din will, upon application of the liable party, appraise[34] the amount of the damages so that if the injured party seized something of greater value, he must return it.

---

the wrongdoer. If the seizure was accomplished by a third party, the prevailing view seems to be that it is as if the injured party had himself done the seizing. Similarly, the injured party may sometimes obtain a beth din protective order to assist him in the seizing, but this may not be done through a heathen court (although there is some authority that permits even this latter form of seizure).

34. There is a prevailing view that the beth din can be asked to assess the amount of the damage prior to the seizure. R. Ramo follows the opposing view that the beth din does not specify for the injured party the amount of his damages, and it is only if the party from whom the property was seized complains that the beth din will determine whether the seizure was valid or whether a surplus was seized.

Chapter 2

EXIGENCY JURISDICTION OF THE BETH DIN

INTRODUCTION

Exigency jurisdiction of the beth din can be exercised only in extraordinary times, in a society in which the halachah is supreme.[1] It

---

1. As was noted in Chapter 1, there were many areas over which the nonordained judges did not have jurisdiction. When ordination was practiced, it was required that the procedure take place only in the Land of Israel, and thus there were many parts of the world where ordained judges were not available. Even where there were ordained judges, cases existed over which even the beth din, the Lesser Sanhedrin, or the Great Sanhedrin would not have regular jurisdiction. Thus there was always the need for exigency jurisdiction over and apart from the regular jurisdiction of the Sanhedrin and beth din.

There are instances of the exercise of exigency jurisdiction in biblical times. Judah exercised exigency jurisdiction when he meted out the death sentence to his daughter-in-law Tamar when he discovered that she was pregnant. (See Sifthai Hahamim on Rashi, Genesis 38:24.) The jurisdiction exercised by Joshua in condemning Achan at Jericho was also in the nature of exigency jurisdiction. (See Baalai haTosafoth on Genesis 38:24.) Ramban (on Genesis 19:18) indicates that the incident of the "concubine at Gibeah" was also under exigency jurisdiction. (See Judges 19.)

In Talmudic times there are recorded instances of the exercise of exigency jurisdiction. For example, Shimon b. Shetah killed eighty witches in one day under exigency jurisdiction. (See Jerusalem Talmud, *Hagigah*, Chapter 2.) Similarly, Rabbi Eliezer b. Jacob's reports that a man was stoned to death for riding a horse on the Sabbath and that another was flogged for having relations with his wife in a semipublic

22

must be exercised by persons who, because of their great stature, could do so without offending the populace.[2]

---

place are examples of exigency jurisdiction. (See *Sanhedrin* 46a. See also *Sanhedrin* 27a, 52a, 58b; *Kiddushin* 81a; *Moed Katan* 17a; *Yebamoth* 25a; *Megillah* 25b.)

All of the codes detail the laws of exigency jurisdiction. The following is an outline of the laws of exigency jurisdiction as it exists today.

2.

I. When may exigency jurisdiction be exercised?

A. There must first be a determination by the beth din that an emergency exists. Before a beth din or the selectmen of the community decide to exercise exigency jurisdiction, they must thoroughly search their souls, for an immediate reaction to an emergency situation often produces an undesirable result. The judges must not only decide that the times require it, but also that the exercise of the exigency jurisdiction will produce the necessary result. This decision must not be taken lightly.

Sometimes the exigency jurisdiction should be exercised to "build a fence around the Torah." Such might be the case if the beth din or the leaders were to enact a rule or law to prevent people from disregarding the laws of the Torah.

An essential question must be asked before exercising exigency jurisdiction: Is the exercise thereof "for the sake of heaven?" If the person or beth din can honestly say that it is being done solely to uphold the laws of the Torah and to ensure that the people uphold the laws of the Torah, then the first test of exercising this jurisdiction has been met. No other reason, no matter how lofty, is a sufficient basis for exercising exigency jurisdiction.

B. Determination by the beth din that a community is dissolute is deemed an emergency. The exigency jurisdiction may be exercised only as long as the exigency exists. Once it is over, then the right to exercise this jurisdiction ceases. There have been times in Jewish history when emergency measures were taken to preserve the religious beliefs of the nation. But the ability to enact emergency measures was all too often lacking, because the community was not influenced by the majority. In such situations a strong, courageous Rabbinic leadership might have been able to sway the people. Instead, the people saw their Rabbinic leaders squabbling among themselves over trivia. All too often the exigency even exists among those who profess to adhere to the words of the Torah. Such people may talk of ideals, but they do not live them. Witnessing this, those who are not Torah-observant become even more disillusioned and alienated. Too often there is no consensus among the leading Rabbis on what the "sake of Heaven" requires at the time. Thus the lack of respect for the Rabbis sometimes creates a lack of respect for Heaven, a result the opposite of that which should be achieved by the exercise of exigency jurisdiction.

C. An individual may be punished by the beth din under its exigency jurisdiction (1) even if the individual is dissolute in a violation other than the violation in which the community is dissolute and (2) even if the individual is not dissolute, but it is feared that his conduct will be a bad example for others.

When the community is dissolute, the beth din must attempt to resolve the violations of law thereby created. In an ideal situation, calling attention to the violation would be sufficient. Ideal situations rarely exist, however. Communities are usually dissolute in their observance of the precepts of the Torah either deliberately or out of having been brought up that way. In such situations there is little likelihood that calling the problem to the community's attention will be sufficient to resolve it. Persuasion is usually the best remedy, coupled with the provision of a clear example of how Jews who are true to the Torah conduct themselves. This is perhaps too much to expect of persons who are allegedly religious, however. The remedy of exigency jurisdiction is rarely effective in a community whose members violate the laws of the Torah. With the coming of the Messiah, there will be more likelihood of exigency jurisdiction coming into play in the event that there will be communities that will still see fit to violate the Torah precepts.

There is also the problem of enforcing Torah law when the individual is the violator. In many tightly knit religious communities, however, both economic and social pressure can be brought to bear on those who violate the community's norms. In an ideal situation the beth din would be able to enforce its edicts against a violator. But because people nowadays move about freely, a person ostracized in one community often takes up residence in another and may even achieve a prominent role in his new community. Again, the best way for a beth din to exercise its legitimate decisions would be by persuasion and education, so that the violator would come to adhere to the decisions of the beth din.

Many members of a community adhere to the confines of the law out of a true, deeply rooted feeling of respect and love for the law, especially Torah law. Sometimes, however, people see others flouting the law and "getting away with it." Otherwise law-abiding citizens become resentful. They feel foolish for observing the law while violators not only seem to profit by refusing to adhere to the law but also often achieve prominent positions in the community despite their violations. In such situations it may become urgent that the beth din exercise its exigency jurisdiction, even if the violator will disregard the attempts to punish him. The violator may become less smug and may come to realize that violations of the law will not be rewarded. Most important, however, is the fact that the beth din's action will show law-abiding citizens that their conduct is preferred and rewarded by the respect of the community. The mere fact that they are obeying the Divine law is sufficient reward to most Torah law–abiding individuals, but seeing that violators do not gain advantage by their violations gives the observant person extra comfort.

II. Over which matters may the beth din exercise exigency jurisdiction? And when it does so, what penalties may it impose?

A. The beth din may exercise exigency jurisdiction even in matters over which the nonordained judges do not ordinarily have jurisdiction. The exigency jurisdiction of the beth din extends to all areas and is not limited to the Land of Israel. This is evident from the many incidents related in the Talmud in which nonordained judges exercised exigency jurisdiction even though they lived outside the Land of Israel, both before and after ordination had lapsed.

There are many discussions of the theoretical exigency jurisdiction of the beth din, including the theoretical power of the beth din to impose the death penalty (see Quint and Hecht, Volume 1, Chapter 2). There was a period in thirteenth-century Spain when beth din exercised exigency jurisdiction, including carrying out of the death penalty. Otherwise, however, the discussions are theoretical, with much authority on both sides of the issue. It seems to this author that in a society in which the beth din has little genuine jurisdiction, it would be foolhardy to say that it may invoke the death penalty. The great codes do give the beth din such jurisdiction. With the early coming of the Messiah and the reintroduction of ordination, there will once again be Sanhedrin to mete out the death penalty, both as regular and as exigency jurisdiction. It is to be remembered that even while ordination was still practiced and the Holy Temple stood, the death penalty had been suspended except in extraordinary situations. (See *Abodah Zarah* 8b, and Tosafoth thereon, beginning words *ela shelo danoo*.)

1. The beth din may impose monetary fines and in appropriate cases direct that the fines be paid to the victim or to charity.
2. The beth din may confiscate the offender's property.
3. The beth din may banish the offender.
4. The beth din may impose corporeal punishment.

There are many recorded instances in which the beth din meted out corporeal punishment, such as flogging or chopping off limbs. This, too, does not seem to be a viable method for use in a largely secular society. The beth din may substitute a monetary fine for an offense for which the punishment is flogging. The offender is more likely to abide by the decision of the beth din if it involves a monetary payment rather than a physical punishment.

III. What is the standard of proof necessary to impose exigency jurisdiction punishments?

A. The beth din does not require the normal standard of competent proof. Witnesses in criminal trials are required to undergo cross-examination and inquiry. This requirement is waived by the beth din when exercising exigency jurisdiction.

In most criminal cases the offender must be warned about ceasing his conduct, and he must be informed about the punishment to be meted out if the conduct does not cease. This may not always be required when the beth din exercises exigency jurisdiction.

Ordinarily, circumstantial evidence is not permitted in a trial before a beth din. In exercising exigency jurisdiction, the beth din may permit circumstantial evidence to prove that the alleged offender is guilty.

The beth din requires only probable cause to impose its punishments.

Even a persistent rumor about the offender may be considered sufficient probable cause. Ordinarily, the rumor must be repeated uninterruptedly to qualify as a persistent rumor. The beth din should attempt to trace its source. If it is found to emanate from an enemy of the alleged offender, it is to be disregarded.

Even witnesses who might otherwise be ineligible to testify may here enable the beth din to render a judgment. Certain disqualifications render a witness ineligible to testify; for example, a witness may not be related to the offender, nor may witnesses be related to each other or to the judges. These disqualifications may be waived when the beth din exercises exigency jurisdiction.

Even hearsay testimony, which ordinarily is not admissible, may be used to prove the guilt or innocence of an alleged violator in situations of exigency jurisdiction. The beth din may also rely on the testimony of only one witness, something which is ordinarily not permitted.

IV. By whom may exigency jurisdiction be exercised, and what are the limitations on its exercise?

A. Exigency jurisdiction may be exercised only by the greatest Sage of the generation, who shall have been appointed by the community to judge the people.

According to Jewish law, a person qualifies as a great Sage when his vast knowledge of Torah is acknowledged to be unparalleled in his generation. It has been the history of the Jewish people that the great Torah Sages became known to the Torah community, no matter how widely they were dispersed.

The basis for permitting exigency jurisdiction to be exercised only by the greatest Sage is obvious. Only a great Sage can decide whether all the requisite conditions have been met and can determine the best method to cope with the exigency. Moreover, all the cases that are described in the Talmud deal with situations in which the greatest Sage (or certainly one of the greatest Sages) rendered the decision to punish the offender.

The requirement that the Sage be appointed for the task of exercising exigency jurisdiction is also apparent from the Talmudic cases, wherein the person exercising such jurisdiction was often appointed by the Exilarch.

B. Exigency jurisdiction may also be exercised by the community selectmen. There is a tradition that if a community appoints seven selectmen to act as its leaders, then this group is endowed with wide-ranging powers to control the lives of the community members. If there are fewer than seven men on the committee, then the scope of their jurisdiction is ordinarily less broad than that of the committee of seven. The committee's powers include the right to exercise exigency jurisdiction in appropriate cases or else to appoint judges who can exercise exigency jurisdiction.

Exigency jurisdiction may not be exercised, if while benefiting some persons it is detrimental to other individuals or detrimental to the group. In addition, the seven selectmen may not change the customs of the community if certain groups would benefit at the expense of other groups or individuals. Thus the rules of venue of a trial may not be changed if the parties were operating under the established rules. For example, a limited partner may not be made liable for the debts of the partnership if this was not the law when he joined the partnership.

Abodah Zarah[3] states that forty years prior to the destruction of the Holy Temple (may it be rebuilt speedily in our days), capital cases were no longer being judged in Israel. When the Great Sanhedrin realized that murders were so numerous that they could not be dealt with properly, they discontinued hearing capital cases rather than risk pronouncing persons guilty without adequate hearings. There are probably many situations that are in desperate need of exigency jurisdiction. However, this jurisdiction should not be assumed by those who are not adequately qualified.

Because of the foregoing, nothing will be gained by elaborating on such jurisdiction here. Therefore, the discussion of this topic has intentionally been limited. For those who wish to study the subject further, a review of *Jewish Jurisprudence*, Volume 1, Chapter 2, as well as the notes to this chapter, will provide additional material.

TEXT

Exigency jurisdiction

The *Shulhan Aruch*, as well as all the codes dealing with the jurisdiction of the beth din, provides for exigency jurisdiction of the

---

C. Exigency jurisdiction may not be exercised if it will be in conflict with Torah law.

D. Exigency jurisdiction exercised by the community selectmen is subject to veto by the outstanding Sage of the community; it is also subject to veto by a judge appointed by the community to deal with such exigencies.

V. The beth din may use outside help in exercising exigency jurisdiction.

A. The outside help may consist of non-Jews.

In stating that the beth din may rely on non-Jews to help it enforce its decrees in exigency jurisdiction cases, it is assumed that the non-Jews represent a greater physical threat to the offender than that which can be mustered by the Jews of the community.

B. The outside help may consist of invoking the jurisdiction of the secular courts.

As will be noted in Chapter 26, the Jewish litigant may ordinarily not avail himself of the secular courts in enforcing his rights. In the case of the beth din exercising its exigency jurisdiction, however, it may avail itself of the secular courts, including the civil courts of the Gentiles, to enforce its decrees.

3. See *Abodah Zarah* 8b.

beth din. This subject has intentionally been omitted here because no beth din is currently qualified to exercise such jurisdiction. If the administrative judges and the heads of all the beth dins and review Beth Dins, together with the political leadership of the nation, believe that an emergency situation has arisen that calls for the exercise of exigency jurisdiction, then the rules of the *Shulhan Aruch* should certainly be followed.

Chapter 3

THE NUMBER OF JUDGES REQUIRED FOR A BETH DIN

INTRODUCTION

This chapter deals with the number of judges required to sit on the beth din. It is assumed that a beth din system as described in Chapter 1 has been implemented. However, not every community desires, or is able to establish that type, or any type, of beth din system. Therefore, the chapter provides for alternative methods of determining the number of judges to sit in the beth din in each case.

TEXT

Agreement on the number of judges

The parties may agree between themselves on the number of judges on the beth din that will judge their dispute. This agreement is binding and may not be altered by any community rules.[1]

---

1. There is a principle in halachah that in monetary matters the parties may come to an agreement upon procedures and even substantive matters and such agreements will be enforced. Of course, this is true only so long as it does not contravene a Torah or Rabbinic law that prohibits such conduct. Thus, for example, the parties may not

The community may establish any beth din system it wishes. The established system is binding on all members of the community, except as stated in the preceding paragraph. The author believes that the beth din system described in Chapter 1 is a viable one for Jewish communities throughout the world, including the Land of Israel. If such a system, or any other type of unified beth din system, is not established, then the following alternatives are suggested.

Traditionally, communities have established beth dins of three members. Many smaller communities have established beth dins consisting of one person, usually the rabbi of the community.

When the parties cannot agree
on the number of judges

If the parties cannot agree on the beth din to judge them and the community has not established a beth din system, then the plaintiff may institute the procedures described in Chapter 13, whereby each of the two litigants selects one judge, and the two judges so selected select the third judge.

If the parties cannot agree between themselves on the composition of the beth din, and the community has not established a beth din system, and the defendant does not respond to a summons to avail himself of the procedure described in Chapter 13, then the plaintiff may invoke a beth din to try his complaint against the defendant. The following rules apply in such a case:

1. The beth din may not consist of fewer than three judges.[2] The

---

decide to charge interest on a loan, since this is prohibited by Torah law. Similarly, the custom of a particular community or trade will be enforced by the beth din so long as it does not contravene a Torah or Rabbinic law. The beth din may not compel the defendant to submit to its jurisdiction if the matter in controversy involves a transaction in a trade in which all controversies are traditionally resolved according to customary procedures within the trade, and the parties have availed themselves of such procedures.

2. There is a difference of opinion in the Talmud as to whether three judges are required by Torah law or whether one judge is sufficient to judge commercial actions. There is also a difference of opinion among the commentators on the Talmud as to whether the three judges or the one judge had to be ordained. As was explained in Chapter 1, there eventually evolved a Rabbinic requirement that every beth din

beth din of three judges will be valid only if at least one of the three judges is knowledgeable in the law.[3] If none of the three is knowledgeable in the law, their judgment is void.[4]

2. A valid beth din may compel the defendant to appear before it to be judged.[5] At this point the defendant may still avail himself of the procedures described in Chapter 13; or he may state that he wants to

---

consist of three nonordained judges. This requirement was enacted so as not to close the door to commerce. The creditor would be reluctant to extend credit, for example, if he knew that he could not enforce his rights in a beth din unless its judges were ordained, because it might be difficult to find such a beth din. The rule permitting nonordained judges was also enacted to prevent wrongdoers from avoiding liability by insisting on being tried by a beth din of ordained judges, which was not always available. Certainly by the time the practice of ordination lapsed in the middle of the fourth century c.e., the requirement that a beth din consist of three nonordained judges was firmly established. What is discussed in this chapter regarding the composition of the beth din applies to all those cases over which the beth din has jurisdiction as stated in Chapter 1. Both R. Karo, in *Shulhan Aruch*, and R. Ramo follow the authorities who hold that absent an agreement of the parties to the contrary, a minimum of three judges is required for a beth din to assume jurisdiction and to compel the defendant to appear before it.

3. All the judges on the panel may be laymen in the law. The only requirement (unless waived by the parties) is that at least one of the members of the panel have some knowledge of the law, which he may have acquired by having read law or by having heard the law from proper sources. He is then deemed knowledgeable. A knowledgeable man is not the same as an expert, who has both a great knowledge of the law and the ability to apply the legal principles to the case before the beth din.

4. If none of the judges is knowledgeable, then there is no one on the beth din who can attempt to teach the others how to decide the case or try to persuade the other members how best to decide the case. The converse is also true. Neither of the litigants may insist that all three judges be knowledgeable. Just as many of the other qualifications required of the judges may be waived (such as permitting relatives of one or of both of the litigants to judge the case), similarly the litigants may agree that all three judges be unlearned. The latter waiver should be explicit rather than inferred from the fact that the litigants appeared before such a beth din. In Chapter 22, R. Ramo states that if the community has appointed a beth din of unlearned judges, the litigants cannot object to such a beth din judging their case.

5. The essence of the judicial system is to provide a forum for the person who feels aggrieved to have his complaints heard. If the defendant can refuse to come before an impartial panel to have the dispute adjudicated, then the complainant will be without recourse, and then all his substantive rights are to no avail. Therefore, it is imperative that there be some way for the complainant to compel the defendant to come to a beth din to adjudicate their differences.

be judged by another beth din in the same community.[6] The
defendant may not avail himself of this procedure if the beth din to
which he has been summoned is the community-appointed beth din.

3. The fact that a beth din consisting of fewer than three judges
rendered an accurate decision does not validate their decision.[7]

4. All proceedings held before a beth din of fewer than three
judges is a nullity.[8] Any pleas, admissions, and testimony taken before
such a beth din are of no legal significance and may be recanted and
changed at a subsequent valid judicial proceeding. Any perjured
testimony given at the invalid proceeding does not affect the credibility in subsequent proceedings of the person who so testified.

---

6. A beth din that is not the regular appointed beth din for the city may not judge
a defendant without his consent, if he agrees to be judged by another beth din in the
same city. If he refuses to appear before another beth din in the same city, then the
first beth din may judge him without his consent. The option of going before another
beth din in the same city is not available to the defendant if he is summoned to appear
before a beth din appointed for the city.

7. If scholars reviewing the decision proved that it was accurate, then it would be
binding; but if the decision was determined to be inaccurate, then it would not be
binding and another trial would be required. This kind of uncertainty would make a
mockery of the entire judicial process. A defendant would not know whether to
answer a summons instituted by this panel, and the process would be void of
certainty and stability.

Shulhan Aruch, after stating that a beth din may not consist of fewer than three
judges, sets forth two exceptions. These two exceptions allay the uncertainty that
may arise from not answering a summons. The first exception is the case in which the
litigants have accepted the panel to adjudicate their dispute. The defendant, by
appearing before this panel and stating that he accepts them to adjudicate the dispute,
removes any concern on the part of the plaintiff that the defendant will raise a
post-trial objection to the jurisdiction of the beth din since it had fewer than three
judges. The defendant, by voluntarily appearing before this panel, has vested the
panel with the same authority as a panel of three judges. The other exception, which
deals with recognized expert judges, has been omitted here because it is not clear that
the concept exists even today in this context. The case is otherwise in the situation
in which the beth din consisted of three judges. Whether a panel of three judges made
a mistake or not is irrelevant; otherwise the rule would be that the defendant would
be compelled to appear before the beth din as a defendant and would find out after
the trial whether the trial was valid.

8. This rule does not apply if the community has appointed the beth din, or if the
parties have agreed between themselves to the number of judges on the beth din that
will adjudicate their case.

5. If the defendant fails to appear in response to a summons in any case, the plaintiff may avail himself of the remedies outlined in Chapter 11.

6. Each of the members of the beth din should (but is not required to) familiarize himself with the abilities and qualifications of the other judges before he agrees to join the panel.[9]

7. Many communities traditionally have a beth din composed of five judges. This custom may apply if the beth din is selected by agreement between the parties, or if the parties avail themselves of the procedure described in Chapter 13. This custom does not apply if the beth din has been appointed by the community.

---

9. The idea of joining only with judges who are qualified and worthy certainly requires no elaboration: it represents an ideal situation toward which every community should strive in appointing a beth din. It is not actually prohibited to sit on a beth din before one knows who the other judges are going to be. The word *prohibited* as used in many of the codes is merely for emphasis. This concept is taken from the Jerusalem Talmud, where it states that the pure-minded of Jerusalem would not sit in judgment unless they first knew who their fellow judges would be. While this is sound advice, a beth din is certainly not disqualified if its members did not follow it.

Chapter 4

SELF-HELP

INTRODUCTION

In this day and age, with modern methods of transportation and communication, there is usually no necessity to employ self-help.[1]

---

1. The concept of self-help, or taking the law into one's own hands, is described in the Talmud as an acceptable legal method. However, there is a difference of opinion in the Talmud as to whether self-help may be employed when the user would not be damaged by waiting to come before the beth din. The most obvious case of self-help is self-defense. A person has the absolute right to defend himself from bodily harm. Does this right extend to protection of property? Does it extend to permitting an aggrieved person to seize an article from a person who allegedly wronged him in order to compensate for the wrong? Does it permit the victim of a robbery to retrieve the stolen article from the robber? Does it permit a lender to seize collateral from the debtor if the debt is not paid on time? Obviously, there are many facets to the concept of self-help.

The authorities cover the entire spectrum of ideas in this area. Some are very liberal in permitting self-help. Others would limit it severely, such as to cases of protecting the very article that is in the process of being stolen. And many authorities find themselves somewhere between the two extremes. It is to be recognized that self-help is in derogation of the principle that the judicial system is the arbiter of the law and the method of settling disputes. Thus a legalist might severely restrict the use of self-help, while a psychologist might permit the alleged victim of wrongs to use self-help to enhance his self-image, even if the victim might have obtained the same result, if not a more favorable one, in the beth din. Finally, a system that permits

Therefore, this chapter takes into account that while there is such a concept in halacha, it should be used only in the most obvious cases, such as in self-defense.

TEXT

Employing self-help

Self-help may be employed for the purpose of self-defense, whether one's person or one's property is threatened. For example, it may be employed if a person sees property that was stolen from him in the hands of the robber. It may also be employed to recover chattel that was deposited as a bailment with another party who now refuses to return it.[2]

Seizure of property

A plaintiff or potential plaintiff may seize a defendant's or potential defendant's chattel if he fears that (1) the defendant will leave the jurisdiction; (2) the defendant will secrete his assets; (3) the defendant will fail to appear before the beth din; (4) the chattels are in the hands of a third party who will aid the defendant in secreting the assets or will return the assets to the defendant, who will then leave the jurisdiction or will refuse to appear before the beth din or will secrete his assets; or (5) if the defendant is holding chattels belonging to plaintiff. In all five of these situations, the seizer should immediately

---

self-help relies to some extent on the principle that might makes right, since the stronger the person, the more likely he is to be successful in availing himself of self-help. (A full discussion of self-help is presented in *Jewish Jurisprudence*, Vol. 2.)

2. As has been noted, there are many opinions regarding the scope of self-help. R. Karo believes in his *Shulhan Aruch* that self-help may be employed to seize property only when the seizer has a clear right to claim it. Self-help may not be used to seize property to satisfy any other claim, whether liquidated or not. According to this view, a person may employ self-help only if he has a claim that he can prove in beth din. If there are no witnesses to the act of self-help, then the one who has employed it is believed if he claims that he seized his own property, even though he is not able to prove it in beth din. (He could have been silent, since there were no witnesses to the act of seizure.)

institute suit in beth din against the defendant and deposit with the beth din the assets that he seized.

Self-help is subject to judicial review

All self-help, whether carried out by an individual or by a community,[3] is subject to judicial review upon the request of either party.

Self-help should be used sparingly. If the free and easy use of self-help were to be permitted, lawlessness in the guise of self-help would be the result. The strong would be in a more favorable position than the weak. Thus the employment of self-help is subject to judicial review. Was it properly used? Was excessive force used? Should the person who employed self-help have waited to go to beth din? These and many other questions can be raised by either or both of the parties. Furthermore, once the parties are before the beth din, the beth din may raise many questions of its own. Most important, the beth din may not only undo the self-help, but it also has the right to fine and otherwise punish the person employing self-help if he overstepped the rules of law. Anyone who employs self-help must realize that there are consequences to its use.

---

3. Self help has several aspects. Self-help can be an end in itself; that is, as the final action in the dispute between the parties unless either party seeks judicial review of the self-help. There is also the right of a party to seize, or to ask the beth din to seize, property so as to enable the parties to be secure in the judgment to be rendered at the end of the trial. There is also the concept of the beth din asking a party to post security to ensure compliance with the judgment of the beth din. If an individual, whether a member of the community or not, contests a tax assessment, the community may insist that he post security to ensure compliance with the judgment of the beth din. The burden of proof rests with the individual to show that his position was the correct one. The community stands in the position of electing to come forward with irrefutable proof, or it may insist that the individual come forward with his proof, which the community will be able to overcome. The community also has the choice of selecting the law most favorable to its position if there is a choice of various laws.

Chapter 5

THE DAYS ON WHICH A TRIAL MAY NOT BE HELD, AND THE DAYS ON WHICH A SUMMONS MAY NOT BE SERVED

INTRODUCTION

In a system of laws based on the Torah, all of the Torah's commandments, which of course include both oral and written commandments and all of the centuries of codes, commentaries, and responsa, must be adhered to. This chapter specifies days on which certain judicial activities, such as the holding of trials or even the serving of summonses, may not take place. The preparation for the Sabbath or a Holy Day takes on some of the solemnity of the Sabbath or the Holy Day itself. Thus, not only may trials not be held on the Sabbath or on Holy Days, but efforts should be made to avoid holding trials on the day before the Sabbath and the day before (and in some instances several days before) Holy Days (see notes 2 and 3).

The same holds true for the serving of a summons. This law was extended to other days because a person might be so busy with his preparations for the Sabbath or the Holy Day that he might forget that he had been served with a summons. This chapter assumes that the community has some beth din system in place, but it also provides for those situations in which there is no beth din.

TEXT

Days on which a trial may not be held

A trial may not be held on the Sabbath or on Holy Days.[1-3]

---

1. In the fifth century B.C.E., Ezra the Scribe enacted ten laws decreeing that: (1) the Torah should be read publicly during the afternoon prayer services on the Sabbath, (2) the Torah be read publicly on Mondays and Thursdays during the morning prayer services, (3) the beth din meet on Mondays and Thursdays, (4) clothes be washed at least every Thursday, (5) garlic be eaten at the Friday night meal, (6) the housewife arise early to bake bread, (7) a woman must wear a *sinar,* (belt) (8) a woman must comb her hair before her ritual immersion, (9) peddlars selling spices be allowed to travel in the towns, and (10) immersion be required of those who had become ritually impure. These are all fully discussed in the end of the seventh chapter of *Baba Kamma.* The enactment dealing with the meeting of the beth din was interwoven with the enactment dealing with the public reading of the Torah. Since people would be coming to town to hear the reading of the Torah on Mondays and Thursdays, it would be a good time to have their disputes adjudicated. With the increase in commerce over the centuries, the practice developed in many communities that the beth din would meet more frequently, and often on every day of the week, except for the days already mentioned. The practice nowadays is for the beth din to meet on any day except those prohibited.

2. As mentioned in note 1, the beth din began meeting on every day of the week. Thereafter the Rabbis prohibited the beth din from holding sessions on the Sabbath and on Holy Days lest the judgment be given in writing. (Writing is prohibited on the Sabbath and on Holy Days.) In case of emergency the beth din may meet on those days, and the decision that they render will be written after the Sabbath or Holy Day. There are some cases in which the beth din will meet not for the purpose of deciding a case, but rather to enable the plaintiff to acquaint them with his claim. An example would be a case in which a bridegroom claims fraud in the inception of his marriage because his bride was not a virgin; in order to preserve his rights, he must make a timely claim.

3. The Sabbath, of course, is Saturday in every week. But in Jewish law and observance, the day commences at sundown the night before. The Sabbath begins a short interval before sundown on Friday night and continues until a short time after sundown on Saturday night, thus lasting approximately 25 hours. After sundown on Saturday night, the next day has legally begun, and it is legally the first day of the week, namely Sunday. Thus Holy Days commence just before sundown on the day before the Holy Day. For example, if the Day of Atonement is on a Monday, it would commence a short interval before sundown on Sunday night and would end a short interval after sundown on Monday night. The months of the Jewish calendar are as follows: the spring months are Nissan, Iyar, and Sivan; the summer months are

Tammuz, Av, and Elul; the fall months are Tishrei, Heshvan, and Kislev; and the winter months are Tebeth, Shevat, and Adar.

The Holy Days referred to in the text are Rosh Hashanah, the New Year, which is observed for two days, although according to Torah law it is only one day. The dates for Rosh Hashanah are the first and second days of the month of Tishrei (approximately the end of September). The next Holy Day is Yom Kippur, the Day of Atonement, which is on the tenth day of Tishrei. These two Holy Days, Rosh Hashanah and Yom Kippur, are generally referred to as the "days of awe" because they are solemn convocations during which people pray to God for forgiveness for past transgressions; they admit their transgressions, feel contrite, and resolve to live a life geared to the observance of the Divine commandments.

The other three Holy Days in the Jewish calendar are days of joy; they celebrate historical events in the formation of the nation during the exodus of the Jewish people from Egypt by the Divine hand and during their movements in the desert on the way to the Holy Land. The first of these is Passover, the feast of unleavened bread. In the Land of Israel, Passover is celebrated for seven days, the first and last days being total Holy Days, while the five intermediate days are semi-holy days in that some necessary work is permitted. Passover celebrates the exodus from Egypt. The Jews had to leave Egypt in a hurry after God wrought His miracles there, and thus they had no time to have their dough leavened and baked into bread. Instead, by baking their dough before it became leavened, they made matzoth. The first and last days of Passover are celebrated on the fifteenth and twenty-first days of the month of Nissan and the intermediate days are from the sixteenth through the twentieth days of Nissan. The month of Nissan is an early spring month. Outside the Land of Israel, Passover is celebrated for eight days, the first two being Holy Days, which are celebrated on the fifteenth and sixteenth days of Nissan. The last two days are celebrated on the twenty-first and twenty-second days of Nissan, and the four (instead of five intermediate) days are celebrated from the seventeenth through the twentieth days of Nissan. Fifty days after the first day of Passover is the holy day of Shevu'oth, or the Feast of Weeks, since it falls seven weeks after the end of the first day of Passover. This Holy Day, which is celebrated on the sixth day of the month of Sivan (on the sixth and seventh days of Sivan outside the Land of Israel), celebrates the giving of the Torah on Mount Sinai to the millions of Jews who were assembled there to hear the word of God. The last Holy Days in the Jewish calendar are around Succoth, or the Feast of Tabernacles, so called because the Jew is commanded by God to eat his meals and to sleep in a tabernacle, which he constructs for himself outdoors. These Holy Days commemorate the fact that the Jews lived in tabernacles on their journeys through the desert on the way to the Holy Land, and clouds of glory spread by God hovered over them like a tabernacle. Succoth consists of a Holy Day at the beginning and a Holy Day at the end, and six intermediate days. The first day is the fifteenth day of the month of Tishrei, and the last day is the twenty-second day of Tishrei.

There are other holidays and fasts that are of Rabbinic origin, such as the festival of Hanukah, which begins on the twenty-fifth day of Kislev and lasts for eight days and which marks the victory of the Jews, led by the Hasmonaeans, over the Syrian-

The beth din shall make its own rules on which other days are not permissible for trials.[4] The beth din should take into account that part

Greeks. The festival of Purim, which marks the victory over Haman in Persia, is celebrated on the fourteenth day of Adar; in Jerusalem it is celebrated on the fifteenth day of Adar. The Fast of Gedalia, which is on the third day of the month of Tishrei, marks the date on which the Jewish governor Gedaliah was killed after the destruction of the first Holy Temple, ending whatever autonomy the Jews in Israel still had at the time. The fast of the tenth day of Tebeth marks the beginning of the final siege of Jerusalem before the destruction of the first Holy Temple. The fast of Esther, on the thirteenth day of Adar (the day before Purim), marks the fact that the Jews fasted prior to doing battle with their enemies during the time of Haman. The fast of the seventeenth day of Tammuz is the historic date on which many calamities befell the Jews: The tablets on which the law was written were shattered by Moses when the people worshipped the golden calf; the regular daily sacrifices were discontinued in the Holy Temple; the Romans breached the walls of Jerusalem during the siege of the city; the wicked Apostomas burned a Torah scroll; and an idol was placed in the Holy Temple. The most severe of the Rabbinic fast days, which falls on the ninth day of Av, commemorates the occurrence of the following events on that date: The spies sent by Moses to explore the Land of Israel brought back a pessimistic report; both the first and the second Holy Temples were destroyed; the city of Bethar, which held the remnants of the first Roman massacres, was captured and destroyed; and the site of the Holy Temple was plowed under by the Roman governor.

In our lifetime, three special days have been added to the calendar. The twenty-seventh day of Nissan marks the remembrance of the Holocaust. The fifth of Iyar marks the independence of the State of Israel in 1948 C.E.; and the twenty-eighth day of Iyar marks the day of the reunification of the Holy City of Jerusalem in 1967 C.E.

4. For reasons already stated in the previous notes, trials may not be held nor summonses served on the day preceding the Sabbath or a holy day. There are several other situations in which such exceptions are required. A bride or bridegroom may not be served with a summons to appear before a beth din during the three days before the wedding celebration nor during the seven days following the wedding celebration. According to Jewish law, the bride and bridegroom may not work during the seven days following their wedding, and on these days special meals are eaten and special blessings are recited at the meals. Naturally, the bride and bridegroom are too preoccupied during this period to attend the beth din.

The circumcision ritual qualifies as another exception. According to Jewish law, a newborn son must be circumcised on the eighth day of his life. Here, too, the father is busy making preparations for the feast which accompanies the circumcision ceremony. Since he is so preoccupied, he is exempt from beth din attendance on the eight days preceding the circumcision and on the day of and the day after the circumcision. Similarly, all others who feel that they should be exempt from attendance at beth din, for whatever reason, are permitted to make an application to the beth din and request an adjournment.

of Friday[5] is used for the Sabbath preparation. Therefore, the beth din session, if held on Friday, should end early enough to provide adequate time for all involved to prepare for the Sabbath. The beth din should also take into account that the days before Holy Days[6] are usually used for preparation, and adequate provision should be made for that.[7]

Time for trials

A beth din organized by the community shall set its own times for trial during the day. Where feasible, there should be sessions for small

---

5. In many communities, cases are not judged on the day before the Sabbath (Friday) nor on the day before a Holy Day because both the litigants and the judges are busy with preparations. Not only should cases not be heard on those days, but judges should not decide cases on these days because they will not have sufficient time to deliberate. In some situations witnesses may decide to submit their pleas or have the witnesses testify on these days, or they may ask the beth din to complete the trial and even render a decision.

6. In those communities where the rules prohibit trials on Fridays or on the day before a Holy Day, the defendant may not be served with a summons requiring him to appear in beth din on these days. The foregoing is true even if the summons was served on an appropriate day. If the return day of the summons is a Friday or the day before a Holy Day, then the defendant may disregard the summons with impunity and will not be held in contempt of beth din for having done so. In many communities, a summons served on a Friday or on the day before a Holy Day requiring attendance on these days is void. One is not punished for disregarding such a summons.

7. As was stated in note 3, Nissan and Tishrei are months within which major Holy Days fall, and the people are as busy with preparation for these days, as they are for the Sabbath. In the case of the Sabbath, there is only one day of preparation, whereas in the case of the Holy Days, there are many days of preparation. Thus many days of the month are as pressing as Fridays are. Therefore, a summons may not be served requiring attendance during the months of Nissan and Tishrei. A limitation is placed on the restriction against requiring attendance during these two months. In some communities, only nonresidents of the community will not be required to attend during these months, whereas the residents of the community will be required to appear in beth din during these months. The nonresidents may, however, be served with a summons during these months requiring attendance before beth din after these months. If a trial was commenced prior to the beginning of Nissan or Tishrei, then the litigants may be compelled to continue the trial during these months. This ruling may have the effect of making the litigants avoid dilatory tactics, since they will want to end the trial as quickly as possible. If the judges see that true justice will not be done by having a trial continue into these months, then they will adjourn the trial until after the Holy Days in these months.

claims in order to accommodate those who find it inconvenient to take time off from their employment to litigate small amounts.

Unless agreed to by the parties, and unless provided for as a small claims beth din, a trial should not be commenced at night. If a trial commences during the day, however, it may continue into the night.[8] There is also an opinion that a trial that commences at night is nevertheless valid. Testimony of the witnesses may never be taken at night without the consent of all the parties.

Where the litigation will be tried before a beth din not organized by the community, the judges and the litigants shall determine such days and times as meet the convenience of the judges and the parties and their counsel.

When a summons may not be served

A summons may not be served on the Sabbath or on a Holy Day.[9]

---

8. There are certain verses in the Torah from which the Rabbis were able to demonstrate that trials may not commence at night, but may commence only during the day. Once a trial has commenced—that is, the testimony has been received and evidence has been admitted—the judges may continue their deliberations at night. As was stated previously, the litigants together with the judges may agree that a trial may commence or that part of the trial may be held at night. All that is said about not commencing a trial at night has no reference to the service of a summons, which may be served at night if it requires attendance in beth din in the daytime.

9. As was stated previously, a person may not be served with a summons that requires him to appear in beth din on certain Holy Days during the months of Nissan or Tishrei, and these days were extended to include the entire month. However, a summons may be served during these months requiring attendance at the beth din at a later time. According to some authorities, the beth din may require attendance immediately after the Holy Days in the month rather than waiting for the next month to begin. The reason that a summons requiring attendance for some other time may not be served on Fridays or on the day before a holy day is that the person so served will be busy with his Sabbath or Holy Day preparations and forget that he was served with the summons, and thus will forget to come to beth din. But if he is served on some other day, albeit during the months of Nissan or Tishrei, he will be apt to remember that he was served with a summons.

A personal query from my good friend Marvin Klitsner: May a summons be served on *Isroo Chag*, the day immediately after a Holy Day, and may a summons be made returnable on that day? According to the opinion that the entire months of Nissan and Tishrei are included in the prohibition of returnable days for the summons, they are already included in the prohibition (except for Shevu'oth, which is only a single Holy Day). According to the other opinion that a summons may be made returnable

The beth din may also establish other days on which a summons may not be served. Rules should be established to prohibit the service of a summons on a Friday or on the day before a Holy Day.

A summons served on the Sabbath or on a Holy Day is a nullity, and the beth din officer who makes such service should be punished according to the dictates of the beth din.

If a summons is served on any of the other days prohibited by the beth din, then the beth din shall make appropriate conditions to deal with the situation, including provisions for leniency if the defendant fails to appear in beth din on the return date or answer the summons as provided in Chapter 11.

---

immediately after the Holy Days, each beth din should make its own rules regarding *Isroo Chag*, although this author would suggest that a summons should not be made returnable on *Isroo Chag*.

Chapter 6

THE MINIMUM
MONETARY JURISDICTION
OF THE BETH DIN

INTRODUCTION

This chapter focuses on the minimum monetary jurisdiction of the beth din. In times like these, when one often does not bother to pick up small change in the street, it might seem that the halachah should adopt a new standard. Rabbi Yechiel Michel Epstein, in his *Aruch HaShulhan*, says that even in his days at the turn of the twentieth century, people were already questioning the many laws that depended upon a small coin called the *perutah*. He states:

> Know that the *perutah* has significance of the locale in all geographic areas and at all times. All of the measurements given by the Sages of blessed memory were received from generation to generation from the time when Moses, may he rest in peace, received the measurements from the Holy One, Blessed Be He, at Sinai. And even now we see in many places that for a *perutah* one may buy a slice of bread or an onion or a needle and similar things, [even though there are] those who scoff at it [*Aruch haShulhan, Hoshen haMishpat*, Volume 7, Chapter 190, p. 4, para. 2].

His remarks are aimed at scoffers who do not realize the significance and grandeur of a tradition of thirty-five centuries, wherein this tiny coin has been the symbol of something small yet valuable. How many people in the world in 5750 crave a *perutah's* worth of food every night! But in addition to stating the law as it applies to the minimum monetary jurisdiction of the beth din, this chapter shows that the law was not unmindful of the concept of minimum monetary jurisdiction. The notes also contain some rules for combining causes of action as well as for asserting counterclaims. Also noted is the concept of the beth din's continuing to exercise jurisdiction once it has acquired such jurisdiction.

TEXT

Monetary requirement at the commencement of the trial

The judges do not begin a trial unless the plaintiff's claim is for at least the value of a *perutah*.[1] If the trial commences[2] for the value of at least a *perutah*,[3] then the trial is completed,[4] even if the judgment

---

1. A trial will not be commenced unless the plaintiff is suing for at least the value of a *perutah*. Once this minimum jurisdictional requirement has been met, the beth din must deal with additional causes of action alleged by the plaintiff and/or counterclaims asserted by the defendant, even if these additional causes of action or counterclaims are for less than a *perutah*.

2. If judgment was rendered in favor of the plaintiff's cause of action, then the plaintiff may not assert additional claims against the defendant for less than a *perutah*. However, the defendant may assert counterclaims even if they are for less than a *perutah*. If judgment was rendered in favor of the defendant on the plaintiff's cause of action, then neither the plaintiff nor the defendant may assert any causes of action for less than a *perutah*.

3. Once the minimum requirement of a *perutah* has been met, the beth din will retain jurisdiction, even if the pleas are subsequently amended to reduce the demand to less than a *perutah*, either because of lack of proof or because the defendant's admissions placed the issue at less than a *perutah*.

4. Two or more plaintiffs may combine their claims to make up the requisite jurisdiction of a *perutah*, if and only if their claims arose from a joint interest, such as a partnership. One plaintiff may join several defendants in his lawsuit to make up the requisite jurisdictional amount of a *perutah*, even if there is no common interest among the defendants or any common questions involved. The beth din, while retaining jurisdiction, should, in the interests of justice, try each claim separately.

will be for a smaller sum.[5]

The defendant may assert a counterclaim, even if it is for less than a *perutah*.

---

5. If a beth din hears a case in which the minimum jurisdictional requirements were not met, its judgment is void. However, the proceedings are valid insofar as admissions made before the beth din and insofar as the proceedings affect the credibility of witnesses who were shown to have perjured themselves during the hearing. The foregoing discussions apply to cases in which a monetary judgment is sought. Cases involving the minimum value of a chattel are discussed in Chapter 88.

Chapter 7

WHO IS ELIGIBLE TO JUDGE AND WHO IS NOT ELIGIBLE TO JUDGE

INTRODUCTION

This chapter will focus on those persons who are ineligible to judge, those who are eligible to judge the case before them, and those who may not judge the case. Thus a judge may be eligible to judge one case, but because of the facts of the case or because of the parties involved, he may not be eligible to judge another case or to participate as a judge of the beth din.

TEXT

The following topics are discussed in this chapter:

The proselyte as a judge
The bastard as a judge
The blind person as a judge
The minimum age of a judge
Women as judges
An intoxicated person as a judge
A witness in the case as a judge in that case
A judge who is inferior in wisdom to the litigant

A judge who is a friend or an enemy of the litigant
Two judges on the same beth din who hate each other
A relative of the litigant as a judge
A judge joining a beth din with a robber as a member
Personal qualities of a judge
A case in which the judge may derive a benefit from the decision
of the beth din

The proselyte as a judge

If a beth din contains a proselyte,[1] it may not judge a Jew.[2] If the

---

1. A Jew is one who is born of a Jewish mother or is properly converted. One who is properly converted is called a proselyte. The child of a proselyte married to a proselyte is still called a proselyte. The child of a proselyte and a Jewish spouse is no longer designated a proselyte. Thus, in this discussion, a proselyte is considered one who has converted to Judaism or whose two parents were proselytes.

According to Torah law there are two types of proselytes. One is the resident stranger, a former heathen who has forsaken the worship of idols and observes the other commandments made obligatory upon the descendants of Noah, but who was not circumcised or immersed. Nowadays, this kind of convert may not be accepted, since he could be accepted only when the law of the Jubilee was in force, and this law has lapsed. As explained by Rambam in Chapter 10 of the *Laws Concerning the Jubilee and Sabbatical Years,* it lapsed when the tribes of Reuben and Gad and half of the tribe of Manasseh were exiled. Rambam also states:

> The Israelites counted seventeen Jubilees from the time they entered
> the Land until they left it. The year in which they left, when the First
> Temple was destroyed, was the year following a Sabbatical year, and
> the thirty-sixth year of that Jubilee period, the First Temple having
> stood for 410 years. When the First Temple was destroyed, this count
> of Jubilees ceased, and from that time the Land remained desolate for
> 70 years. The Second Temple was then built and stood for 420 years.
> In the 7th year after its rebuilding, Ezra went to the Land, and this is
> called the second entrance into the Promised Land. From that year
> the Israelites began a new count and declared the 13th year after the
> building of the Second Temple a Sabbatical year. They then counted
> 7 septennates and hallowed the following 50th year. Even though the
> Jubilee was not in force during the time of the Second Temple, it was
> nevertheless counted in order to hallow the Sabbatical years.

Rambam, writing in the year 1176 C.E., notes that according to the reckoning of the Geonim it was the year following the Sabbatical year. It is this counting upon which

proselyte's mother or father was Jewish,[3] then he may judge a Jew.[4] A proselyte may judge another proselyte, even if neither his father nor his mother was Jewish.

The bastard as a judge

A beth din containing one, two, or three bastards is a valid beth din and may judge monetary cases.[5]

Israel depends in formulating the Sabbatical years. Hopefully it will not be too long, with the advent of the Messiah and the ingathering of all of the exiles, before the Great Sanhedrin, sitting once again in the Chamber of Hewn Stone on the Temple grounds, will once again count the Jubilee years.

The second type of proselyte exists even today. As stated by Rambam in *Laws Concerning Forbidden Intercourse*, when a heathen wishes to enter into the covenant and assume the yoke of the Torah, including acceptance of all of the commandments, he requires circumcision, immersion, and the offering of an acceptable sacrifice. Until the Temple is rebuilt, which we pray will be within our days, the necessity for the sacrifice does not exist. Thus men require circumcision and immersion, while women require immersion only. The procedure for conversion can be entrusted only to those fully conversant with and accepting of halachah, and all alleged conversions by those who pretend to have a smattering of halachah or who disavow its binding nature are of no value, except to cause confusion among the Jewish people.

2. In those situations in which a proselyte may not judge, if he sits on a beth din of three, then the entire beth din is unfit. In those situations in which a proselyte may judge, the proceedings are valid even if all three judges of the court are proselytes.

3. The most important line in genealogy is that of the mother. If she was Jewish, then the child is Jewish. For other purposes, the father's genealogy is followed. Thus if he is a Kohen (a descendant of a priestly family) or a Levite (a descendant of the tribe of Levi, who fulfilled certain functions in the Holy Temple) or an Israelite (one who is neither a Kohen nor a Levite), then his progeny are the same. After R. Karo writes in Chapter 7, para. 1 the exception that a proselyte whose mother was Jewish may judge, Ramo adds "or his father." R. Ramo's comments are a logical conclusion, for if the mother's being Jewish makes the child eligible to be a judge, it should be that much more so if the father was Jewish.

4. All of the foregoing notes apply *only* if the proselyte judge wishes to exercise jurisdiction by compulsion. If the Jewish litigant voluntarily submits to the jurisdiction of the proselyte judge, then he has jurisdiction even if neither of his parents was Jewish.

5. Rambam, in Chapter 15 of *Laws Concerning Forbidden Intercourse*, states:

> Who is considered a bastard as designated in the Torah? The offspring by any of the forbidden unions, except by a menstruant, whose child is considered impaired, but not a bastard. If a man has

The blind person as a judge

A person who is blind in only one eye may judge monetary cases in the first instance. A person who is totally blind may not be a judge. But if he did act as a judge, his participation is valid.[6]

---

intercourse with a woman of any of the other forbidden unions, whether by force or by consent, whether willfully or by error, the child born of that union is regarded as a bastard, and both male and female are eternally forbidden to marry into Israel. There are three classes of bastards: an assured bastard, a doubtful bastard, and a bastard on the authority of the Scribes. Who is deemed an assured bastard? The offspring of an undoubtedly forbidden union. A doubtful bastard is the offspring of a doubtfully forbidden union—for instance, if a man had intercourse with a woman whose betrothal to another man or whose divorce is doubtful. Similar considerations apply to a bastard on the authority of the Scribes. For instance, if a woman, having heard that her husband had died, remarries, and thereafter it comes to light that her first husband is still living, and if he then has intercourse with her while she is still wed to the second man, the resulting child is deemed a bastard on the authority of the Scribes. If an unmarried woman becomes pregnant by way of adultery, she should be asked, "What is this expected child" or "this newborn child?" If she says, "It is legitimate, for I had intercourse with an Israelite," she is believed, and the child is to be considered legitimate, even if the majority of the inhabitants of the city in which she committed fornication are such as she could not lawfully marry.

6. It is to be noted that a blind man should not ritually slaughter an animal in the first instance unless he was observed by others to see that he performed according to the laws and rules governing kosher slaughtering. Nevertheless, if the blind person *did* slaughter without being observed, his slaughtering is post facto valid. The slaughtering of an animal according to kosher laws is quite complicated; yet the act is post facto valid. If the blind person can be observed, there is ample authority to say that it may even be done in the first instance. There is some authority for believing that these laws apply to a person who at one time did have vision but later lost it; but if he never had vision, then even post facto, his slaughtering is not valid.

In the case of judging, by contrast, the law seems to be more strict regarding the blind. Of course, the Torah is the ultimate source of the law, and there is an underlying Torah law that equates judgment of monetary cases with declaration of a person to be a leper. Just as the latter case requires a person who is able to see and examine the leper, so it is in the case of judging. It is to be remembered that jurisprudence in Torah is only one part of the overall body of Jewish law, which embraces every facet of life. Nonjurisprudential concepts are often introduced to prove jurisprudential points. It is not difficult to understand that a judge should be able to see. He must be able to observe the demeanor of the people who are testifying, and he should also be able to see the evidence.

The parties may accept a person who is totally blind to judge their case. Even those authorities who hold that a totally blind judge may not judge would hold that the blind person may assist in explaining the law to the judges.

A person who uses eyeglasses to help him see is considered as eligible as a person with good vision.

The minimum age of a judge

There are those who hold that a man[7] is eligible to judge if he has attained the age of 13.[8] It seems to this author that the better view is held by those who believe that a man should not be eligible to judge until he has attained the age of 18.[9]

---

7. The law regarding kosher slaughtering of animals is that a minor who knows how to move his hands to control the act of slaughtering may slaughter even in the first instance if other knowledgeable adults observe him. But if he slaughtered without being observed by others, his act is invalid. He is considered a minor for these purposes until he has attained the age of 13 years and a day. There are those who hold that a person should not receive certification to slaughter until he has reached the age of 18 years, for at that time he becomes more mature and is more careful. But as the commentaries explain, such capability depends upon the astuteness of the individual. Certainly in the case of acting as a judge, the litigants will be loath to appear before a person tender in years unless they have confidence in his ability to judge.

8. There is a difference of opinion in the Talmud regarding when a minor becomes of age. One opinion holds that males mature earlier than females, so that a male reaches maturity at the age of 12 years, and a female at the age of 13 years. The prevailing view, however, is that females mature earlier; this opinion holds that females reach maturity at 12 years, and males at 13 years. Rambam discusses the definition of a minor and an adult in Chapter 2 of *Laws of Marriage*.

> A male child is called a minor or a little boy from his birth until he becomes 13 years old. Even if he grows many hairs within this period of time, they do not constitute a token, but are considered the same as a mole. If after he becomes 13 years and 1 day old, he grows two hairs in the nether part of the body, in the places known for the growth of hair, he is considered an adult and is called a man.
> The rules for a female are similar to those for a male, except that the age is 12 years instead of 13 years.

9. A person may be a judge in monetary matters from the age of 13 and onward if he is well versed in the law; otherwise he should not be appointed a judge until the age of 18. Judges in capital cases should be at least 20 years of age. In matters affecting real estate, there is authority that a person should not be appointed a judge until he has grown two pubic hairs and has attained his 13th birthday. Regarding the

Women as judges

A woman is not eligible[10] to judge.[11] Although she is not eligible to be a judge, she may, however, judge cases if the litigants ask her to judge their case. She may also assist the judges in arriving at a judgment.

An intoxicated person as a judge

One who has had an intoxicating drink may not be a judge in a capital case.

In monetary matters, one who is drunk may not be a judge.[12] But

---

appointment of a permanent judge for a community, there are those who hold that he should be at least 20 years of age, and that if he is to be the sole judge he should be at least 40 years of age, unless he is the greatest Sage in the community.

10. This statement applies to those situations in which the judge has the authority and power to compel litigants to appear before the beth din against their will.

11. In the finality of the statement that women may not judge, there is a question that troubles many of the greatest talmudic commentators and codifiers regarding the role of Deborah. As related in Judges 4, the Israelites were being oppressed by Jabin, king of Canaan, whose general was the famed Sisera. The Israelites cried out to God for help. Deborah was a "prophetess, the wife of Lappidoth, she judged Israel at that time" (Judges 4:4). She summoned Barak to command an army and to engage the Canaanites in battle. When Barak requested that Deborah accompany the army to battle, she replied, "I will surely go with thee; notwithstanding the journey that thou takest shall not be for thy honor; for the Lord will give Sisera over to a woman" (Judges 4:9). As Deborah predicted, the enemy was vanquished, and thereafter Deborah composed her triumphal ode, found in Judges 5.

What concerns the commentators is the phrase that "she judged Israel at that time." Several explanations are given. One is that perhaps women are actually not excluded from judging. Or perhaps Deborah's case is unique because she was judging at the Divine command. Or perhaps she was not actually judging but rather merely advising the judges. Adding to the controversy is a view in Tosafoth (see *Niddah* 50, Tosafoth introductory words *kul hakasher*) and a strong view in *Sefer Hachinuch*, commandment 77, that women may indeed judge. Clearly, the question of whether women should be permitted to judge merits more study. (This matter is more fully discussed in the Appendix.)

12. There is a statement in the Talmud that if one has reached the stage of Lot's drunkenness he should be exempt from all responsibilities (*Erubin* 65a). We find a description of Lot's drunkenness in the Torah. After the destruction by God of Sodom and Gomorrah is described, the following passages appear:

> And Lot went up out of Zoar, and dwelt in the mountain, and his two daughters with him; and he feared to dwell in Zoar; and he dwelt in a

if he has had some liquor and still knows how to judge, he may join with other judges to form a beth din.[13] The better practice would be for him not to judge a case by himself.[14]

---

cave, he and his two daughters. And the first-born said unto the younger: "Our father is old, and there is not a man in the earth to come unto us in the manner of all the earth. Come let us make our father drink wine, and we will lie with him, that we may preserve seed of our father. And they made their father drink wine that night. And the first-born went in and lay with her father, and he knew not when she lay down, nor when she arose. And it came to pass on the morrow, that the first-born said to the younger: "Behold I lay last night with my father. Let us make him drink wine this night also; and go thou in, and lie with him, that we may preserve seed of our father." And they made their father drink wine that night also. And the younger arose, and lay with him; and he knew not when she lay down, nor when she arose. Thus were both the daughters of Lot with child by their father. [Genesis 18:30–36]

13. In the opening passages of the first chapter of the *Book of Temple Service* Rambam states:

(1) Any priest fit to minister was forbidden to enter to the place of the Altar and inward if he drank wine. If he entered and ministered, his ministry was invalid; and he was punishable with death by the hand of Heaven; for it is said: *that ye die not* (Leviticus 10:9). This was so only if he drank a fourth of unmixed wine at one time, of wine that was at least forty days old. But if he drank less than a fourth, or if he drank a fourth but with interruption, or if he mixed it with water, or if he drank more than a fourth of wine but it was within forty days from his press, he was exempt from penalty and did not profane his ministry. If he drank more than a fourth of wine, even though it was mixed and even though he interrupted his drinking and drank it little by little, he incurred the penalty of death and rendered his ministry invalid. (3) Just as a priest was forbidden to enter the sanctuary when drunk, so is every person, whether priest or lay Israelite, forbidden to render a decision when drunk. (4) Furthermore, one who is drunk may teach the law, including even legal passages and textual interpretations, provided that he does not render actual decisions. But if he is a scholar appointed to make decisions, he may not teach in such condition, for his teaching is tantamount to an actual decision.

A *fourth* refers to one-quarter of a *log* (almost a pint), a liquid measurement used in halachah. A fourth is equal to approximately 3.5 ounces.

14. Regarding a person who is slaughtering animals or fowl according to the details of the halachah, *Shulhan Aruch, Yoreh De'ah,* Chapter 1, para. 8, states: "One who is as drunk as Lot has the same legal status as an imbecile. If he has not reached that

A witness in the case as a judge in that case

A witness who has testified in a case may not also be a judge in that case.[15] If he has not testified in the case, he may act as a judge in the case, even if he witnessed the event with the view of being a witness to testify in the case.[16]

If all three judges of the beth din saw the event in the daytime, they may decide the case on the basis of their own observations and need not have any additional testimony or evidence or witnesses presented to the beth din.[17] If they witnessed the event in the nightime, they may either act as witnesses before another beth din or act as judges

---

state of drunkenness as Lot, he may slaughter in the first instance." R. Ramo, in his emendations to R. Karo, adds: "A drunken person should not slaughter, because he is not apt to slaughter according to the halachah."

15. If a person, or even all the members of the beth din, witnessed an event, and he or they did not testify to that event in a beth din, then he or they may judge that event. This rule applies only to monetary cases and does not apply to capital cases, and it holds true even if the judge or judges intended to act as witnesses to the event and thus to be able to testify to the event in beth din; so long as they did not actually testify to the event, they may act as judges of the event.

16. One might logically ask how, if a judge relies on his own opinion of what he saw, he can receive testimony from other witnesses with an open mind. Furthermore, he cannot be cross-examined. The adversarial system of justice, wherein judges recuse themselves if they are familiar with the case, depends upon the adversaries presenting the case, and the judges acting as arbiters to see that all of the rules are followed, and then rendering a decision based on what they have learned from the pleadings, evidence, and testimony presented. But even then the judge may take into consideration his own impression of the demeanor of a witness. Thus the judge's impressions go a long way toward helping him render a decision.

The halachic system does not contemplate this type of cross-examination (see Chapter 30). Furthermore, the judge hears all of the testimony in order to arrive at the facts, but if he actually witnessed the event, he already knows the facts. The caliber and integrity of the judges who serve on the beth din is such that it is unlikely that they would be close-minded and not allow the testimony of the witnesses to convince them that their first impression may have been mistaken.

17. If the three judges saw the event and have not testified before a beth din, they may act as judges based merely on their own observation of the event; they need not have any other independent testimony on which to base their decision. This is permitted because if they have not testified, they have the dual status of witness and judge. They maintain this dual status only as long as they have not breached it by testifying before a beth din, at which time they become exclusively witnesses and may never again act as judges in this matter.

and base their decision solely on the testimony of other witnesses and not on their own observations.[18]

If the matter being judged by the beth din is based on Rabbinic law, a person who testified in a case may still be a member of that beth din to decide that case.[19]

A judge who is inferior in wisdom to the litigant

The judges may not compel a litigant who is superior to them in wisdom to appear before them.[20-22] Rather, the beth din convenes a

---

18. The judges may maintain this dual status of being both witness and judge if they had this dual status when they witnessed the event. In the situation in which the judges could not have acted as judges when they witnessed the event (at night, for example) they do not have the dual status of both witnesses and judges. They may act as witnesses before another beth din, or they may act as judges if other witnesses to the event testify before them. The difference between witnessing an event at night and in the daytime is that a beth din may commence its sessions during the daytime but may not do so at night, as set forth in Chapter 5. Presumably the same would hold true for other times when the beth din may not hold sessions.

19. All of the foregoing rules apply only if the matter to be judged is a dispute based upon Torah laws regarding conduct between two persons. If the matter in dispute is based upon a law of Rabbinic origin, however, such as would be the case if a signature on a document were being questioned, the person who has testified regarding the signature may also judge as to the validity of the signature.

20. A Sage may be summoned to beth din. If the Sage believes that the judge of the beth din (or even all three judges combined) is inferior to him in wisdom, he has two options. He may waive his privilege (see note 21) and appear before the beth din, or he may object to appearing. In the latter event, the scholars of the community decide how to handle the matter.

21. Judging was often a secondary obligation thrust upon the judges; their first and foremost obligation was the study of Torah. Torah study was acknowledged to be the highest attainment, and the more proficient one was in the study of Torah, the more one was respected. One who respects the Torah must honor those who study it, especially the Sages. To compel a man to appear before another who is inferior to him in some manner raises the summoner to the same level as the Sage. There may be instances in which it would be tantamount to putting the Torah to shame to require the Sage to appear before a particular beth din. The Sage is thus given the option to refuse to appear if he believes that such refusal will enhance the status of Torah in the community.

22. A person need not always take advantage of his superior position. In fact, it is often laudable for such a person to waive the privilege, unless he believes that doing so would defeat the purpose of the privilege granted by the Torah. Examples of such

meeting of all of the community's scholars, who decide how to proceed. At the convened meeting, the scholars may decide that the

---

privileges are the rights granted to a parent, to a Sage, to the president of a tribe, and to the king of Israel.

Regarding the commandment to honor a parent, Rambam, in *Laws of Rebels*, states in Chapter 4:

> (1) The honoring of father and mother is a weighty positive commandment; so too is reverence for them. The Torah attaches to the duty of honoring and revering parents an importance equal to that which it attaches to the duty of honoring and revering God.

After a detailed explanation of the duties of honoring and revering, Rambam states:

> (8) Although children are commanded to go to the above-mentioned great lengths, the father is forbidden to impose too heavy a yoke upon them, to be too exacting with them in matters pertaining to his honor, lest he cause them to stumble. He should forgive them and shut his eyes; for a father has the right to forego the honor due to him.

Regarding the duty to honor a teacher or rabbi, Rambam writes in *Laws of Talmud Torah*, Chapter 5:

> (1) Just as a person is commanded to honor and revere his father, so is he under an obligation to honor and revere his teacher even to a greater extent than his father; for his father gave him life in this world, while his teacher who instructs him in wisdom secures for him life in the world to come.... There is no honor higher than that which is due to the teacher; no reverence profounder than that which should be paid to him.
>
> (11) If one's chief teacher wishes to excuse all his pupils or any of them from all or any of these observances, he may do so. But even then the disciple must show courtesy to him, even at the moment that he explicitly dispenses with it.

Regarding the president of the Sanhedrin, Rambam writes in Chapter 6 of *Laws of Talmud Torah*:

> (6) On seeing the president, one rises as soon as he is seen, and does not sit down till he is seated in his place or has passed out of sight. If the president desires to dispense with the honor due to him, he may do so. When the president enters an assembly, all present rise and do not sit down till he tells them "sit."

Regarding a king, Rambam writes in Chapter 2 of the *Laws Concerning Kings and Wars*:

Sage must appear before the beth din, in which event he must obey. Or they may advise him that he need not appear before the beth din, and the scholars will adjudicate the dispute between the Sage and the other litigant.

A judge who is a friend or enemy of the litigant

It is essential that both litigants be equal in the eyes and hearts of the judges.[23] It is best if the judges do not know either of the litigants.

It is prohibited for a person to judge a litigant whom he loves, or who is his friend, or whom he hates. A beth din that is disqualified on account of enmity or friendship may select a different beth din of eligible judges to judge the case. Authorities have expressed conflicting opinions as to the validity of a judgment if the judge nevertheless did judge in such situations. It depends upon the facts in each case as it is brought up for review.[24]

He is permitted to be one of the selected judges in a situation in

---

(1) The king is to be accorded great honor. The attitude of his subjects toward him should be one of awe and reverence...

(3)...for in the case of a king, if he renounces the honor due him, it is not remitted.

The Talmud explains that the king may not remit the honor due to him because the Torah states "thou shalt surely set a king over thee" (Deuteronomy 17:15).

23. The purpose of the adjudication in every case is to arrive at a decision that is as close to justice as humanly possible. A person who has a preconceived notion about a case is unlikely to be swayed by the evidence. It is in the way of human nature for a judge to be partial when one of the litigants is closer to him than the other litigant. Even Moses, the greatest judge of all time, did not judge a case if he thought that the litigant had made a statement that might have prejudiced him. Thus, in the Torah, there is described the situation in which the daughters of Zelophe had come to Moses and asked that they be given the right to inherit the property of their father, who died without any sons. Moses might very well have heard their pleas by himself, but they introduced their request to him by saying, "Our father died in the wilderness, and he was not among the company of them that gathered themselves against the Lord in the company of Korah, but he died in his own sin, and he had no sons" (Numbers 27:3). As soon as they mentioned that their father was not part of Korah's rebellion against the Divine commandments as transmitted through Moses, he realized that his impartiality would be compromised. Moses acted piously in refusing to decide their claim and instead taking their claim before the Almighty to decide.

24. There are situations in which a judge may legally adjudicate a case but wishes

which each selects one judge (as described in Chapter 13), since each litigant will select one whom he likes.[25]

A litigant who alleges that the judge is prejudiced because he hates him or loves the other litigant is not believed on his mere word, but must prove his allegation.[26]

Two judges on the same beth din who hate each other

Two scholars who hate each other[27] are prohibited from sitting on the

---

to refrain from doing so out of piety. Some examples of such situations are a teacher judging his disciple, a man judging a neighbor with whom he has a close relationship, a host judging his guest, and a man judging the father of his son-in-law or daughter-in-law. If the judge is an appointed judge of the community, however, then he need not out of piety refrain from judging such a case.

25. Chapter 13 sets forth the procedure for having three judges sit as a beth din. Each litigant selects one of the judges, and the two judges so selected then select the third judge. In this situation the law assumes that each litigant will select a judge who will be partial to him. However, if a litigant abuses this system and selects a very close friend who cannot possibly retain his objectivity, then the judge can be disqualified by the other litigant.

26. The question of prejudice may be raised by the litigant on a prima facie showing that prejudice may result. A determination should be made by a recognized impartial expert or experts whose decision on this question will be binding to all parties. It may be made binding by a kinyan (a legally binding acceptance by the parties). (See Chapter 195.) Once the case has begun, objection may not be raised except if the evidence of extreme close relationship could not possibly have been known before.

27. The concept that two scholars can hate each other, which appears in halachah, is perplexing. There is an injunction in the Torah that a person must not hate another: "Thou shalt not hate thy brother in thy heart" (Leviticus 19:17). Perhaps the reference in the halachah is not to an actual scholar, but rather to a learned person, as we find in Kiddushin 49b, where it is taught that if a man betrothed a woman and added the condition " 'On condition that I am a talmid' [disciple], we do not say such as Simeon b. Azzai and Simeon b. Zoma, but one who when asked a single question on his studies in any place can answer it, even in Kallah. 'On condition that I am a Sage,' then we do not say, like the sages of Yavneh [a great academy] or like Rabbi. Akiva [one of the great sages of all time] and his companions, but one who can be asked a matter where he must apply logic and he can answer it."

Alternatively, perhaps the reference is to the type of competitiveness found in Sanhedrin p. 24a, where it is stated that the scholars in Babylonia hurt one anothers' feelings when discussing halachah. Thus, rathern than endeavoring to arrive at a just decision, each member of the beth din would try to outwit the other by showing his

same case before the beth din.[28] If two judges who hated each other did sit on the same beth din,[29] the judgment of the beth din is not valid.[30]

Similarly, two judges who are very different in temperament should not sit on the same beth din.

A relative of the litigant as a judge

A person ineligible[31] to testify on account of kinship[32] or because of

---

erudition. (My son-in-law, Robert Silverman suggested that perhaps the word *scholar* did not actually refer to a true scholar, but rather was a name for a member of the beth din, since ideally the members of the beth din *should* be scholars.)

28. When two judges who sit together on a beth din hate each other, they prevent the obtaining of justice. Each is more concerned with contradicting the other's view than with ensuring a just decision.

29. A scholar who hates one of the judges should not even be present in the courtroom when the judges are deliberating, since he may try to influence the beth din by contradicting that judge, thus misleading the other judges.

30. Some commentators have said that, similarly, two judges who love each other should not sit on the same beth din, since neither will be able to render an independent judgment. Just as two judges who hate each other will lose sight of the truth in their effort to contradict each other, two judges who love each other will agree with each other, even if one does not truly believe that the other is right. This author thinks that the two situations are not similar. If two judges love and respect each other, each will be open to the words of the other, and if one believes that the other is incorrect, he will say so and the other will listen with great heed to the words of his beloved friend. What is more, their love for each other will enable them to cast opposing votes without arousing the other's animosity. Such a situation can make for a more diligent search for the truth, more honest deliberations, and a greater opportunity for justice.

31. Generally, whoever may judge may testify. However, there are those who may testify but may not judge. Thus it is clear that all judges are included in the class of witnesses, but not all witnesses are included in the class of judges. Therefore, one who may not testify certainly may not judge. However, the fact that women may not testify does not in itself disqualify them from judging. Tosafoth explains that the aforementioned rules may apply only to men and not to women.

32. There are certain persons who may not testify because of kinship. Chapter 33 lists the relatives who are disqualified from testifying. If such a degree of kinship exists between any of the judges, or between any of the judges and any witnesses, or between any of the judges and any of the litigants, then that judge may not act as a judge in the matter.

sin[33] is disqualified to sit on the beth din. (See Chapters 33 and 34 for details regarding those who are ineligible to testify.) The judges should be related neither to each other nor to the witnesses nor to the litigants.

If one of the judges on the beth din is disqualified because he is either a relative or a sinner, then the entire proceeding is a nullity and a new case must be started. If a litigant is aware of the fact that the opposing litigant is related to one or more of the judges and nevertheless continues in the litigation, then the disqualification is waived.[34]

---

33. Where sin as a disqualifier is concerned, judges are held to a stricter standard than witnesses. A judge is disqualified to judge a case if he is a sinner, even if the laws that he has violated are those promulgated by the Rabbis.

34. As has been noted, a litigant may waive the disqualification of the other litigant's being related to one or more of the judges. But there are two other types of kinship disqualifications—that of the judges being related to the witnesses or to each other. Is a waiver effective regarding these disqualifications? Regarding a judge who is related to one of the witnesses, the cause for alarm is not as great as it is when a judge (or judges) is related to the opposing litigant. Since a litigant may waive the disqualification based on the relationship between the judge and opposing litigant, he should certainly be able to waive the disqualification based on kinship between a judge and a witness. Regarding the disqualification based on two or more judges being related to each other, it seems that this too should be an easy matter to decide. However, there may be a flat prohibition in such a case. There is a dispute in *Sanhedrin* (p. 22a) about kinsmen testifying regarding the new moon. In a Mishnah, it is stated by R. Simeon that a father and son may testify regarding the sighting of the new moon so that the Sanhedrin may sanctify the new month based on their testimony. However, the sages prohibit father and son from testifying in the same case. The Talmud, explaining the Mishnah, states:

> Levi said, What is the reason of R. Simeon? Because it is written "And the Lord spoke unto Moses and Aaron in the Land of Egypt saying, This month shall be unto you the beginning of months," which implies that this testimony shall be valid when given by you [Moses and Aaron, who were brothers]. And the Sages? This verses implies that this evidence shall be entrusted to you [the leaders of the community, the Sanhedrin].

If Moses and Aaron, two great sages whose credibility was never questioned, could not be joined in witnessing and thus not in judging, it is clear that there could be no waiver, since the judicial system did not lend itself to waiver for this disqualification.

The fact that a litigant can waive the disqualification of a judge's being related to the other litigant is based upon the fact that a person may also abandon his moneys. The

A judge joining a beth din that contains a robber

A judge may not join a judicial panel with a person or persons whom he knows are robbers, wicked persons, or violators of the law.[35] The aforementioned prohibition applies even if the beth din will arrive at a just decision.[36] The prohibition also applies in an arbitration proceeding.

Personal qualities required of a judge

Ideally, each of the members of the beth din should possess the following seven characteristics:[37-39] (1) wisdom, (2) humility, (3) fear

---

beth din was not a disqualified beth din. It was only because one of the judges happened to be related to one of the litigants that an otherwise qualified beth din was disqualified in this case. Such temporary disqualification can be waived. But if two judges are related to each other, then the beth din is disqualified regardless of the identity of the litigants. This is a permanent disqualification and may not be waived. To hold otherwise would breach the judicial system. A litigant may waive his rights to have a judge related to the other litigant recuse himself. But the litigant may not be asked to permit two relatives to act as judges, once this does not involve his rights, but rather goes to the qualifications of the judicial system.

35. This law is to be compared with the law in Chapter 3, para. 4, of *Shulhan Aruch* where R. Karo states that a person should not join a judicial panel until he knows who the members are, lest he find them unworthy. It can be simply said that there are two distinct standards. In Chapter 3 there is a higher standard, which states that one should know specifically the identity of the judges he may be joining. In this chapter, however, the judge need not adhere to such a high standard and may join with others unless he knows that they are wicked or do not abide by the law. More complicated answers are given by many of the later commentators. This author believes that the judge should in the first instance attempt to adhere to a higher standard and know at the outset who the other judges of the beth din are. Are they judges with whom he would be proud to sit? If it is not possible to investigate the matter throughly, however, then it is sufficient if the judge knows that none of the other members of the beth din is a transgressor of the laws of the Torah.

36. What if the litigants agreed to have the wicked person serve on the beth din? May the other judges join in with him? While there is authority on both sides, it would seem that the better practice would be to avoid joining with the wicked judge and to explain the decision to the litigants. If the declining judge is not certain of his facts, he should refuse to serve but should not offer this explanation.

37. A judge of a beth din should possess seven characteristics:

1. Wisdom—he should have knowledge of the law and be able to apply it to the facts of the case.

of God, (4) disdain for ill-gotten money, (5) love for the truth; (6)
esteem of their fellow men; and (7) a good reputation.

A case in which a judge may derive benefits
from the decision of the beth din

A judge may not judge any case in which he or any close relative has
an interest in the outcome.[40-43] Cases involving taxes or any other

---

2. Humility—he should realize that there are greater scholars and more learned
judges than he.

3. Fear of God—he should realize that he is judging persons created in the image
of God and that he will eventually have to account for his actions to the
Supreme Judge.

4. Disdain of gain—he should not only be relatively unconcerned with his own
material wealth, but he should also in no manner or form think of the gain that
he would realize by rendering a judgment in favor of one of the litigants.

5. Love of truth—he should realize that in judging he is attempting to ascertain
the true facts, because the truth (which is probably unattainable) is the goal
of man.

6. The love of his fellow men—he should be such an exemplary person that his
decision will be respected by both litigants.

7. A good reputation—he should be known in the community as the ideal
person to adjudicate a lawsuit fairly and intelligently.

38. If the entire panel of judges does not collectively possess these characteristics
to at least the degree that the community believes appropriate, then all proceedings
before such a beth din are a nullity, for there was no beth din present.

39. The characteristics described are those required for the judges of the beth din.
Of course, the standards were more stringent for the judges of the Great Sanhedrin
and of the Lesser Sanhedrin. Rambam sets forth many intellectual criteria, including
the requirement that they have a knowledge of many secular disciplines so that they
can judge such cases. They also had to possess certain physical traits so that they
would inspire the respect of the persons appearing before them. In addition, they had
to be articulate and fluent in foreign languages so as not to have to rely on interpreters. They also had to be understanding and sympathetic.

40. A judge may not preside over any matter in which he stands to benefit from the
result. He may, however, in an appropriate case and prior to the commencement of
the trial, renounce any potential benefit that he may have realized from the result of
the trial.

41. That which has been said about the judge having an interest in the outcome of
the litigation also applies to any interest that a close relative of his has in the outcome.

42. Sometimes the entire beth din of a city is disqualified; such would be the case
if the result of the trial would benefit the city and thus also directly or indirectly
benefit the judges. An example of this would be where the city is one of the parties

monetary matters in which the city is one of the litigants may not be judged by a judge who resides in that city.[44]

If the city has made a decree,[45] or if there is a custom[46] in the city that the judges in the city adjudicate tax matters or other monetary matters in which the city is a litigant, their judgment is binding.

---

to the dispute, as where the title to a Torah scroll is being disputed by the city and an individual. A decision in favor of the individual might result in the judge's not being able to hear the reading of the Torah in the city synagogue, if that were the only Torah in the synagogue. In this situation, too, the judge could permanently renounce his membership in this synagogue and become a member of another synagogue. Similarly, the beth din of a city may not adjudicate tax disputes between the city and the citizens of that city, since they would be affected by the outcome of the dispute. If they were to find in favor of the individual, then their own tax rates would be raised to make up the deficit. However, if the tax was merely a temporary levy for a fixed sum, then the judges could pay the fixed sum and then adjudicate cases, since they would no longer be affected by the outcome of the trial.

43. The foundation of any judicial system is impartial administration of the law. Needless to say, if the judge or a close relative of his had the potential to directly or even indirectly benefit from the outcome of the litigation, the judge could not be impartial. The law goes even a step further and tells the judge that his impartiality is compromised if a group of which he is a part might benefit from the outcome of the litigation. This benefit need not be limited to direct financial gain; it could be an indirect benefit, such as a friend's obtaining a job or a contract as a result of the judgment. In any case in which the judge has even the slightest thought that he might be affected by the outcome of the judgment, he should immediately disqualify himself.

44. The judge may have a conflict of interest because if he decides in favor of the taxpayer and against the city, the city will have to find other means of raising the lost taxes and the judge may find his taxes increased as a result of his decision.

45. A city may enact a decree that the judges may adjudicate all disputes in the city, including disputes to which the city is a party.

46. The custom has grown up in most communities that the beth din of the city may adjudicate disputes between the city and individuals. This custom is binding on the inhabitants of the city.

Chapter 8

THE APPOINTMENT OF JUDGES

INTRODUCTION

This chapter continues the discussion that began in Chapter 7 and focused on the criteria of ineligibility. But there is more to appointing a judge than ensuring that he is not ineligible. He must meet higher criteria. This chapter deals with some of the qualities that raise the judge above the average person. It is also addressed directly to the judge and tells him of the great reward that flows from adhering to the standard of justice. In rendering just decisions, the judge becomes aligned with the Almighty in sustaining the universe.

TEXT

To appoint worthy judges

One who appoints a judge who is not worthy[1] or who is not wise in the knowledge of Torah[2] or who is ineligible to be a judge[3] trans-

---

1. A judge who has a bad reputation is certainly not worthy.
2. The *Midrash Rabbah* (Deuteronomy 5:6) gives the following account:

gresses the negative commandment "You shalt not respect persons in judgment" (Deuteronomy 1:17).

It is prohibited to appoint an ignorant person as a judge[4] on reliance that he will consult a wise man each time a case comes before him.[5] Cities that do not contain men who are wise and worthy and eligible should appoint the wisest among them to be judges.[6] Since the community has accepted them as judges, no one in the city may object to their judgments.[7] Every community may accept judges who

---

Rabbi Acha said that King Solomon's throne had six steps as it is written "There were six steps to the throne" (1 Kings 10:19). In the section of the Torah dealing with the appointment of judges there are six applicable verses, all found in Deuteronomy, end of Chapter 16 and beginning of Chapter 17: (1) "Thou shalt not wrest judgment." (2) "Thou shalt not respect persons." (3) "Neither shalt thou take a gift." (4) "Thou shalt not plant thee an Ashera" [which is taken to mean that an unfit judge should not be appointed]. (5) "Neither shalt thou set thee up a pillar" [which also refers to appointing an unfit judge]. (6) "Thou shalt not sacrifice to the Lord thy God an ox or a sheep wherein is a blemish" [this too deals with the judiciary because of the special punishment to be meted out by the judges]. A herald stood in front of King Solomon's throne, and as King Solomon ascended the first step to the throne to mete out justice, the herald pronounced the first verse "Thou shalt not wrest judgment." The same procedure was followed as he mounted each step, so that by the time he reached the throne of judging, all the verses dealing with the appointment of an unfit judge were recited.

If the wisest of all men needed a constant reminder of how important it is to judge wisely, how much more do ordinary men need such a reminder when they are called upon to judge?

3. Persons who are ineligible to judge include minors, those totally blind, and proselytes, as discussed in Chapter 7.

4. A community may not appoint an ignorant person as a permanent judge in reliance on the possibility that he might consult a scholar every time he has a difficult question to decide. He may neglect to consult, or he may not frame the question properly for the scholar.

5. If an ignorant person was appointed to judge a single trial and he did consult with a scholar before rendering a judgment, his judgment is valid.

6. The failure to appoint judges may result in the litigants availing themselves of the secular courts.

7. In communities where none of the inhabitants possess the qualifications to be judges, and if there are no visiting judges who will judge the cases (either because they will not come to the community or because they wish to be paid and the

do not meet the Torah standard for judges.

It is forbidden to appear before any judge who was appointed because of a money payment[8] or other consideration.[9] It is incumbent upon the inhabitants of such a community to ridicule him.

Conduct of the judges

While the judges are in the beth din,[10] they must sit in fear of the Almighty and in a serious manner.[11] It is forbidden to act lightheadedly or to sit and engage in idle talk in the beth din. The judge should see himself as if a sword were lying on his neck and as if purgatory were open beneath him.[12]

The judge should know whom he is judging,[13] and before Whom he will be required to give an accounting in the future if he perverts the cause of justice.

---

community cannot afford to pay them), the community, with the consent of the citizens, may appoint its best members to be the judges of the beth din.

8. A judge may not be appointed by any kind of a conspiracy or guile. He certainly may not be appointed by a direct or indirect bribe. Judgment by any judge so appointed is prohibited. If anything, such a judge should be reviled until the community appoints a fit judge.

9. There is, of course, Torah basis for the prohibition against appointing a judge through guile, deception, or direct bribe: "Gods of silver or gods of gold thou shalt not make unto you" (Exodus 20:20). But it can also be seen that if a judge believes that he can be appointed for a bribe, then the entire concept of bribery has no importance as a prohibition to be devoutly avoided. The next logical step for such a judge is to accept a bribe to render a decision in favor of the briber. The opening wedge that the judge himself drove is the breakdown of the judicial system.

10. A judge who delivers a judgment in perfect truth causes the Divine presence to dwell in Israel. A judge who does not deliver judgments in perfect truth causes the Divine presence to depart from the midst of Israel.

11. In days gone by, men wore their phylacteries and prayer shawls throughout the day. This was in keeping with the Divine command to wear phylacteries and fringes, which are at the corners of the prayer shawls. When men became busy with earning a living, this beautiful custom ceased to be widely practiced. In some yeshivoth, however, there are some students and teachers who still follow it. This author believes that the dignity of the beth din would be enhanced if the judges wore their prayer shawls and their phylacteries.

12. The Lord will take the life of a judge who wrongfully takes the possessions of one and gives them to another. For this reason a judge should always envision himself with a sword hanging over his head and purgatory gaping under him.

13. The judge is judging the children of God.

Any judge who does not render a truthful judgment causes the Divine presence to depart from the people Israel.[14] Every judge who intentionally[15] and wrongfully causes money to be taken from one litigant and to be given to the other litigant will in turn be judged by the Almighty and pay with his own life. Every judge who judges a truthful judgment even if only for one hour causes the Divine presence to dwell among the people Israel and is equivalent to perfecting the entire world.[16]

---

14. A judge should not ask himself why he needs all this trouble and responsibility. Scripture advises him: "He is with you in giving judgment" (2 Chronicles 19:6).

15. Although the codes do not mention the word *intentionally*, the drastic penalty noted—that of losing one's life—is probably intended only if the wrongful judgment was deliberate, reckless, or thoughtless.

16. Tur, in his opening statements to *Hoshen haMishpat*, cites a teaching that discusses two *Mishnayoth* in *Aboth*. In Chapter 1, Mishnah 2, there is the teaching of Simon the Just that the world rests upon three things: Torah, the sacrificial services in the Holy Temple, and acts of kindness. In that chapter in Mishnah 18, R. Simeon b. Gamliel is quoted as saying that the world rests upon three things: judgment, truth, and peace. If the world rests upon the three things mentioned by Simon the Just, why the necessity for the three things mentioned by R. Simeon b. Gamliel? The commentaries provide many answers, both long before Tur wrote in the fourteenth century c.e. and after Tur, down to this very day.

This author believes that with the destruction of the Holy Temple, may it be rebuilt speedily and in our days, none of the matters mentioned by Simon the Just can be fully achieved (see Beth Yosef on Tur). Thus mankind is relegated to the things that it can fulfill even before the Holy Temple is rebuilt. Truth takes the place of the Temple service, because visiting the Holy Temple, especially to offer a sacrifice, and even more especially to offer a sin sacrifice, was a moment of truth for the visitor. One may be able to fool one's fellow man, but one cannot fool the Knower of all of man's innermost thoughts.

Peace substitutes for acts of kindness. Living with one's neighbor in peace is the greatest act of loving kindness one can exhibit. It is to be noted in passing that "Truth" and "Peace" are also names for God.

As for judgment, it stands in the place of the proper fulfillment of the observance of the Torah. If a person deviates from the observance of the Divine commandments, whether those between man and man or those between man and God, it is the system of judgment which brings him back into line. Just as the other two, *Truth* and *Peace*, are names for God, so is *Judgment* His name. In fact, the Days of Awe contain many prayers in which there are references to judgment not only as an attribute of God but also as a name of God. *Judgment* is His name is connected with with the statement in the Talmud that if a judge delivers a judgment in perfect truth, if even for one hour, Scripture considers him a partner with the Lord in the creation of the world (see *Shabboth* 10a). He is a partner in sustaining the world by firming up one of the three pillars upon which it stands.

The earlier sages sought as much as possible to avoid appointment to any office, including that of being a judge.[17] They agreed to serve only if they were convinced that there was no one else capable of serving, and then only with much community pressure.[18]

A judge is forbidden to act in an arrogant manner with the community.[19] The judge should act with humility and restraint.[20,21] The judge should be patient with the troubles and burdens of the community.

Respect for the judge

It is incumbent upon the community to treat the judge with respect and honor. As soon as one is appointed a judge in the community, he should engage only in occupations that the community finds suitable

---

17. One should not pursue the office of judge.

18. However, if the community believes that the Sage is capable of the task, and if they want him to act as their judge, then in order to maintain the tradition of a competent judiciary selected by the community, the Sage should accept the community's wish.

19. Every person appointed to a position of authority in a community should realize that all of his actions should be for the sake of Heaven. This is true for no one more than for the judge, because he is responsible for meting out justice.

20. The function of the judicial system is to settle monetary disputes among individuals and between individuals and the community. In so doing, the beth din stands in the place of Moses, who settled the disputes between the people. A judge must realize that he stands on this lofty level. The members of the community should treat him with the respect that befits the importance of his function. For the people to treat the judge with disrespect would be to show contempt for the entire system, which would turn the community lawless. All too often, however, judges remember the respect due to them but forget two equally important considerations. First, they must reciprocate the respect. Honor and respect flow in two directions. A person who would like to see it flow in his direction must ensure that it flows from him even more abundantly. Second, the person to be respected must warrant that respect. It is not enough that he holds an important position; he must fulfill the role of a model leader. The outstanding Jewish halachic leaders were always the most esteemed role models of the community.

21. A judge must not act in a disrespectful, haughty, or arrogant manner to those outside or inside the beth din. He should treat others with humility and respect, regardless of their station in life. To do otherwise would subject him to the admonition in the Book of Job (37:24): "Therefore if men fear him [the judge], he shall not see [among his sons] any wise of heart."

for a judge.[22] The judge should not act in an irreligious manner or become rude or drunk in public.

It is forbidden to slight the messenger of the beth din.[23,24] If a person vexes the messenger of the beth din, the messenger should report it back to the beth din so that they may take appropriate action to punish the offender.[25]

---

22. In both his personal life and his professional life, the judge must never behave in a manner that would cause others to disrespect him. Everything connected with him—his work, his leisure pursuits, his friends and associates—must be respectable. Optimally, the community will be able to support the judge of the beth din in a manner such that he will not have to seek other employment. Where this is not possible, the community should attempt to find employment for him that is in keeping with his capabilities and in keeping with the community's standards for a respectable position.

23. The judicial system is composed of the judges, the officers, and all other beth din personnel. Each deserves respect if the system is to function well. Like the judge, the messenger of the beth din must warrant the community's respect and must treat others with respect.

24. The messenger of the beth din is to be treated with respect when he is carrying out the assignments of the beth din. If a litigant behaves disrespectfully toward him, the messenger may tell the judges of the incident, and in reliance upon his testimony, they may inflict corporeal punishment upon the litigant. They may even inflict a more severe punishment, that of placing him under a ban.

25. In an extreme case, the messenger of the beth din is authorized to inflict corporeal punishment upon the offending litigant.

Chapter 9

THE PROHIBITION AGAINST TAKING BRIBES: HOW JUDGES MAY BE COMPENSATED

INTRODUCTION

In establishing a judicial system, the question arises of how to pay the judges who are the heart and soul of the judicial process. This chapter deals with this question. Also to be discussed is the related problem of some judges finding their own method of compensation—by accepting bribes or gifts. The latter problem stems from the fact that some litigants believe that there is no justice in the judicial system, and that the only way to obtain justice is to bribe a judge. Only when the judiciary is above reproach will the litigants have confidence that justice will prevail. The entire code of law is a nullity unless the substantive rights of the litigants can be honestly enforced.

TEXT

Prohibition against taking bribes

It is exceedingly, exceedingly[1] prohibited for a judge[2] to take a bribe.[3]

---

1. All the codes double the term *exceedingly* in this instance and also in two other instances regarding prohibited conduct—that of exacting usury from a borrower and that of engaging in licentious behavior. In all these instances greed or lust may be overwhelming; hence the double exhortation against such behavior.
2. The prohibition against taking a bribe applies to all public officials.

The judge may not take a bribe even to decide the case truthfully. The judge may not take equal bribes from both parties. The judge must not accept a gift from either side after the trial.

A judge who has taken a bribe must return it whether or not he has already decided the case. The better practice is to return the bribe even if the bribe-giver has not yet demanded its return. The bribe should be returned even if it was given by the winner of the case who should rightfully have won the case without giving a bribe. The bribe must in all events be returned to the briber if he demands it.[4]

It is prohibited to give a bribe to a judge[5,6] The prohibition against giving and receiving a bribe does not apply only to money or things that have monetary value; it applies equally to a bribe of words,[7] such as giving a judge a compliment. A loan to a judge may constitute a bribe.[8]

---

3. The prohibition against taking a bribe appears in the verse "Thou shalt take no gift" (Exodus 23:8). This is a much stricter and more easily enforced standard than is the usual standard in those systems of law that prohibit only a bribe defined as a thing of value intended to influence official action. A gift, whether so intended or not, is prohibited. This verse prohibits the taking of a bribe even if the judge would have decided the case according to true legal principles and in favor of the party who should rightfully win the case. The prohibition against finding in favor of the wrong party is already stated in the verse "Thou shalt not wrest judgment" (Deuteronomy 16:19).

4. The briber may sue the bribe-taker for return of the bribe unless the briber has forgiven the amount of the bribe.

5. The prohibition also applies to bribing a non-Jewish judge of the secular courts. The reason for this is that the Gentiles are commanded by halachah to set up a judicial system. This is one of the seven Noahide laws which the Torah requires all Gentiles to observe. The other six commandments given to all Gentiles are those against (1) idolatry, (2) blasphemy, (3) adultery, (4) murder, (5) robbery, and (6) eating a limb torn from a live animal.

6. Whoever gives a bribe to a judge contravenes the negative commandment "Nor put a stumbling block before the blind" (Leviticus 19:14).

7. Rambam, in *Laws of Sanhedrin,* Chapter 23, para. 3, states: "Not only may a judge not receive a bribe of money, he may not be given a bribe of words. A judge was once crossing a river on a small boat when a person stretched out his hand and helped the judge to get ashore. When the judge found out that the man who helped him had a case before him, the judge disqualified himself."

8. The prohibition against borrowing from a litigant would seem from the codes to apply only to the situation in which the judge is borrowing from the litigant as an isolated event, and the judge has nothing to lend to the litigant, should the latter want to borrow from him. Although there seem to be exceptions in the codes and the

A gift given to a judge prior to the commencement of the litigation may constitute a bribe.[9]

Payment to the judge

The judge may not burden the community or the litigants with excessive fees to be paid to beth din functionaries.

A judge may not be paid by the litigants. If he is paid by the litigants, his judgment is void.[10] In extraordinary cases if both litigants ask a judge to decide their case and if he takes time from his paid occupation to do so, both litigants may equally pay to the judge the money he lost by not pursuing his actual occupation.[11]

In the situation of each litigant selecting a judge and the two judges then selecting a third judge, the better practice would be for each litigant to pay an equal fee to the beth din; then the panel would divide the fees as the beth din sees fit.

Where a beth din system is functioning, the ideal procedure is for the community to pay the judges from a fund budgeted for this purpose at the commencement of the fiscal year. The salaries of the judges and the other beth din functionaries should be determined by the seven members of the city council.[12] If necessary, a special tax should be levied by the community, with all of its members contributing equal amounts. If necessary, the community may levy fees on the litigants.

---

commentaries, the better practice might be for a judge to recuse himself from a case if he knows the litigant well enough to borrow things from him.

9. Although the codes and commentaries make exceptions, it seems that the better practice would be for a judge to recuse himself when he has recently received a gift from the litigant, even if it can be shown that the gift was not given in contemplation of the lawsuit.

10. Not only is the judgment for which he took payment void, but all his prior judgments are suspect, unless it can be shown that he did not receive payment for those lawsuits.

11. A judge may be reimbursed for his transportation to reach the place of trial.

12. In some communities the organization that sponsors the beth din instructs the litigants to pay the appointed judge. The better practice is to have the litigants pay the city or the organization that sponsors the beth din and have them pay the judges. The establishment of a functioning beth din system supported by tax revenues, as is the practice in the Rabbinic beth din in the State of Israel today, would alleviate many of the problems.

Chapter 10

THE JUDGE SHOULD
BE DELIBERATE
IN JUDGMENT

INTRODUCTION

The focus of Chapter 9 was the admonition to the judge not to take a bribe nor to be paid by the litigants. This chapter further admonishes the judge to avoid rendering hasty decisions. Rather, the judge should be deliberate, giving each case the consideration it deserves.

TEXT

The judge should be deliberate in judgment

The judge should be deliberate in arriving at his decision.[1] He should think the matter through thoroughly and should render his decision

---

1. This rule of law is based on a piece of advice given in the tractate of the Mishnah known as the *Ethics of the Fathers (Aboth)*. The opening Mishnah discusses the handing down of the halachic tradition from Mount Sinai. Thereafter, the first substantive statement is that a judge should be deliberate in judgment. The first Mishnah states that: Moses received the Torah (both the written Torah and the oral Torah) from Sinai and transmitted it to Joshua, and Joshua to the Elders, and the Elders to the Prophets, and the Prophets to the men of the Great Assembly. They said three things: (1) be deliberate in judgment; (2) raise up many disciples; and (3) make a fence around the Torah.

only when it is perfectly clear to him. He should not act with undue haste, and he should try to avoid giving a decision immediately at the conclusion of the trial.[2] He also should not unduly delay the rendering of his decision.[3]

If a judge is uncertain on a point of law, he should not rely on expert advice that he might once have sought for a similar case; instead, he should once again seek expert advice.

Small cases should be given the same consideration as large cases

In the eyes of a judge, a lawsuit for a *perutah*[4] should be as important as a case for a hundred *maneh*.[5]

---

2. The judge should not try to show off his erudition and intellectual capacity by making a hasty decision. The litigants will inevitably suffer from such haste.

3. The litigants come to the beth din so that the plaintiff can have a quick adjudication of his claim. A long delay will frustrate the purpose of bringing the lawsuit. It also engenders disrespect for the judicial system if justice is continually delayed.

4. A case for a *perutah* is as important to the poor person as the case for the *maneh* is for a rich person. The judicial system should be available to all, regardless of financial status. In Chapter 6 it is stated that the smallest amount for which the beth din's jurisdiction will be invoked is the *perutah*.

5. A *maneh* is worth 19,200 *perutahs*.

Chapter 11

COMMENCEMENT
OF A LAWSUIT:
PLEADINGS

INTRODUCTION

In this chapter, an effort will be made to combine the old procedures with a few suggestions for some later procedures. Three types of beth din will be considered: (1) the established beth din, as suggested in Chapter 1; (2) the beth din sponsored by a rabbinic organization, which is presently used in a few disputes; and (3) the practice whereby both parties select a judge and the two judges so selected select the third judge, as described in Chapter 13.

An innovative feature that is introduced in this chapter is the concept of a default judgment. Such a procedure does not seem to be considered in halachah, although it has been discussed in various commentaries.

As noted Chapters 11 and 26, if the defendant fails to appear after being served with a summons, the beth din has two options. It may place the defendant under a ban and/or it may under certain conditions permit the plaintiff to pursue a remedy in the secular courts. (Under ordinary circumstances, invocation of the jurisdiction of the secular courts is prohibited. See Chapter 26.)

In Chapter 13, para. 6, the *Shulhan Aruch, Hoshen haMishpat* states: "... it is required that the litigants be present before the beth din." In Chapter 18, para. 6, it states: "The beth din may render its decision in monetary matters in the absence of the litigants." These two laws seem to contradict each other; the former requires the presence of the litigants, while the latter permits the rendering of the decision in their absence. The great classical commentaries on *Shulhan Aruch, Hoshen haMishpat, Sma*[1] and *Schach*,[2] hold that the latter law merely permits the rendering of a decision in the absence of the litigants after they have already appeared in beth din and presented their pleas and evidence. According to this view, there can be no default judgment based on the failure of the defendant to appear in response to a summons.

Bach,[3] in his commentary on *Tur Hoshen haMishpat*, states that the apparent contradiction in the statements need not be reconciled. Rather, he states that if the defendant is available he should be served with the summons, and this is the first-instance procedure. If, however, the defendant is beyond the reach of the beth din, then the law becomes post facto, and the case may be heard post facto by the beth din even if the defendant has not appeared. *Tummim*[4] cites *Bach* and agrees that in the first instance the defendant should be required to appear, but if he does not appear, then the case can proceed without him. *Kzoth*[5] cites the views of both *Sma* and *Bach* and concludes that *Bach's* view is preferable: Where it is not practical to serve the defendant, it is as if the law has entered the post facto stage, and the beth din may proceed to hear the case even if the defendant has not appeared.

Maharam Schick[6] had this question presented to him when a town had passed a decree permitting its beth din to render default judgments if the defendant failed to appear pursuant to a summons served upon him. Citing *Sma* and *Schach* on one side and the holdings

---

1. *Sefer Meiroth Ainayim*, by Rabbi Joshua Falk, who lived in Poland, 1555–1614. See comment 13 on Chapter 18, *Shulhan Aruch, Hoshen haMishpat*.

2. *Siphtai Cohen*, by Rabbi Shabtai Cohen, who lived in Vilna and Germany, 1622–1663. See comment 8 on Chapter 13, *Shulhan Aruch, Hoshen haMishpat*.

3. *Bayit Chadash*, by Rabbi Joel Sirkis, who lived in Poland, 1570–1641. See end of comments on *Tur Hoshen haMishpat*, Chapter 13.

4. *Tummim*, by Rabbi Jonathan Eybeschutz, who lived in Poland and Germany, 1690–1764. See comment 4 on Chapter 13, *Shulhan Aruch, Hoshen haMishpat*.

5. *Kezoth haChoshen*, by Rabbi Aryeh Leib Heller, who lived in Poland, 1745–1813. See comment 1 on Chapter 11, *Shulhan Aruch, Hoshen haMishpat*.

6. Responsum of Rabbi Moses Schick, who lived in Hungary, 1807–1879. See *Hoshen haMishpat*, responsum 2.

of *Bach* and *Kezoth* on the other side, he adduces the various proofs that had been used to support the decree; he then concludes that all of these proofs are inadequate for the proposition that the beth din may render a default judgment. He concludes, however, that default judgment may be permitted under the law as stated in Chapter 2—that is, under the exigency powers of the beth din. This was the first specific breakthrough in a particular decree permitting default judgments.

The beth din system in the State of Israel has the following rule:

Rule 92. If the plaintiff appeared and the defendant failed to appear, after being properly summoned, the beth din may, on the basis of the clarity of the complaint, decide in favor of the plaintiff in the absence of the defendant and render a judgment, or postpone the sitting of the beth din to another day.

The source given for this law is the holding of the *Kezoth*.

In view of the fact that *Bach, Tummim, Kezoth*, Maharam Schick, and the Israeli beth din permit this procedure, is what I have set forth here new? According to the statements of *Bach, Tummim*, and *Kezoth*, the procedure for a default judgment is only post facto or in cases that are treated as post facto; thus there are many cases to which default judgment is not applicable. The statement of Maharam Schick is also limited to those situations in which an exigency exists, and thus the beth din will always have to declare such an exigency before it can invoke the procedure. As for the rule of the beth din system in Israel, there may be a special reason for it. Under Israeli law the beth din is given exclusive jurisdiction over certain personal matters, including marriage and divorce. The remedy of granting the plaintiff permission to invoke the secular courts based on the defendant's nonappearance will not benefit the plaintiff in any way, since the secular courts do not have jurisdiction in those matters over which the beth din has exclusive jurisdiction; thus the secular courts will send the case back to the beth din, which had just given the plaintiff the right to sue in the secular court. Therefore, the case of the Israeli beth din may be unique because of the exclusive jurisdiction of the beth din in matters over which the secular courts have no jurisdiction.

Because of the foregoing, perhaps there should be a rule permitting the beth din to grant a default judgment. The rationale for this suggestion is based on Chapters 2 and 18, along with evidence from *Bach, Kezoth,* Maharam Schick, and the Israeli beth din system. There are also a few other factors that tend to point in the direction of permitting default judgment, none of which, taken by themselves, are necessarily conclusive, but when taken together and in combination with the statements of the aforementioned authorities may support this conclusion.

The law is that the beth din may not hear the pleas of the plaintiff or his witnesses unless the defendant is present in the beth din. As will be shown in Chapter 28, however, there are exceptions to this law. An exception may be made, for example, if the litigant is ill, if the witnesses are ill, if the witnesses are about to depart for a foreign country, or if the witnesses are in another city and the other litigant does not wish to go to that city to hear their testimony. Thus there are procedural exceptions even in situations that seem to be ironclad.

As noted in Chapter 124, there are also exceptions that permit a sage or a modest woman to have his or her pleadings taken by deposition. In Chapter 106 it is stated that an authenticated instrument of debt may be enforced even in the absence of the debtor being sued. In Chapter 13 it is stated that a potential litigant may state his case to the person whom he wants as one of his judges, even though it is not permissible to discuss the case with a judge before the case starts because a judge may only hear the pleas of one of the litigants in the presence of the other litigant. In Chapter 46 it is stated that a creditor may have his note of indebtedness authenticated even if the debtor is not present. Rabbi Yehiel Epstein[7] states that if the defendant does not appear at the beth din in response to a summons, the beth din may grant permission for the plaintiff to invoke the jurisdiction of the Gentile courts. Before doing so, however, the plaintiff would have to prove to the beth din that he had a *prima facie* case. He could do this by documentation or, if that was not possible, by producing proof and witnesses to the beth din. Thus this is another instance in which the beth din will hear a plaintiff's case without the defendant's ever having appeared. (The difference is that if a default judgment were available, the beth din could grant judgment on the

---

7. *Aruch haShulhan, Hoshen haMishpat,* by Rabbi Yehiel Epstein, who lived in Russia, 1829–1908. See Chapter 26, para. 2.

basis of the *prima facie* showing, without having to send the litigants to the Gentile courts.)

Clearly, then, the idea of instituting a policy permitting default judgment is consistent with the other exceptions. The ban imposed on the defendant often does not serve as an adequate deterrent. In addition, the plaintiff may be given permission to pursue a remedy in the secular courts. This policy presupposes that the judicial system is powerless to act and relegates its enforcement authority by turning the recalcitrant defendant over to secular authorities (which is exactly where a defendant who would defy the summons of a beth din might want to be). Most important, it presupposes a system that can function only in a secular society that has secular courts with power over defendants. The halachic judicial system is designed for a functioning Jewish society in which the reign of halachah is complete and there is no necessity for a secular court system. Thus the threat of being sent to the secular courts is not significant in the ideal halachic system. For these reasons, the entire concept of default judgment should be examined to determine whether it should be made available to a beth din.

Some may argue that if the defendant does not care about being placed under a ban, he will not be concerned about a default judgment. However, many people are much more concerned about their reputations in commerce than their spiritual reputations. Moreover, the concept of default judgment would be part of a judicial system wherein the beth din would be a functioning body in a society in which it would be able to enforce its judgments and decrees.

Another topic discussed in this chapter is whether a summons must be accompanied by a written complaint or at least by a statement of facts upon which the plaintiff bases his allegation that he is entitled to a judgment against the defendant. In Chapter 13 of *Shulhan Aruch, Hoshen haMishpat* it is stated: "A person may not be compelled to reduce his pleas to writing. A judge should not receive the pleas in writing but should rather hear the pleas orally and then order the stenographer to reduce them to writing, if both litigants agree to this, and both pay the stenographer's fees." The glosses add: "However, both litigants may agree to present their pleas in writing, and whatever they set down in writing they cannot thereafter retract."[8] As is clear

---

8. Several reasons are given for not reducing pleas to writing: (1) The other party

from the accompanying note, there are several reasons that the parties might object to reducing their pleas to writing. One of the main reasons is that the judges must hear the pleas orally and not from a written statement. This rule can be overcome by the opening statements which are made at the commencement of the trial. *Maznai'im Lamishpat*[9] states that if the custom of the community beth din is to reduce the pleas to writing, then the custom should be followed, and the prohibition in the *Shulhan Aruch* based on a Mishnah in *Baba Bathra* 167b is applicable only if it is not customary to reduce the pleas to writing.

Another reason that is sometimes offered for objecting to reducing the pleas to writing is that the party may not want to pay the scribe's fee. It is suggested here that an indigent person may apply to the beth din for financial assistance. Rabbi Mordechai Yaffe, in his *Eer Shushan*, Chapter 13, para. 3,[10] writes that the judges may instruct the stenographer to reduce the pleas to writing after they have been stated in beth din. Also, Rabbi Yehiel Epstein, in his *Aruch haShulhan, Hoshen haMishpat*, Chapter 13, para. 8,[11] states that after hearing the pleas orally, the judges may reduce the pleas to writing in order to stimulate

---

may then falsify his pleas in response to the other party's precise written pleas. (2) The written plea is not easily amended or explained if inimical to the claim of the party. (3) The judges must decide the case on the basis of testimony given in beth din, where the demeanor of the litigants can be observed.

These reasons do not seem to be of such importance that either party should be able to prevent the pleas from being placed in writing. There is no reason that each litigant should not have full knowledge of the pleas and defenses of the other party so that they can be responded to logically and precisely. The judges will, during the course of the trial, determine whether there has been any falsification. The parties should be bound by their pleas and should not be able to change them except in conformity with the rules outlined in Chapter 80. The rule that the judges must decide the case on the basis of the testimony presented in the beth din is not overridden by their receiving written pleas, since the litigant and his witnesses will still have to testify in beth din. In addition, the opening statements of the parties fulfill the role of the oral pleading in beth din. There is also strong authority that the requirement that the judges take into account only the oral testimony applies solely to witnesses and has no application to the testimony or pleas of the parties.

9. See Chapter 13, para. 5.

10. Rabbi Mordechai Yaffe (1536–1612) wrote a code following the style of Rabbi Yosef Karo's *Shulhan Aruch*.

11. Rabbi Yehiel Epstein (1829–1908) wrote a code/commentary following the order of Rabbi Yosef Karo's *Shulhan Aruch*.

their recollection. With this in mind, this chapter provides for written pleas in the procedure to be followed when a beth din is organized as described in Chapter 1. Alternate procedures wherein the litigants retain the option to plead orally are also provided. Of course, this presupposes that the defendant will not insist on knowing what the plaintiff's pleas will be before answering them, as stated in the following paragraph in reference to the procedure to be followed when a party desires to know the other party's pleas.

The following statement appears in Rabbi Yehiel Epstein's *Aruch haShulhan*, Chapter 11, para. 2: "The defendant may say to the plaintiff before the defendant goes to beth din, 'Tell me what is the basis of your lawsuit against me.' If the plaintiff responds that he will not disclose the claim to him until they arrive in beth din, the defendant may then respond...that he...will not go to beth din until the plaintiff tells him."

Based on Rabbi Epstein's statement, a section is included here whereby the defendant may make a demand for a bill of the particulars of the plaintiff's complaint.

TEXT

Commencement of the lawsuit

Procedure A

In a beth din system as described in Chapter 1, a lawsuit is started when the plaintiff files his complaint with the clerk of the beth din.[12] At that time, the plaintiff must pay the clerk whatever fees[13] are

---

12. There does not seem to be much authority on when a lawsuit is considered to have started. In Chapter 5 it was stated that a trial is deemed begun at a certain point in time, but nothing is said about when a lawsuit is deemed begun. There are times when it may make a difference, as when a landowner brings action to evict the current occupier of the land (see Chapter 140). Is it within three years from the time the occupier commenced to occupy the land? Since the commencement of the lawsuit in beth din is deemed to bring public attention to the facts stated in the plaintiff's complaint, the filing of the complaint will be deemed to be within the three-year period if begun within three years of the occupier's commencement to occupy.

13. Each beth din shall make provision for those litigants who are unable to pay all

required for the clerk to prepare a summons based on the complaint[14] and for the filing and service of the summons and complaint; the plaintiff must also pay any other fees designated by the beth din.[15]

A party who claims that he is indigent may apply to the beth din for financial assistance or to have the clerk of the beth din assist him without charge. If the plaintiff is unable to prepare his own complaint, the clerk of the beth din shall assist him in the preparation.

The summons is written in the name of the entire beth din and signed by the chief judge of the beth din or by all three judges.[16]

Procedure B

Where there is no community-appointed beth din, and if there is a beth din sponsored by a recognized rabbinic organization, the plaintiff will appear before an official of the organization to commence the lawsuit. The official, in the name of the rabbinic organization, sends a summons to the defendant to appear before its beth din.

Procedure C

Where there is neither a community-appointed beth din nor a recognized rabbinic organization, the plaintiff will usually avail himself of the procedures stated in Chapter 13. The judge selected by the plaintiff will send a summons to the defendant to commence the procedure of selecting the judges.

---

or part of the required fees. It would be in keeping with thousands of years of Jewish tradition for the halachah to be charitable to those who require it. On the other hand, there is a Mishnah in *Peah* that states in part: "And anyone who is not in need of taking and does take will not die before he is dependent on others."

14. This chapter has followed those systems of law that have the clerk of the beth din prepare the summons, since there will be uniformity throughout such systems. Of course, the beth din may provide that the plaintiff or his counsel prepare the summons, but this imposes a burden on those plaintiffs who wish to appear *pro se*.

15. See Chapter 9, where the judges and the beth din are admonished to refrain from imposing high fees on the litigants.

16. This is the traditional method of issuing a summons (see Chapter 11 of *Shulhan Aruch, Hoshen haMishpat*). Each beth din should have the authority to devise another way to have the summons signed, such as by a chief clerk.

Contents of the summons

Under procedure A, the summons will contain the names and addresses of the parties, the name of the beth din, and the name and address of the plaintiff's attorney, if any. The summons will also state the last day for the defendant to appear and the notification that if he does not appear in the action by such date, default judgment will be entered against him as demanded in the complaint. He should also be notified of all other sanctions, such as the potential to be placed under a ban.

Under procedure B, the notice will state the name, address, and telephone number of the rabbinic organization whose beth din has been called upon to try the lawsuit, the names of the parties, the nature of the plaintiff's claim, the date by which the beth din expects the defendant to respond to the summons, and the person at the beth din to be contacted by the defendant or his representative.

Under procedure C, the summons will state the names of the parties, the name, address, and telephone number of the judge selected by the plaintiff, the nature of the claim, and the last date by which the judge expects to hear from the defendant or from the judge he has selected.

Service of the summons

Under procedure A, the summons and the written complaint must be served personally on the defendant by the beth din officer.[17]

---

17. Regarding the summons, the rules of the Israeli beth din provide the following:

Rule 31. Every summons to a party shall be in writing except in those instances where these rules provide otherwise.

Rule 32.

(1) A written summons must contain the name and location of the beth din, the index number of the case, the names of the litigants, the nature of the case for which the summons is being served, the name and address of the the person summoned, and the date and hour when the party must appear.

(2) The summons must be sealed with the seal of the beth din and with the seal of the clerk and must bear the date on which it was written.

Rule 33. Each written summons shall be produced in two identical forms, one of which the beth din agent shall leave with the party summoned and the second of which shall be returned to the beth din when it is signed by the party summoned, and thereon the agent of the beth din shall certify by his signature that the summons was served and the time of service.

If the defendant cannot be served personally, then the beth din officer may leave the summons and complaint at the defendant's home with a person of suitable age and understanding, with the request that the person give the summons to the defendant when he returns home.[18]

If the defendant is deaf or mute, or incompetent, or a minor, then

---

Rule 34.

(1) The agent of the beth din shall deliver the summons to the person to be summoned in any place where he finds or meets him.

(2) If the person to be served refuses to accept the summons from the agent of the beth din, or if he accepts and refuses to sign, the agent shall endorse the refusal in writing on the copy that he returns to the beth din.

(3) If the agent of the beth din does not find the person to be summoned, he may leave the summons at the residence of the party to be summoned with an adult member of his family, or at his place of business with a person who is employed there, or with one of his neighbors; the person accepting the summons shall sign and endorse thereon his full name and his kinship or relationship to the person to be summoned and the time of delivery.

(4) In no event shall the agent of the beth din deliver the summons to the adversary of the person to be served.

Rule 35. If the litigant to be served does not reside in the vicinity of the beth din, the summons shall be sent to the beth din near the litigant's residence. If there is no beth din there, the summons shall be sent to the rabbi or to the public authorities of the locale, and the service shall be made by agent in conformity with Rule 34.

Rule 36. If it is impossible to serve the summons in one of the ways just stated, the beth din shall determine the method of service of the summons on the party; they may send it by registered mail with return receipt or publish it in the newspapers or use any other method that they deem appropriate.

Rule 37. Beth din shall not decide to summon the litigant by publication of the summons except upon a declaration by the person seeking the service of the summons that he does not know the whereabouts of the person to be served and that he unsuccessfully did all that he could do to locate him, including investigating and searching in places of records.

Rule 38. In all instances where the summons has not been personally served upon the litigant, the beth din may for good cause decide that attempted delivery of the summons was insufficient.

Rule 39. Notification of a part by beth din of the day of a session, which is endorsed on the record, is the equivalent of a written summons delivered to the party.

Rule 40. The delivery of a written claim, judgment, or all other writings designated for a party shall be carried out in the same manner as was previously described for the service of summons.

18. Some legal systems permit the service of a summons by mail, if the attempt at personal service fails. The concept of substituted service as stated in the halachah from time immemorial is certainly to be preferred.

the summons must be served to the defendant's guardian.[19] If no guardian has been appointed, then the plaintiff may avail himself of the procedure for such appointment as described in Chapter 290.

If the defendant is a partnership or corporation, a copy of the summons and complaint must be left with a partner, a general partner of a limited partnership, or an officer of the corporation. If such a person cannot be served, then the managing agent or general agent of the partnership or corporation may be served.

Under procedure B, the notice shall be sent by registered mail, with return receipt requested where available. The signing of the receipt by the defendant will signal the commencement of the lawsuit.

Under procedure C, the notice shall be sent by registered mail, with return receipt requested if available.

Regardless of the procedure followed, if the summons is personally served on a day or date prohibited for such service, as stated in Chapter 5, then the service is a nullity. If the summons is served by mail, and if the defendant advises the person delivering the notice that he cannot accept any mail on the day the summons was delivered because it is a day or date on which he may not sign for such mail, then the service shall not be deemed made until it is redelivered on a day or date when the defendant is able to sign for it.

Contents of the complaints

Under procedure A, the complaint and all other pleadings shall be phrased in plain, concise statements in separately numbered paragraphs and containing, as far as practicable, a single allegation.[20]

---

19. There are three types of legally disabled individuals who are often mentioned together in halachah: the *heresh*, the *shotah*, and the *katan*, the deaf-mute, the incompetent, and the minor, respectively. That which applies to one often applies to the other two.

20. Regarding the complaint, the rules of the Israeli beth din provide the following:

Rule 23. Every claim shall be presented by the delivery of a written complaint to the clerk of the beth din.

Rule 24. Each complaint shall include the following:

(1) The name of the beth din where the the claim is presented

(2) The full name of the plaintiff and his address, and the name and address of his counsel if he is so represented

(3) The full name of the defendant

The complaint shall set forth a plain, concise statement of the complaint showing that the plaintiff is entitled to relief and demanding the relief to which he deems himself entitled.[21]

Under procedures B and C, the complaint need consist only of a general statement of the allegations on which the plaintiff is basing his complaint. Similarly, the answer need set forth only the facts that serve as a denial of the complaint.

The plaintiff has the option to advise the person who sends out the

---

(4) The facts that constitute the basis of the claim

(5) The demand made by the plaintiff; if the demand is for the payment of a sum of money, he must specify the exact sum or approximately the sum if he is not able to exactly specify the sum at the time the complaint is presented

Rule 25. The plaintiff may include in one complaint several claims that arise from different and unrelated facts, but they shall each be stated separately.

Rule 26.

(1) The written complaint must be signed by the plaintiff or, if he does not know how to sign, with his fingerprint.

(2) If the complaint is signed by the counsel for the plaintiff, the counsel shall annex to the complaint a written authorization according to the rules.

Rule 27.

(1) The plaintiff shall present one copy of the written complaint for the beth din and also one copy for each defendant.

(2) A copy of the written complaint shall be delivered to each defendant together with the summons, in accordance with the rules relating to the service of the summons.

Rule 28. The clerk shall receive the written complaint together with the copies referred to in the preceding rule and note on the written complaint the date on which to it); similarly, the defendant may during the course of the proceedings bring a counterclaim against the plaintiff. to it); similarly, the defendant may during the course of the proceedings bring a counterclaim against the plaintiff.

Rule 29. In fixing dates for trials, the clerk shall set the dates in the order in which the complaints are received, unless written instructions to the contrary are given by the beth din.

Rule 30.

(1) During the course of the proceedings, the plaintiff may bring forth incidental claims (that is, claims that are connected to the main claim or are somehow related to it); similarly, the defendant may during the course of the proceedings bring a counterclaim against the plaintiff.

(2) If such claims are presented during a hearing, they need not be presented in writing; it is sufficient for them to be recorded in the transcript, unless the beth din directs otherwise.

(3) The beth din has the authority to decide that incidental claims or counterclaim may not be added to the main claim, but must give the reason for its decision.

summons not to include a description of the plaintiff's claim. In response to the defendant's inquiry, the judge will explain to the defendant that he will be advised of the complaint when he appears before the beth din. The defendant may at this point avail himself of the option to refuse to appear in beth din until he knows the nature of plaintiff's claim.

The pleadings shall be construed to do substantial justice.

Answer to the summons and complaint

Under procedure A, the defendant shall serve his answer within twenty days after the service of the summons and complaint. If the twentieth day is named in Chapter 5 as a day or date on which the beth din may not meet, then the answer must be served no later than the second business day thereafter. The answer shall be sent to the plaintiff or to the plaintiff's counsel if the plaintiff is so represented.

Under procedures B or C, the defendant shall answer the notice of the beth din or judge selected by the plaintiff within the time stated in the notice or within twenty days, whichever is later. If the twentieth day is named in Chapter 5 as a day or date on which the beth din may not meet, then the answer must be served no later than the second business day thereafter.

Contents of the answer

Under procedure A, the answer shall set forth every defense available, in law or in fact, to the claims of the plaintiff. It may also set forth any counterclaims or setoffs that the defendant has available. It may also set forth those matters that may be set up by motion according to Chapter 14. If the answer asserts a counterclaim against the plaintiff, the reply to the counterclaim must be served on the defendant or his counsel within twenty days after the answer has been served. If the twentieth day is named in Chapter 5 as a day or date on which the beth din may not meet, then the reply must be served no later than the second business day thereafter.

---

21. See Chapter 80 regarding the amending of pleadings.

Default by defendant

Under procedure A, if the defendant does not appear in beth din on the return date of the summons, then the beth din officer re-serves him, and if he still does not appear, he is served a third time.[22]

Under procedures B and C, if the defendant does not respond to the summons of the beth din or of the judge, then a second summons is sent to him, and if he still does not respond, then a third summons is sent to him.[23]

Under any of the procedures, if the defendant does not answer or appear after the the third summons is delivered or received by mail, then the beth din may, at the end of the last day to appear or thereafter,[24] upon application of the plaintiff, hold the defendant in contempt of the beth din.[25] As punishment, the defendant is placed under a ban until he purges himself of the contempt charge.[26] A defendant served by substituted service cannot be held in contempt of beth din for failing to appear.[27]

---

22. There used to be a distinction in the halachah between those situations in which the defendant resided in the same city as the beth din and those in which he was a nonresident. A resident would be held in contempt of the beth din if he did not appear after he was served the first time, whereas a nonresident had to be served three times before he could be held in contempt of the beth din for his failure to appear.

23. See note 22.

24. The authorities state that the plaintiff should not be held in contempt of beth din until the next day in order to give the defendant the advantage of an entire day to appear. As was explained in Chapter 5, the next day according to the halacha starts at sundown, and thus the beth din should be able to declare the defendant in contempt at sundown. It seems, however, that most authorities would have the beth din wait until the next morning to declare him in contempt of beth din.

25. The officer of the beth din is generally believed by the beth din, if he states that he served the defendant. He is also believed if he tells the beth din that the defendant acted contemptuously against him or against the beth din or both. In such event, the defendant may be held in contempt of the beth din even after the first service of the summons. Of course, if the defendant can prove to the beth din that he was not properly served with the summons, he will not be held in contempt.

26. See Chapter 1, where this subject is discussed. Despite the procedure, many persons were not affected by the fact that they were under a ban. Thus there must often be other methods of punishment for being in contempt of the beth din.

27. The person who actually serves the summons is not equal to the beth din officer with respect to the degree of credibility accorded to his statement that he served the defendant.

The beth din may give the plaintiff permission to pursue a remedy in a secular court, as stated in Chapter 26.

It seems to this author that the seven selectmen of the community should have the authority to issue a decree that if a defendant fails to appear in the beth din after being served three times with a summons, the beth din may enter a default judgment against him pursuant to an application by the plaintiff to award him such judgment for the relief that he sought in the complaint. The beth din should have the authority to award such judgment upon a *prima facie* showing that the plaintiff is entitled to the relief that he seeks or, if it shall so require, upon a full evidentiary hearing.

If the defendant is deaf or mute, or incompetent, or a minor, then the beth din must appoint a guardian for the defendant if one has not already been appointed. The guardian must be given notice of the hearing and must appear and explain why he has defaulted in answering the complaint.

All of the foregoing and any rules that the beth din may make for default judgments should apply equally in the event that the plaintiff fails to reply to a counterclaim asserted in the defendant's answer.

A default judgment may be set aside by the beth din for good cause shown within such time as the beth din may by rule prescribe.

Purging of contempt

The better practice seems to be that the defendant not be purged of the contempt charge and that the ban not be removed until the defendant appears in the beth din and is ready to proceed to trial.[28] His mere promise to appear should ordinarily not be sufficient to purge him of contempt for failing to appear in response to the summons.

In other situations of contempt of the beth din, the promise to abide by its terms may be sufficient to purge the defendant of contempt. Before it allows the defendant to be purged of the charge, the beth din

---

28. Although there are many people who are not affected by being held in contempt of beth din and being placed under a ban, there are many others who *are* affected by the ban. It may affect their religious lives, their social lives, and even their economic lives. They would therefore wish to be relieved of the ban and purged of its effects.

may impose costs on the defendant, including the costs to the plaintiff to compel the appearance of the defendant in beth din. If the plaintiff is successful, he will obtain all his costs. If the defendant wins the lawsuit and the beth din determines that the plaintiff's claim was frivolous, the plaintiff will not be awarded any costs. If the defendant wins the lawsuit but the beth din concludes that the plaintiff's lawsuit was not frivolous, it may award the plaintiff all or part of the costs incurred to bring the defendant to beth din.

If the defendant disputes the contempt charge, the plaintiff must prove the contempt before he will be awarded the costs of bringing the defendant to beth din. If the plaintiff cannot prove the defendant's contempt, the defendant is required to take an oath that he was not in contempt; he is then purged of the contempt charge without costs.

If the plaintiff had to invoke the secular courts, as provided in Chapter 26, then all his expenses are paid by the defendant. The same holds true if the plaintiff had to invoke the secular courts to enforce a judgment of the beth din.

Demand for a bill of particulars

Each beth din shall establish rules regarding the demanding of and the furnishing of bills of particulars. They may provide for a written demand upon the other party or for a demand made by motion. They may provide for the scope of the bill of particulars and for sanctions to be imposed if a party does not comply with the demand or order for the bill of particulars.

Chapter 12

ARBITRATION

INTRODUCTION

The laws described in this chapter are those of arbitration. The halachah as it appears in *Shulhan Aruch* deals almost exclusively with the obligation of the beth din to recommend arbitration as a method of settling a lawsuit that has already commenced. As commerce and industry have grown, so have the number of agreements between parties, or within industries, that contain arbitration clauses. The scope of this chapter has been expanded to include both situations.

Most arbitrations are not involved in the judicial process. The parties, either by prior agreement or when a dispute arises, may agree to arbitrate their dispute. They will follow either the arbitration procedure provided for in the arbitration agreement or the procedures described in Chapter 13, wherein each party selects one of the arbitrators, and the two arbitrators thus selected then select the third arbitrator. Many of the laws of this chapter are applicable even in arbitration agreements that never enter the judicial process. Especially so are the laws of *kinyan* that bind the parties to their agreement to arbitrate. (The word *kinyan* means "acquisition" and perhaps even "acquisition and ownership.") The laws of *kinyan* are more fully set forth in Chapters 195, 201, and 203 and are briefly described in this chapter insofar as they are applicable here.

There may also be recourse to the judicial system to enforce arbitration agreements or to prevent a party from proceeding in beth din because of an arbitration agreement. Finally, at the end of the arbitration process, there may be resort to the beth din to enforce the arbitration award.

Some of the advantages to arbitration are the speed and modest fees of the process. Also, if difficult questions arise the arbitrator can be an expert in the field, whereas judges may not be experts in the particular field involved in the dispute.

TEXT

Duty of beth din to recommend arbitration

Every beth din should have a panel of arbitrators available to arbitrate disputes. Such a panel may be part of the beth din and may consist of judges or nonjudges, or both. The beth din should also have available names of arbitrators, or organizations devoted to arbitration, to recommend to litigants who wish to arbitrate their disputes outside of the beth din system.

The judges of the beth din are duty bound, and it is a praiseworthy act on their part, to attempt to persuade the litigants to have their lawsuit settled by the rules of arbitration rather than by strictly legal principles.[1] If the parties agree to arbitration, the process may take place before an arbitrator or arbitrators who are part of any of the aforesaid classes of arbitrators. The parties may insist that the judge or beth din before whom the case was to have been tried be the arbitrator or arbitrators. The parties will usually avail themselves of the

---

1. There is a difference of opinion as to how much persuasion the judges must use so that the parties will submit their differences to arbitration. A great effort should be made when justice, and even more so when equity, demands that the matter be arbitrated because adherence to strict legal principles may deprive one of the parties of equitable treatment. For example, if the strict law would deny the plaintiff any recovery because he was not able to produce all the evidence required, and if the defendant is unjustly enriched by such a result, then the arbitration process should be strongly urged on the defendant.

procedure described in Chapter 13 for the selection of a beth din and will apply that procedure for the selection of the arbitrators.

Any party may make application to the beth din to stay all proceedings there because the parties have, by *kinyan*, bound themselves to arbitrate either the dispute in question or all disputes that may arise between them. Upon such application, the beth din will examine the alleged arbitration agreement, and if it finds that it is binding, will order the dispute to arbitration, and will set such terms as give full effect to the arbitration clause or agreement.

Any person may bring an action in the beth din to compel arbitration of a dispute on the grounds that the other party to the dispute has entered into a valid arbitration agreement by *kinyan*. If the beth din finds that such a valid arbitration agreement does in fact exist, it may issue an order directing the parties to arbitrate as set forth in the agreement or upon such terms as the beth din shall determine.

The admonition directed against judges to refrain from perverting justice also applies to arbitrators.[2]

The beth din may advocate arbitration at any time during the legal proceedings up until a verdict has been announced.[3] Once the judge or the beth din has announced its verdict, it may no longer suggest arbitration. However, a third party outside of the room of the beth din

---

2. The arbitration process does not permit the arbitrators to disregard legal principles; rather, it allows them to be somewhat flexible in trying to achieve that which is equitable. There is a mistaken belief held by many that arbitration is used to achieve a result that is midway between both claims. Thus, for example, if the plaintiff seeks $100 and the defendant admits $50, then the plaintiff will be awarded $75, the midpoint of the dispute. In fact, the award may sometimes turn out to be $75. More often, however, the award will be closer to the amount that would have been determined if the case had been decided along strictly legal grounds. It has even been suggested that the arbitrators may not deviate by more than a third from the sum that would have been decided upon if the case had been tried according to strict legal principles. In a case in which the parties agreed to arbitration in order to avoid the taking of an oath by one of the parties, the value to the party who did not take the oath may also be taken into account in determining the award. Even in an arbitration, if the pleas of the plaintiff or defendant are without any substance whatsoever, the result through arbitration would be the same as if the case were judged according to strict legal principles.

3. A case can still be arbitrated if a beth din is asked to arbitrate even after the decision is announced, since the beth din does not lose jurisdiction over the case by announcing its verdict.

may suggest arbitration even after a verdict has been announced.[4]

The beth din may compel arbitration if the necessity for one or both of the litigants to take an oath exists.[5] Even after the judges have announced their verdict, they may request that the winning party reduce the amount of the verdict.

The beth din may suggest arbitration even to orphans who have a strong legal position if the beth din believes that in the long run it will avoid problems.[6] In such situations the beth din may order that the arbitration award be adhered to by the orphans when they reach majority. If the administrator of the orphans' affairs wishes to submit to arbitration a dispute involving them, the better practice would be for him to obtain permission from the beth din.

In cases in which the beth din does not know how to decide a case according to strict legal principles, they may apply arbitration procedures.[7]

Authorities differ in their opinions about whether the judge or the beth din may compel one or both of the litigants to act in an equitable manner beyond the requirements of the strict law. Such action is known as *lifnim mishurath hadin*.[8] This author believes that the view that denies the judge or the beth din the right to compel a person to act *lifnim mishurath hadin* should be followed.[9]

---

4. A third party's suggesting arbitration while inside the beth din room might serve to embarrass the beth din, since they were not able to persuade the litigants to submit to arbitration. Also, the implication may be that the suggestion is being made with the tacit consent of the beth din judges, and at this stage of the proceedings the judges should no longer be espousing arbitration.

5. There are five types of oaths, as stated in Chapter 87: (1) an oath required by Torah law; (2) an oath instituted by the Sages of the Mishnah; (3) an oath instituted by the Sages of the Talmud (a *hesseth* oath); (4) an oath instituted by the Gaonim; and (5) an oath that accompanies another required oath. (See Chapter 87.)

6. The beth din may suggest arbitration for a case involving orphans only when it feels that the orphans will benefit thereby.

7. A beth din that does not know how to decide a case according to strict legal principles may use one of two methods to render its verdict. It may apply arbitration principles, or it may use its broad discretionary powers. This applies if the beth din is frustrated because of the actions of the defendant. However, if it is the plaintiff who is frustrating their attempts to reach a sound legal decision, then the beth din may dismiss his case. In all of these situations the beth din does not require the consent of the parties to arbitrate, but may do so on its own initiative.

8. See the author's article on *Lifnim Mishurath Hadin, Annual Volume of Young Israel Rabbis in Israel,* Vol. 2, Jerusalem (1988).

Binding oneself to arbitrate

The parties are not bound to proceed to arbitration[10] and/or to adhere to the arbitrated decision[11] unless they have bound themselves by a *kinyan*.[12] This applies whether the parties have agreed to arbitrate at

---

9. The authorities who discuss this law are of the opinion that it would be ideal for the litigants to act beyond the strict legal requirements and thus work out their differences by each making compromises to some extent. There is probably nothing wrong with the judge's *suggesting* such ideal conduct to the litigants, but to *require* the winning party to waive some of his rights based on equitable principles seems to exceed the power of the judges. Even those who would advocate giving the judges such power would limit it to those situations in which the winning party is wealthy and the losing party is poor, or in which the winning party is an important person who it would behoove to go beyond the requirements of the law. Similarly, if the winning party is a sage, it would set an example for others in acting *lifnim mishurath hadin*. (Of course, status has no bearing in determining who should win the case. We are speaking here of the time either before or after the trial when the judge may suggest acting beyond the strict requirements of the law. One of the facts to consider in attempting to impose such conduct on a party is the cost to him. If there is no cost or the cost is negligible, there may be reason for requiring such conduct.)

10. If either party wishes to withdraw from arbitration or to refuse to abide by the decision of the arbitrators because there was no *kinyan*, he must submit to the beth din to have the case judged there. If he threatens to go to the secular courts then the award of the arbitrators is not vacated, even without a *kinyan*.

11. If the arbitration is before all or even three of the seven elders of the city council, then their decision is binding even without a *kinyan*.

12. The laws of *kinyan* are fully discussed in Chapters 195, 201, and 203. Transfer of property from one owner to another may be carried out only by means of a legally binding *kinyan*. However, the term *kinyan* has come to apply to one particular means of acquisition—that whereby the acquirer hands over a handkerchief (or something similar) to the grantor and as soon as the grantor takes hold of the handkerchief, the acquisition is complete. For example, if the grantor is selling a book or a piece of realty to the acquirer, as soon as the purchaser hands the handkerchief to the seller, the book or land belongs to the purchaser, regardless of the purchase price. Of course, the seller would not complete the *kinyan* process unless he also simultaneously receives the agreed-upon consideration. In the arbitration process, the plaintiff, by accepting the defendant's handkerchief, binds himself to abide by the arbitrators' decision, even if it is for a lesser sum than he had been seeking. The plaintiff then hands his handkerchief to the defendant, who, by accepting it, binds himself to pay to the plaintiff the award determined by the arbitrators. Thus, by handing his handkerchief to the other, each party binds himself to the decision of the arbitrators. If the dispute is about personalty that each party claims is his, then when the defendant hands his handkerchief to the plaintiff, the plaintiff agrees to relinquish to the defendant whatever ownership or part ownership is agreed upon by the arbitrators. Likewise,

the urging of the beth din or by a prior agreement. If the dispute is regarding personalty, then the defendant agrees in the *kinyan* process that the personalty in dispute belongs to the plaintiff, and the plaintiff agrees to forgive whatever rights he may have to the personalty. Thus, regardless of the arbitrators' decision, the parties have already laid the legal groundwork for the effectiveness of the award. Ordinarily, forgiveness of an indebtedness does not require a *kinyan*.[13] (See Chapter 241.)

If the dispute is a monetary one, the defendant binds himself in the *kinyan* process to pay the amount specified by the arbitration decision of the beth din.[14]

A written agreement embodying other matters, such as a partnership agreement that contains a clause stating that the signatories agree to be bound by arbitration in the event of a dispute, is binding without a further *kinyan*.[15] This will be true only if the embodying agreement became binding by *kinyan*. Such agreement may or may not name the arbitrators. If it does not name them, then the general rules of the trade or the community are followed in naming arbitrators, or application may be made to the beth din to name the arbitrator or arbitrators.

If the parties have carried out the arbitrators' decision, or have so acted in reliance thereon that it will no longer be equitable to rescind

---

when the plaintiff hands his handkerchief to the the defendant, the defendant agrees to be bound by the decision of the arbitrators. Although there may not ordinarily be a *kinyan* unless the exact amount of the price is known, here, where neither party knows what the award will be, the *kinyan* is nonetheless binding.

13. This case of a party's forgiving part of a debt in the arbitration proceeding is different from the ordinary forgiveness of a debt. In the case of arbitration, the fear exists that the forgiving party may later claim that he really did not intend to forgive the debt or part of it but was talked into it by the arbitrators. This fear does not exist in the ordinary situation in which a person voluntarily forgives a debt. It has therefore been suggested that if the party forgives the debt after the decision of the arbitrators has been announced, the forgiveness is binding on the forgiving litigant even if there was no *kinyan* at the outset.

14. The defendant must be very explicit about what he binds himself to do. A mere statement that he will abide by the arbitrators' decision may not suffice. The better practice would be to say that he will pay whatever amount the arbitrators decide.

15. When the parties formed the partnership they had a *kinyan* to bind themselves as partners. See Chapter 176.

the decision, then the decision is binding even if there was no *kinyan* made.

The arbitration procedure

There should be a written submission to the arbitrators setting forth the positions of each side and, if possible, the submission shall frame the issues involved. The written submission to arbitrate must name the arbitrators; otherwise the beth din will name the arbitrators. This written submission does not take the place of the *kinyan*. The current practice in many communities is to have just a written submission. This author believes that there should always be a *kinyan* accepting the arbitration and the arbitrators.[16] The written submission can spell out many of the details of the arbitration. If the submission bound the parties to pay a penalty for failing to abide by the decision of the arbitrators, and if either party pays the penalty, he must still abide by the decision.[17] A *kinyan* or agreement to be bound by Gentile arbitrators is not binding on the parties, and either one may cancel the *kinyan*.

In an arbitration case, unlike a law case, the arbitrators may testify and still decide the case.[18] The arbitrator may conduct the arbitration hearings in an informal manner. The arbitrator is not bound by either procedural law or substantive law. The rules of evidence are also generally not applicable to arbitration proceedings. The parties have a right to be heard at the arbitration proceeding and to be represented by counsel.

An arbitrator may find a solution other than that requested by either of the parties. The arbitrators' decision must be unanimous. The usual practice is for the parties to waive this requirement and permit

16. Too many practices that were borrowed from the Gentiles under the guise of following the law of the land or following the law merchant have crept into the halachah and are now accepted. Since so much of commercial halachah is bound up with the concept of *kinyan*, the concept ought not be bypassed lightly.

17. If the submission states that the party may choose either the decision or the penalty, then if a litigant pays the penalty, he need not also pay the amount awarded.

18. The question of whether judges may also be witnesses in a case is discussed in Chapter 7.

a majority decision. Once the decision is announced to the litigants, it may not be amended by the arbitrators, since their jurisdiction is terminated once the decision is announced. Their jurisdiction is also terminated if they have rendered a written decision to the parties.

If the decision of the arbitrators does not specify a time for making the award, then it must be done immediately. If a time is specified for such an award, then all the rules as to time mentioned in Chapter 78 apply.

If one of the parties does not abide by the arbitration award, then the second party need not abide and may commence an action before beth din to have the award enforced as a judgment of the beth din.

Vacating the award

Either party may move in beth din to have an arbitration award set aside on any of the following grounds:

1. If either party submitted to arbitration because of threats, extortion, or duress, he may prove this fact to the beth din and the arbitration proceeding will be set aside on his evidence.
2. An arbitration award in favor of a defendant should not be enforced, if the defendant had a weak case and intimidated the plaintiff into submitting to arbitration.
3. If a party submitted to arbitration because he could not locate his witnesses or his evidence, and he thereafter locates them, the proceeding may be set aside. The author suggests that this rule be governed by the rules of Chapter 20.
4. If there was corruption, fraud, or misconduct in procuring the award, then the award is void.
5. If it can be shown that an arbitrator was partial to one side, then the proceeding can be set aside.[19]
6. If the beth din finds that the award is irrational, arbitrary, and capricious, then the award shall be void.

---

19. The fact that a majority of the impartial arbitrators agreed with the position of the partial arbitrator will not affect the right of the aggrieved party to have the arbitration proceeding set aside.

7. If the award is illusory in that it does not settle the controversy, then the award need not be honored.
8. If the award orders an illegal act to be carried out, then the award may be set aside.[20]
9. If an obvious mistake was made in calculation of figures or in the description of any person, item, or property referred to in the award, then the award may be set aside.

---

20. The illegal act may be any act that is prohibited by Torah or Rabbinic law. It may or may not be in the field of jurisprudence. An example would be to order a party to make the award on the Sabbath when such activity is prohibited.

Chapter 13

SELECTING JUDGES TO ADJUDICATE A DISPUTE

INTRODUCTION

This chapter focuses on those situations in which the parties participate in selecting the judges who will adjudicate their case. Even the beth din system described in Chapter 1 will have room for the procedure outlined in this chapter. This system is the one with which most people who have been involved with beth din litigation are familiar. It has been a true friend of all observant Jews through the ages. The system described in this chapter is applicable even in an organized beth din system. The beth din is obligated to recommend that the parties submit their differences to arbitration. This chapter describes how the parties can participate in the selection of the arbitrators. This chapter is also applicable in those situations in which an agreement, whether between individuals or between an industry and its workers, calls for disputes to be settled by arbitration. The possibilities are many. Of course, if a plaintiff or defendant demands to have his dispute adjudicated in the regularly appointed community beth din, then this chapter will not apply. Similarly, if the plaintiff and defendant agree on the judge or judges to adjudicate or arbitrate their dispute, then their agreement is binding and the procedure described in this chapter does not apply.

TEXT

Commencement of the procedure

The procedure begins with the plaintiff selecting a person who will act as a judge to adjudicate his dispute with the proposed defendant. Although the general rule is that the judges may not hear testimony from one of the litigants if the other litigant is not present, it has become the accepted practice to make an exception when each litigant appoints one of the judges.[1]

The judge selected by the plaintiff notifies the defendant in writing that he has been asked to adjudicate the dispute.[2] The defendant then has the option to agree to having the dispute judged or arbitrated by this judge; or, the defendant may appoint a judge, who then communicates with the judge appointed by the plaintiff.[3]

If the defendant appoints a judge, then the two judges so appointed appoint a third judge. In times gone by, the third judge did not require the approval of the parties, but the current practice is that the third judge should be approved by the parties. The parties cannot appoint a third judge without the approval of the two judges.[4] If the judge appointed by the defendant is related to the judge appointed by the plaintiff, they may not sit together on the beth din; then the plaintiff must appoint another judge.

---

1. See Chapter 28, where it is stated that the judges may not hear testimony unless the litigants are present in the beth din. The practice described in this chapter is considered an exception. There is really no method whereby the plaintiff can request the assistance of the person he wants to appoint as a judge without familiarizing him with the case. Similarly, the defendant, in appointing his judge, must tell him what the case is about before he will consent to act. Although some of the commentators state that this is an exception that developed gradually, this author believes that it is actually not an exception. The rules of Chapter 28 apply to a beth din or judge appointed by the community or trade. They also apply to direct testimony of the litigants or witnesses during the judicial proceeding.

2. See Chapter 11, where this procedure is briefly described.

3. If the defendant does not reply, there are certain demands that the plaintiff may make on the judge whom he has selected. As noted in Chapter 11, this may include the right to ask for a default judgment.

4. See Chapter 3.

If the two judges and the litigants cannot agree on the third judge, then the community procedure for appointing the third judge should be followed or the leaders of the community should appoint the third judge. If there is an established beth din, then the beth din will appoint the third judge. If there is no community procedure for appointing a third judge and the community leaders will not appoint a third judge, then the plaintiff may convene a beth din of three persons who will then summon the defendant to appear before them.

If the plaintiff appoints a judge who is disqualified to act, because of relationship *to* the plaintiff, the defendant's appointed judge should in writing so notify the plaintiff and unless the plaintiff disputes the fact, the judge he appointed is disqualified and the defendant is under no further obligation to appear.

If the defendant appoints a judge who is not qualified to act, then the plaintiff may convene a beth din of three judges, who will then summon the defendant to appear before them.

If either party wishes to disqualify the selected judge, then the party must prove his allegation with two other competent witnesses.[5]

As was stated in Chapter 9 the better practice is for the litigants to pay the judges' fees to the beth din and not directly to the judges. In those communities where the litigants do pay the judges directly, however, the fee must be paid whether the litigant wins or loses. If payment were to depend upon the result of the litigation, the judge would become an interested party in the trial's result.

Either of the litigants may insist that he will appoint two judges and the other litigant will appoint two judges, and the four so appointed will appoint a fifth judge.

---

5. Some authorities have suggested that the party alleging the disqualification must produce two independent witnesses to prove the disqualification of the other party's judge only if the trial has already started. Before the trial has started the party alleging the disqualification is not yet an interested party, and therefore he together with only one other witness should be able to disqualify the other's judge. These authorities would thus limit the rule stated to those situations in which the trial is in progress and is going badly for the person alleging the disqualification; he now becomes an interested party as regards discontinuation of the trial, and he therefore may not testify against the other's judge. It seems to this author that this distinction is not valid, since the litigant is always an interested party; therefore, two other witnesses should be required.

Binding oneself to the procedure

Either litigant may recant and appoint another judge, unless he has bound himself in one of three ways, after which he may no longer state that he does not want to be bound by the choice he has made, nor may he thereafter ask that additional judges be appointed to the beth din.[6]

The litigants may become bound by a written submission in which both sides name the judges they have selected. The cost of preparing this submission is borne equally by both parties.

The parties may become bound by performing a *kinyan* whereby they agree to be bound by the judges' decision and either pay that which the judges determine is due or forgive that amount which the judges decide is not due.[7] The parties also become bound once either party has commenced to plead before the judges.[8]

Function of the selected judges

During the trial or hearing, each judge may point out to the two other judges the strong points in the case of the party who selected him. It is a grave miscarriage of justice for a judge selected by one of the

---

6. Some authorities hold that the judges may add additional judges once the parties are bound. This author contends that the litigants should be consulted before that occurs in this type of procedure. This is unlike the case in which a community has an appointed beth din that may judge the parties even without their consent. Such a beth din is certainly free to add additional judges if they believe that such action will result in a more just decision. However, if the parties have deliberately selected the first two judges and not the first four judges, then they meant for the case to be decided by just three, not five judges.

7. The rules and method of *kinyan* are set forth in Chapters 12, 195, and 203.

8. Some authorities state that if one of the parties has begun his plea before the judges but the second litigant has not yet pled, then the second litigant may still recant on his choice of judge. It seems, however, that this puts the plaintiff at a distinct disadvantage. This author believes that the preferred view would be that if one of the litigants is bound, then the other litigant should also be bound. The rule has therefore been stated that both parties are bound as soon as one of the parties has begun his pleas before the judges.

litigants to falsify evidence or to use guile or other dubious methods to enhance the position of the party who appointed him.[9]

If the judge appointed by a litigant is convinced, after hearing the testimony and the evidence, that the other party is correct, then he must find for the other party.

If either party has selected a judge who may be called as a witness in favor of the other party, he should refuse to serve and should act as a witness when called. If the judge refuses to resign and if the other party refuses to appoint another judge, then the matter should be brought before the leaders of the community to decide if the judge can continue to serve in this case. There may be situations in which the lawyer appointed by one of the litigants is to be called as a witness by the other party. This discussion begins in Chapter 122.

Procedure to be followed in difficult cases

If the appointed judges believe that the case is too difficult for them to decide, they may request the advice of more learned authorities. However, the decision in the case must come from the original beth din and not from the consulted authority, even if the consulted authority is a well-known beth din.[10] (Consult footnote 11 for a discussion of those situations in which a beth din may decide to hear a case in the absence of one or more of the litigants and of how the procedure described in this chapter differs from the procedure described in other chapters.[11])

---

9. All of the admonitions and rewards promised to the judge who judges impartially and to the best of his ability come into play in this procedure. The judges are not the lawyers for the parties who appointed them. There is a natural inclination for each judge to draw the best possible inferences from the testimony and the evidence put forward by the party who appointed him. However, the judge may not dispense with his obligations to search for the truth in the case.

10. There are many reasons why the decision must be rendered by the original beth din and not by the authority consulted. Primary among them is that the oral testimony was given before the original beth din, so only they are able to judge the demeanor of the litigants and the witnesses during testimony. A more basic reason is that the ultimate responsibility for the decision rests with the original beth din, and all of the rules of Chapter 25 dealing with a mistake made by a beth din would not apply in a case in which the consulted authority has no privity with the litigants.

11. The law concerning the authority of the beth din or of a judge to try a case and/or to decide a case in the absence of either one or both of the litigants appears

in Chapters 11, 13, 14, and 19. (This in addition to the reference in Chapter 8, where there is mentioned the unlearned judge who seeks guidance from a learned person; this reference is actually an application of Chapter 13.) It is thus not a decision made in the absence of the litigants but a consulting procedure. There is also the procedure described by Rabbi Yehiel Epstein in his *Aruch haShulhan, Hosen haMishpat,* Chapter 26, para. 2, that if the defendant fails to appear in response to a summons, then the plaintiff would be given permission to invoke the jurisdiction of the Gentile courts. Before doing so, however, he would have to prove to the beth din that he had a *prima facie* case. Thus this is another instance of the beth din's hearing testimony in the absence of a party who has not appeared in the litigation. Of course, in this instance the beth din is granting not a judgment, but only permission to appear in the Gentile courts.

Chapter 11 introduces the concept of a default judgment. The defendant failed to appear in response to a summons. There, the jurisdiction of the beth din was invoked by the plaintiff, and the defendant flouts this jurisdiction. It is expedient for the administration of justice if the beth din is permitted to exercise its jurisdiction even if one of the parties is not present. The plaintiff's pleadings and his witnesses and evidence are heard in the absence of the defendant. The entire case, from the pleadings to the decision and judgment, is conducted in the defendant's absence.

In Chapter 13, a situation is discussed in which both of the parties are before the judge or the beth din, and the beth din is not able to decide the case without outside guidance from either a superior beth din or some great Sage or Sages. In this situation, the superior beth din or sage or sages reply to the beth din trying the case. The beth din trying the case then makes its decision, taking into account the advice it has been given. The superior beth din is not authorized to decide the case because the litigants have not appeared before it, and it may not judge a case unless the litigants confer such jurisdiction. This is certainly not like the situation described in Chapter 11, in which the jurisdiction of the beth din was properly invoked but one of the parties failed to appear. In this situation the superior beth din must abide by the general law that a beth din may not judge a case in which the parties have not appeared before it if neither party has invoked its jurisdiction. This is actually a consulting procedure.

In Chapter 14, once again a beth din or sage is asked to examine pleadings and evidence and to decide a case. Some of the great commentators on the *Shulhan Aruch, Hoshen haMishpat,* such as Yonathan Falk and Shabbtai Cohen, comment that this situation is exactly the same as the one that appears in Chapter 13. A reading of the text in *Shulhan Aruch* certainly supports such a contention, but it seems superfluous for Karo to have repeated in Chapter 14 the exact law that he stated in the previous chapter. Yechiel Epstein, in his *Aruch haShulhan* dealing with *Hoshen haMishpat,* states in Chapter 14, para. 6: "If the two litigants desire a beth din in another city and they do not desire to appear personally in that beth din, they send their pleas in writing ..." (literal translation from the Hebrew). This reading of Karo's meaning is also sustained by a reading of his text in the *Shulhan Aruch.* Thus there is procedure for a beth din to decide a case if the litigants are physically absent but have invoked the jurisdiction of the beth din and have consented to the beth din's deciding the case. This situation differs substantially from the ones in both Chapter 11 and Chapter 13.

In those situations in which the third judge was selected without consulting the parties, it is not necessary for the original beth din to consult the parties before looking to more learned authority for guidance on how to decide the case. If the third judge was selected with the consent of the parties, there are opinions that the beth din must consult with the parties before consulting other authorities, and there are opinions to the contrary. This author believes that the beth din does not have to consult with the parties.

In Chapter 13, the litigants did not invoke the jurisdiction of the second beth din and did not submit themselves to its jurisdiction, something which they did in the procedure stated in Chapter 14. In Chapter 11, the defendant did not appear at all before the beth din.

The law stated in Chapter 19 is that the beth din may announce its decision even if one or both of the parties are not present. That situation is different from the situations described in Chapters 11, 13, and 14. In Chapter 11, the defendant never submitted to the jurisdiction of the beth din. In Chapter 13, the litigants never submitted to the jurisdiction of the second beth din. In Chapter 14, the parties submitted to the jurisdiction of the beth din and consented to its reaching a decision in their controversy; although they were not physically present, they were before the beth din. In Chapter 19, the parties not only invoked the jurisdiction of the beth din, but they appeared before it and presented their pleadings, their evidence and their witnesses. After the actual trial was concluded, the judges retired to conduct their deliberations. When the judges returned to the beth din to announce their decision, one or both of the litigants were not present to hear it. Such a situation does not amount to trying a case in the absence of the litigants.

Chapter 14

TRIAL VENUE AND MOTION PRACTICE

INTRODUCTION

Two major topics are set forth in this chapter: trial venue and motion practice. The topic of trial venue is divided into three parts. The first part is the status of the law as it existed in post-Talmudic times—that is, a three-tiered beth din system consisting of the local beth din, the Beth Vaad, and the Beth Din Hagadol.[1]

---

1. Post-Talmudic Law
   A. Under post-Talmudic law there was a three-tiered beth din system regarding venue. (This three-tiered system is not to be confused with the three-tiered system of courts described in Chapter 1. In that chapter the three-tiered system referred to the composition and types of courts and their jurisdiction: the Great Sanhedrin, the Lesser Sanhedrin, and the beth din. In this chapter we are dealing only with the beth din. Even within this category there are different types of beth dins based on their degree of expertise.)
     1. There was the local beth din, composed of the judges of the community.
     2. There was a beth din that comprised reputed expert judges, known as a Beth Vaad, in major cities only.
     3. The most scholarly beth din in the Land of Israel was known as Beth Din Hagadol.
   B. The plaintiff had the option to commence his lawsuit in the local beth din, the Beth Vaad, or the Beth Din Hagadol.

Thereafter the chapter sets forth two types of systems. The first section introduces a beth din system such as the one proposed in Chapter 1; the second section states the current law as it appears in halachah literature based on *Shulhan Aruch* and the subsequent commentaries, responsa, and codes.

1. If the plaintiff selected the Beth Vaad or the Beth Din Hagadol as his venue, and if these were not located in his community, he had to first prove to the local beth din that he had a *prima facie* case before the defendant would be required to journey to the Beth Vaad or the Beth Din Hagadol for the trial.

The Beth Din Hagadol was acknowledged to be superior to the ordinary beth din and even to the Beth Vaad because of the quality of its judges. It was felt that if the facts of the case or the questions of law warranted it, the case should be heard by a superior beth din, either the Beth Vaad or the Beth Din Hagadol.

The danger always existed that a plaintiff would institute suit and demand that the case be heard in the Beth Vaad or the Beth Din Hagadol, which might be a great distance from the defendant's residence; thus the defendant might rather pay the plaintiff than go to the trouble of traveling to these distant courts. It was to prevent this type of extortion that the plaintiff had to first prove to the local beth din that he had a *prima facie* case. Unless he could prove this, he was not permitted to move the venue to the Beth Vaad or the Beth Din Hagadol.

There are a few authorities who hold that the plaintiff, in addition to showing a *prima facie* case, also had to prove to the local beth din that the case was so complicated that the local beth din could not handle it. However, most authorities did not make this a condition for moving the venue to the Beth Din Hagadol.

2. The plaintiff could not choose to go to the Beth Vaad or the Beth Din Hagadol if it could be shown that he was doing this for his personal convenience, as would be the case if, for example, it was known that he was going to be in that location independently of the lawsuit against the defendant.

C. The defendant did not have the option of selecting the venue for the trial. (There are some authorities who hold that if there was more than one beth din in a city, then the defendant could select which beth din in that city would try the case.)

1. The defendant could move the venue to either the Beth Vaad or the Beth Din Hagadol if he was able to show that the plaintiff would have gone there for some other reason.

2. There are some authorities who hold that the defendant always had the option of moving the venue to the Beth Din Hagadol. (The better view would seem to be that if the defendant was given the option of moving the trial to the Beth Din Hagadol, then he should be required to furnish an undertaking to abide by the decision of the Beth Din Hagadol.)

D. In those situations in which the burden of proof rested with neither party and thus both were equally obligated to prove their cases, neither party had the option of moving the trial to the Beth Vaad or the Beth Din Hagadol.

The discussion of venue in the first section presupposes a system of beth dins in each city and in each district. It also presupposes the concept of geographic jurisdiction and subject matter jurisdiction.

The third, fourth, and fifth sections introduce what is perhaps a new concept in halachah—motion practice in the beth din, the forerunner of which appears in Rabbi Yechiel Epstein's *Aruch haShulhan*.[2] He describes a procedure that is actually a motion made jointly by the parties for judgment on the pleadings. This procedure presumes a situation in which there is a dispute not about the facts, but about the legal consequences of the facts as alleged. This concept should be expanded to provide procedures for motions to dismiss and motions for summary judgment. Epstein's concept of a joint motion can be expanded to permit one party to make a motion before the beth din for the types of relief here described.

Shulhan Aruch includes in this chapter laws concerning circumstances under which a litigant may request that the beth din issue a written decision. I have included these laws in Chapter 19, which deals with the written decisions of the beth din.

I have intentionally omitted the subject of motions for judgment on the pleadings and the hearings held thereon, since the codes treat this as a substantive matter rather than a procedural matter; it is included in Chapters 75 through 88.

The rules of the Israeli Rabbinic beth din system include many of the matters discussed in this chapter.

TEXT

Venue where there is an organized beth din

All trials must take place in the beth din of the city (or district) where both the plaintiff and the defendant reside.[13] If both parties are from

---

2. *Aruch haShulchan*, Rabbi Yechiel Michel Epstein, Vol. 7, dealing with *Hoshen haMishpat*, Chapter 14, para. 6.

3. See Chapter 1 for the structure of the beth din that this author has proposed. It is to be composed of at least one beth din in every city. In those rural communities that are not large enough to sustain a beth din, a district beth din has been suggested. Similarly, each city should have a Review Beth Din. In those communities where it is not feasible to have a Review Beth Din, there would be a Review Beth Din for the district.

the same city, neither the plaintiff nor the defendant may demand that the trial take place in another city, even if the latter beth din is known to be superior in learning to the local beth din.

If a lawsuit is commenced in a city other than the one where both parties reside, the case will be remanded to the city where both parties reside. If either party believes that he would not receive a fair trial in the other party's city, he may make a motion for a change in venue.[4]

If the resident plaintiff serves a summons upon a nonresident defendant in the plaintiff's city, then the trial will be held there.

If the plaintiff is unable to serve the summons on the defendant in the plaintiff's city, then the plaintiff must initiate the summons in the defendant's city and the trial will be held there.[5-8] If the plaintiff finds that the defendant owns property in his city that may be attached in accordance with the rules stated in Chapter 73, then the plaintiff may obtain an attachment. He must then immediately notify the defendant, and the trial will be held in the plaintiff's city.[9] If the transaction began in the plaintiff's city, or if both parties resided in the plaintiff's city when the transaction began, then the trial will be held in the plaintiff's city.

---

4. For example, the nonavailability of witnesses and experts at the place where the action was commenced.

5. The defendant may waive the provision made for his benefit to have the venue in his city and insist that the trial take place in the plaintiff's city.

6. If the plaintiff is afraid to come to defendant's city, then the beth din in the plaintiff's city may, upon proper showing, request that the trial be held there. An example would be if the plaintiff is afraid of being arrested for a matter unrelated to the trial.

7. The trial is held in the defendant's city even if the plaintiff states that he would pay the expenses of the defendant's coming to the plaintiff's city. The burden of going to the plaintiff's beth din may be an equally great objection to the defendant.

8. Either party believes that he would not receive a fair trial in the other party's city. The plaintiff has available to him all of the remedies that a party who claims prejudice has available to disqualify the beth din from trying the case. For example, the judge had already heard the pleas from the defendant prior to the trial, which might preclude his being a judge in the matter, as stated in Chapter 17.

9. If the plaintiff finds in another city property of the defendant on which he is permitted to make a levy in compliance with the rules of Chapter 73, then the trial should be held in that city and not in the cities of plaintiff or defendant.

The foregoing rules do not apply in the following situations:

1. If a parent and his child are in litigation, then the trial is held in the parent's city even if the child is the plaintiff.[10,11]
2. If a Rabbi and his disciple are in litigation, then the trial is held in the Rabbi's city even if the disciple is the plaintiff.[12]
3. If either litigant is a very powerful or influential person in the city and the local judges fear him, then the trial is moved to a place where he is not feared.
4. If either litigant is highly respected by the members of the community, then the judges will decide in each case if there can be a fair trial or if the venue of the trial should be changed.

The parties may agree between themselves upon the venue for their trial. Unless the beth din that they have selected finds cogent reason not to try their case, their agreement should be followed. The parties may agree between themselves that instead of a trial they will jointly send their pleadings to a beth din or sage for decision, whether they are in that city or elsewhere.[13] The parties may agree between themselves that the case be tried according to the procedure detailed in Chapter 13, whereby each party selects one judge and those two judges select the third judge. The parties may agree between themselves that the case be tried by one or more persons whom they have selected.

---

10. The trial is held in the parent's city even if the law is more favorable to the parent there. Sometimes through local custom the law may favor a plaintiff or defendant.

11. The parent has to pay the expenses for the son to have the trial in the parent's city.

12. This applies only if the relationship between the Rabbi and his disciple is a special one. For example, it would apply if the disciple feels that the Rabbi was his greatest teacher and is the leader to whom he always turns for advice.

13. This sending of pleas to the Sage or the beth din is not related to a similar sending of pleas by the beth din to a Beth Din Hashuv or Sage when the local beth din is not sure of the law. (In the procedures suggested here, such questions would be presented to the Review Beth Din. See Chapter 13 and notes thereto.) In this chapter the decision should be made by the Beth Din Hashuv or the sage, while in Chapter 13 the decision should be made by the local beth din, taking into account the guidance presented to them by the sage or more learned beth din.

Current practice where
there is no organized beth din

Beth dins designated as Beth Vaad or Beth Din Hagadol no longer exist. In their place are ordinary beth dins and, in a few places, superior beth dins, sometimes designated *Beth Din Hashuv,* or "Superior in Knowledge Beth Din."[14] In most communities there is a great Sage who takes the place of the Beth Din Hashuv.

All trials must take place in the local beth din. If both parties are from the local city, then neither the plaintiff nor the defendant may demand that the trial take place before a Beth Din Hashuv or before the great Sage. If a lawsuit was commenced in a city other than that in which both parties reside, then the case will be remanded to the city in which both parties reside. If the beth din concludes that it is not equitable to send the parties back to their own city for trial, then it will retain jurisdiction over the case. If a resident plaintiff serves a summons upon a nonresident defendant in the plaintiff's city, then the trial will be held where the defendant is served.

If the plaintiff is unable to serve the summons on the defendant in the plaintiff's city, then the plaintiff must initiate the summons in the defendant's city and the trial will be held there.[15-18] If the plaintiff finds that the defendant owns property in his city that may be attached in accordance with the rules stated in Chapter 73, then the plaintiff may obtain an attachment. He must then immediately notify the

---

14. At the present time there is no beth din that is actually designated as a Beth Din Hashuv. Within certain communities there has evolved a recognition of who among the members is a sage and which beth din deserves to be recognized as a Beth Din Hashuv. This is usually based on the stature of the judges on that beth din or on the published works and decisions and acceptability by the halachic community. The sage is usually more readily accepted and recognized than a Beth Din Hashuv. All that has been said regarding requests for review and advice from a Beth Din Hashuv is more applicable to the recognized sage. The time has come for all Torah communities to organize their beth din systems to include a Review Beth Din to consider decisions of the local beth din, as is the practice in Israel's Rabbinic Beth Din system. (See Chapter 1 and Chapter 25.)

15. See note 5.

16. See note 6.

17. See note 7.

18. See note 8.

defendant, and the trial will be held in the plaintiff's city.[19] If the transaction began in the plaintiff's city, or if both parties resided in the plaintiff's city when the transaction began, then the trial will be held in the plaintiff's city. If the town of residence is small and does not have a beth din, then the trial will be held in the closest town that has a beth din.

The foregoing rules do not apply in the following special situations:

1. If a parent and his child are in litigation, then the trial is held in the parent's city[20] even if the child is the plaintiff.[21] Grandparents and older siblings are not part of this exception.
2. If a Rabbi and his disciple are in litigation, then the trial is held in the Rabbi's city even if the disciple is the plaintiff.[22] This exception does not apply to a Sage and an unlearned person who are in litigation against each other.
3. This exception does not apply to a husband and wife who are in litigation against each other.
4. If either litigant is a very powerful or influential person in the city and the local judges fear him, then the trial is moved to a place where he is not feared.
5. If either litigant is highly respected by the members of the community, then the judges will decide in each case if there can be a fair trial or if the venue for the trial should be changed.

The parties may agree between themselves upon the venue for their trial. Unless the beth din that they have selected finds cogent reason not to try their case, their agreement should be followed. The parties may agree between themselves that instead of a trial they will jointly send their pleadings to a beth din or sage for decision, whether they are in that city or elsewhere.[23] The parties may agree between themselves that the case be tried according to the procedure detailed in Chapter 13, whereby each party selects one judge and those two judges select the third judge. The parties may agree between themselves that the case be tried by one or more persons whom they have selected.

---

19. See note 9.
20. See note 10.
21. See note 11.
22. See note 12.
23. See note 13.

Motion Practice

A motion is an application to the judge or beth din for certain kinds of relief.[24] The motion should be made to the beth din or judge where the action is pending.[25] Each beth din, whether in a city or in a district, may designate a department for the determination of motions.[26] Alternatively, the beth din may decide that the judge who is handling a case should also decide all motions in that case.[27]

The motion papers should contain a notice of motion,[28] affidavits,[29] and any other documents or evidence necessary to support the requested relief.

Each beth din or judge should keep a calender of dates on which

---

24. A motion is ordinarily made after the litigation has commenced. It helps keep the litigation within certain parameters and enables the parties to receive justice according to halacha.

25. If a city has more than one beth din, then the beth din where the action is pending should decide the motion. The rules of venue have no application once the action has begun, unless the motion is a request for dismissal because the action was brought to the wrong beth din.

26. If one judge is assigned to just motion practice, he will be able to dispose of motions while leaving the other judges of the beth din available for trial work. This author has spoken to many judges in the secular courts, and they are almost equally divided on the issue of whether justice can be better administered by a specific motion department or by an individual judge who is in charge of the case from beginning to end.

27. See previous note.

28. The notice of motion should apprise the other party of the time and place where the motion will be heard and the relief sought. It should also list the documents annexed to the notice of motion so that if any papers were inadvertently omitted from the set of motion documents sent to the adversary or the beth din, the moving party will be notified that the papers were not annexed. If the moving party relies on a section in the *Hoshen haMishpat* or other code, such as Rambam, *Aruch haShulhan*, or any responsa, it should be so noted on the notice of motion. No papers may be submitted to the beth din unless they were served on the adversary as part of the motion papers. The motion papers (as well as the answering papers) may request that the adversary submit to the beth din papers that are in the possession of the adversary. A memorandum of halachah may also be submitted by any party wishing to do so. The beth din may require that a halachah memorandum be submitted.

29. The concept of affidavits is not widely familiar in halachah.

motions may be heard.[30] The motion should be made at least ten days before the return date thereof.[31] The motion is deemed made when the party to whom it is addressed receives the motion papers.[32] Motion papers must be delivered to the opposing counsel or to the opposing party if he is not represented by counsel. Delivery may be made personally or by mail, FAX, or any other method available.[33] If the motion papers are served at least fifteen days before the return date of the motion, the moving party may request answering papers at least five days before the return date so that he may reply. After the motion has been made, the other party may make a cross-motion, returnable on the same date.[34]

The original motion papers should be filed with the judge or the beth din according to the rules of the beth din so that it may be placed on the motion calendar for the return date. The original moving papers filed with the beth din must contain an affidavit stating that a copy was served on the other side, together with the date and method of service.

On the return date, the beth din or judge may require oral arguments on the motion. Each beth din and judge should formulate

---

30. The dates must comply with the rules stated in Chapter 5.

31. Adequate time should be allowed for the party receiving the motion papers to respond. The rules stated in Chapter 5 should be used as a guide. If a party receiving motion papers requires additional time in which to respond, either the parties may arrange an extension between themselves or the requesting party may make an application to the beth din for additional time. In the latter event the beth din will determine whether to grant his request, and if so, how much of an extension to grant.

32. In some legal systems a motion is deemed made when mailed. With the current state of the mail, it seems the better practice would be to deem the time for answering papers to be served to commence to run from the time the motion papers are received.

33. Modern methods of technology continually bring new methods of communication. The beth din's rules regarding the service of papers should take into consideration the fact that not everyone has all the newest equipment.

34. It is not required that the other party's motion be by cross-motion. The other party may make an independent motion following the same rules. The convenience of a cross-motion is that it ordinarily puts all matters that may be decided by motion before the beth din at one time; the judges may thus treat them together and obtain a better perspective of the entire case and the issues. If the other party makes an independent motion, an application may be made to the beth din to combine the return dates of both motions to the same date and to hear the motions at the same time.

rules specifying whether oral arguments will be required on the return date or whether the motion will be decided solely on the basis of the moving papers, answering papers, and reply papers, if any.

The beth din or judge who hears the motion should make a decision on the motion within thirty days after the return date.[35] The better practice is for the beth din to prepare its own order based on its decision on the motion and to mail a copy to each side.[36]

Motion to dismiss

A motion to dismiss may be brought by either party—by the defendant against the plaintiff's complaint, or by the plaintiff against the defendant's defenses or counterclaim. The motion to dismiss may be directed against the entire pleading or against only part of the pleading.[37] A motion to dismiss should be made during the time that the answering pleading could have been served. The party may, instead of moving on the grounds set forth in this chapter, include such grounds in his answer or reply.

A motion to dismiss may be made on the following grounds:

1. The beth din does not have jurisdiction over the subject matter of the complaint.[38]

---

35. It is rare that a judge can be compelled to hurry a decision. The word *should* has been used intentionally here instead of *is required*. There is very little that the party or his attorney can do to speed the process of justice without antagonizing the judge or the beth din. And try as they might, the judge or beth din will never forget the party who tried to rush him. There should be some review by the administrative judge of motions that have not been promptly disposed.

36. In many courts the attorneys draw up the orders, and sometimes the orders are not completely in accord with the judge's decision. This leads to the proposal of counter-orders, and the judge then has to decide anew which order to sign, sometimes long after he has decided the motion. Then there is also the delay in the judge's signing the submitted order. The best practice is for the judge or the beth din to annex the order to its decision.

37. For example, if a complaint contains several causes of action, the motion to dismiss may be directed either against the entire complaint or against one or a few of the several causes of action. By having even a few of the causes of action dismissed by motion, the defendant diminishes the amount of preparation needed for trial and his exposure at the trial.

38. In Chapter 1, matters that are not under the jurisdiction of the beth din are listed. If a plaintiff were to bring a complaint based on any of these matters, the defendant could move to dismiss the complaint under this section.

2. The beth din does not have jurisdiction over the defendant.[39]
3. The plaintiff lacks the capacity to sue.[40]
4. There is another action pending.[41]
5. There is a basis for an affirmative defense, such as payment,[42] release,[43] *res judicata*,[44] statute of limitations,[45] or disability of the moving party.[46]
6. The complaint fails to state a cause of action.[47]
7. The answer does not state a proper defense.

Summary judgment

The motion for summary judgment may be made at any time after the service of the answer.[48,49] The motion may be made in any action pending in the beth din.[50]

---

39. If the defendant is served outside the geographic area of the jurisdiction of the beth din, or if the summons was not properly served on the defendant, or if it was served on a day when service is not valid, there would be a lack of jurisdiction.

40. The prime examples in halachah of persons who do not have the capacity to sue are the *heresh, shotah,* and *katan,* the person who is deaf and mute, the imbecile, and the minor, respectively. The beth din must appoint a guardian to sue on their behalf.

41. This motion may be made if the parties are the same and the two causes of action are essentially the same.

42. Payment of indebtedness is discussed in Chapter 47.

43. Release from indebtedness is discussed in Chapter 66.

44. *Res judicata* is a defense that the case has already been decided.

45. There are certain situations in which a case may not be brought after a certain period of time. For example, a person who is known to have owned land that a second person is now occupying has only three years to bring an action to dispossess him or to protest against him. If the action is not started nor the protest made during this three-year period, the case will be dismissed (see Chapter 146).

46. See note 40.

47. The plaintiff may believe that the defendant has wronged him or owes him money. However, the facts may be such that there is no liability on the part of the defendant, assuming all the facts of the complaint to be true.

48. Summary judgment should not be granted unless the beth din feels very strongly that there is no triable issue of fact. Summary judgment may be divided into two parts. The beth din may consider that there is really no issue of fact and that judgment should be granted to the plaintiff. Or, the beth din may not be able to ascertain from the motion papers and accompanying memoranda the degree of damage suffered by the plaintiff. In such event, it may order an immediate trial concerning the amount of damages to be awarded to the plaintiff. An issue of fact may exist in the minds of the beth din, if the facts presented lend themselves to more than one logical inference.

49. The motion for counterclaim may be made at any time after the plaintiff has

The parties may offer any type of proof available to show that a triable issue of fact exists. They may offer pleas, affidavits, exhibits consisting of all types of evidence, documents, admissions, confessions, or whatever else a party believes will help his motion or defeat the other party's motion. The proof used must be admissible at a trial. If the proffered proof would not have been admissible at a trial, then it is not admissible for the motion for summary judgment.

The beth din may grant partial or complete summary judgment.

---

served his reply to the counterclaim contained in the answer.

50. Each beth din may exclude from the scope of the motion for summary judgment such matters that it believes should be tried.

Chapter 15

BETH DIN CALENDARS AND SUSPECTED FRAUDULENT CLAIMS

INTRODUCTION

In Chapter 15, the *Shulhan Aruch* joins two topics: (1) priority of trials and (2) the action to be taken by a judge if he suspects that the claims of either party are fraudulent. There is a definite connection between the two topics. As envisioned in halachah, the plaintiff would describe his complaint to the officer of the beth din, who would tell the judge, who would issue a summons. The beth din officer would serve the summons on the same day, and a trial was contemplated for that day. During this expedited procedure the judge would very quickly be able to ascertain whether the pleas were false. The procedure that has been suggested here for the beth din system does not lend itself to such quick disposal. That is not to say that it was not the best system for its day. And it may well be the best system for our day! But whether fortunately or unfortunately, society has become more complex, and the wheels of justice generally grind more slowly, although not necessarily more effectively. Thus the simple notion that the first case to appear in beth din on a given day should be the first case heard no longer holds true. Even under that system there was a prioritization of cases. The priorities stated in the *Shulhan Aruch* have been incorporated here, along with the subsequent commentaries, responsa, and codes.

119

Fraudulent pleas have been treated here as a post-trial motion for judgment. This may be appropriate when the judge or beth din know but cannot prove that the testimony or pleas of one side are unbelievable or contrived and fraudulent. Whether or not intellectually provable, the instinctive opinion of the experienced judge may tell him such treatment is called for.

TEXT

Calendar practice

Every beth din should set a calendar practice for itself that will meet its own needs.[1]

Each new case should be given a number.[2]

A calendar should be set for each day of the sitting of the beth din.[3]

---

1. When rules are established for prioritizing the cases to be heard by the beth din, the litigants will not feel that they are being shunted aside in favor of those who are more powerful or have more influence. The litigants' first contact with the beth din is on the day they arrive to have their case heard. If a litigant sees that another who arrived in the beth din room after he did is having his case tried first, he will feel uneasy about the entire beth din system of justice. If he realizes, however, that there is an established, objective list of priorities, he will be less resentful that his case is not being taken first. A good procedure would be for the clerk of the beth din to give each litigant (or his counsel if he is so represented) a list of the priorities when he first comes to the beth din. Such a list should also be posted in beth din.

2. The number assigned to the case will be used by the parties throughout the history of the case. It will enable the clerk of the beth din to establish the daily calendar, and it will allow an administrative judge to calculate the length of time that a case has been pending. The case number will also be used by the judges in granting or denying adjournments, and it will enable the clerk of the beth din to follow the paperwork. Most important, it will help establish priorities in the event that litigants complain that another case that arrived after theirs is being heard first. Rule 29 of the Israeli Beth Din states the following: "In setting the order of the cases, the clerk shall follow the principle that first in time is first in docket number; except if he receives other written instructions from the beth din."

3. A clerk of the beth din or the chief judge or administrative judge should, where possible, stagger the cases throughout the day and thus obviate the need for litigants and their counsel to sit around waiting for the prior case to terminate. It is also on the first call of the calendar for the day that those parties who seek an adjournment may make such application to the beth din. A better practice would be for the litigants and

Cases should be added to the calendar in accordance with the consecutive calendar numbers, which are issued by the clerk of the beth din when either party certifies to the clerk that the case is ready for trial.[4]

Each beth din may establish a list of cases that will be given priority for trial.[5] The following are some suggested priorities:

A matrimonial case in which there is hope of reconciling the parties[6]

A case involving a minor orphan[7]

A case involving a widow[8]

A case involving a sage or his wife[9]

---

their counsel to attempt to arrange adjournments before they come to the beth din, preferably several days in advance. If an adjournment cannot be agreed upon in advance, there should be an early calendar call for the application.

4. Where possible, the clerk of the beth din should advise the litigants' counsel (or the litigants themselves if they have no counsel) some time in advance that the case will appear on the calendar on a particular date.

5. The list is gleaned from various codes and commentaries. There is by no means agreement upon the items that have been included here, and certainly no agreement on the priorities.

6. Since successful reconciliation of matrimonial cases very often depends upon perfect timing—that is, upon approaching the husband and wife when both are in a receptive mood—such cases should receive priority. The priority would extend to all aspects of a matrimonial case, including child custody, alimony, and child support payments.

7. The priority would be the same if the minor's parents had abandoned him.

8. The Torah is replete with references to doing justice to the orphan and widow. One way to show consideration for them is to avoid their having to sit in a beth din waiting for their case to be heard.

9. There seems to be a wide divergence of opinion on the issue of whether the priority for Sages is applicable in this day and age. There was a time when Sages were involved in the study and teaching of Torah to the exclusion of all else. Thus, their spending time in the beth din waiting for their cases to be tried would be a tremendous waste of time that could be better spent in the study of Torah, which, of course, is the ultimate goal of all. The differences of opinion seem to rest on whether today's sages are of sufficiently high caliber that taking them away from their study would have such a negative impact on the community's knowledge of Torah. There is also some question about whether the required respect for the sage in granting him priority also extends to his wife and other relatives. In this author's opinion, the sage can set an example of true Torah living by waiving whatever priority might be granted to him and publicly stating that he will take his turn together with all other litigants.

A case involving a woman[10]

A short case before a lengthy case[11]

An uncomplicated case before a highly complicated case

A case involving a poor worker who is losing time from work and his wages[12]

A case of a person who is ill or aged and who should be allowed to return home as quickly as possible[13]

Every beth din shall set up procedures for pretrial conferences to attempt to settle either the case or the trial issues.

Suspected fraudulent cases

Sometimes a judge[14] or a beth din may feel that a complaint or a defense is fraudulent. They may not be able to point to any particular

---

There is no reason that the sage cannot bring a tome with him to the beth din and study there in a waiting area set aside for the study of Torah.

10. The reason for giving priority to a case involving a woman is that it is not proper to have a woman sitting for long periods in the beth din together with all the men who are waiting to have their cases tried.

11. The reason for having a short case tried first is that the beth din can show respect for the litigants by not forcing them to wait to have their relatively short cases tried while long cases are being heard. The same reasoning applies to the simple case's being tried before a complicated case. Often a long case is also a complicated case and a short case is a simple case.

12. In an ideal situation, the beth din would set up a department for poor persons with claims involving small amounts of money. A special department should also be set up for wage claims. If possible, these departments should hold sessions at times most convenient for workers in order to minimize their time lost from work.

13. Each beth din should be able to establish its own list of priorities according to the guidance provided by its own experience. A periodic examination of these priorities will show the community members that the beth din is making an effort to dispense justice with the convenience of the public in mind. Too often judges do that which suits their own convenience without giving much thought to the needs of the public. The entire thrust of Torah law is to help litigants obtain justice in a quick and dignified manner.

14. The most important thing that a judge must remember when he is judging cases is that he will someday have to give an accounting to the Judge of all mankind. Therefore, the judge should be very circumspect in wielding his judicial powers. When a judge faces a case in which he feels that a party or a witness or a document is not genuine, and there is no proof before him to corroborate his feeling, he should attempt to ferret out the truth with all the wisdom and ability he possesses. If he is still

witness or statement or plea that makes them feel that a fraud is being perpetrated, but their experience and great wisdom have convinced them of this.[15]

If it is the plaintiff or his case that is suspect, the judge or the beth din may, upon motion of the defendant, either dismiss the case with prejudice against the plaintiff from reinstituting suit on the case again, or if the judge or the beth din is not quite certain enough to dismiss the case, the judge or the beth din may recuse itself from hearing the case.[16]

If it is the defendant or his case or witnesses that are suspect, the judge or beth din should, upon motion of the plaintiff, render a judgment in favor of the plaintiff.[17]

The judge or the beth din should act in the same manner on all requests for adjournments and for additional time to produce evi-

---

not able to show any technical reason for his incredulity, he may still exercise his judicial authority and find for the party who on seemingly pure legal grounds should lose the case. Thus the mere fact that the judge is not able to technically exclude a witness whom he suspects is not telling the truth does not imply that he cannot exercise his judicial discretion and exclude such evidence and testimony from his mind when rendering his decision. This power should not be taken lightly and certainly should be used sparingly and only if the judge is absolutely convinced that he is doing the right thing. There are those authorities who hold that these powers given to the judge under this chapter should not be used at all nowadays, because our judges are not as learned as the judges of bygone days. However, this seems to contradict the rule of law that the judge can judge only in his own time and that the judge in his time takes the place of the greatest judge of bygone times.

15. The qualms that some authorities have with this is that the judge is permitted to disregard that which seems to be valid evidence and testimony and to decide the case based on his feeling certain that a fraud is being perpetrated. As was previously stated, however, only a judge who is truly God-fearing can avail himself of this power.

16. If the judge or the beth din recuse themselves from the trial, they may still state that in the event that the case is again brought, the new judge or new beth din should be aware of their reason for not completing the case.

17. If the judge feels that the defendant is perpetrating a fraud on the beth din, then the judge must find in favor of the plaintiff. In this situation the judge will not be serving justice if he recuses himself, since the only winner will be the fraudulent defendant. The judge should attempt as much as possible, through cross-examination and even by innuendo, to let the defendant know how he feels. Such action on the part of the judge may well lead to the defendant's admitting the truth of all or at least part of the plaintiff's claim.

dence or witnesses if they feel that the request is not made in good faith.[18]

Although the situations in which oaths are required in trials are limited, as explained in Chapter 87, the judge or the beth din may impose oaths upon the suspected party to compel him to tell the truth. The judges and the beth din should also avail themselves of strict cross-examination, which is usually reserved for capital crime cases.[19]

There are times when the judge may be convinced that the defendant did indeed rob or steal from the plaintiff, but sufficient proof is not produced at the trial. The judge may in such a case put the defendant under a ban so that no one may do business with him until he makes restitution to the plaintiff.[20] If the defendant in such a case is an unmarried woman, the men of the town may be advised not to marry her until she makes restitution to the plaintiff. If the defendant in such a case is an unmarried man, the women of the town may be advised not to marry him until he makes restitution to the plaintiff.

---

18. See Chapter 16 regarding extensions of time to plead.

19. The oath mentioned here is not the type of oath taken in other judicial systems, whereby a person who is about to testify swears that he will tell the truth. The oath mentioned here applies to the person (usually the defendant), who takes the oath and is found not to be liable. In some situations the plaintiff is required to take an oath, and if he does he wins the case. These rules are explained in Chapter 87. Jews in some countries have become so accustomed to the oath to tell the truth as it exists in the secular courts that they feel the need for it. In such a situation the beth din should consider this type of an oath if it believes that it will deter the perpetration of fraud on the beth din.

20. Once again it is necessary to stress that the judge must be thoroughly convinced of the rightness of his belief. He is taking a very grave responsibility upon himself in deciding a case against the weight of the evidence. In some situations it is best for the judge to recuse himself, since the judge who replaces him may be more successful in obtaining the truth.

Chapter 16

EXTENSION OF TIME TO PLEAD OR TO PRESENT EVIDENCE PRIORITIZATION OF CASES SUBPOENA FOR EVIDENCE

INTRODUCTION

Chapter 11 provides the rules for the forms of complaints under procedures A, B, and C, the forms of answers, and the time sequences for serving answers and replies. There, procedure A provides for a full written complaint, and procedures B and C provide for less than a full written complaint and even an oral complaint.

There may be times when a defendant requires additional time to answer a complaint or the plaintiff requires additional time to reply to a counterclaim. Or, a litigant may find himself in need of additional time to gather his witnesses or evidence after the trial has already commenced. The subject of time extensions is discussed in the first part of this chapter.

The second part of this chapter sets forth some of the rules of subpoenaing witnesses and evidence. Although the subpoenaing of witnesses appears in *Shulhan Aruch* in Chapter 28, both of these topics have been combined here.

TEXT

Extensions of time to plead

If the defendant requires additional time to plead, or if the plaintiff requires additional time to reply to a counterclaim, then the parties, or their counsel if they are so represented, may by written stipulation extend the time periods.[1]

If the parties are not able to submit a written stipulation, and if the defendant requires additional time to answer the complaint, he or his counsel[2] should apply to the beth din upon notice[3] to the plaintiff's counsel, or if he is not represented by counsel, to the plaintiff. The beth din should determine whether the defendant really requires the extension or is merely using the application to delay the case.[4]

If the plaintiff's cause of action is based on an instrument barring extensions of time to plead, the defendant should not be given an extension unless he claims that the written instrument is a forgery,[5] in which event the barring of extensions would not apply.[6]

The same procedures should be followed in requests made by the plaintiff to reply to the counterclaims of the defendant.

---

1. The written stipulation will serve to avoid any questions about whether an extension was granted, and if so, for how long. A written document is also more reliable for presentation to a beth din in the event that any questions arise as to the timeliness of an answer or a reply. This author also believes that if there is a written stipulation, then no formal kinyan will be required to effect that stipulation (see Chapter 195).

2. The rules for appointing representatives or counsel for the litigants is discussed in Chapters 122, 123, and 124.

3. In giving notice of the application, the defendant or his counsel should ascertain the time when the beth din will be sitting to hear the application. He should notify the plaintiff or his counsel that he will make an application at that time and the place where the beth din or one of its members designated to hear the application will be sitting. Alternatively, in the case of the litigants' selecting their own judges as described in Chapter 13, the judge selected by the litigant will probably inform him about the procedure to be used in seeking an extension of time.

4. The beth din is granted broad discretion in deciding matters of extension for either party. The members of the beth din should ensure that they are not being used by either litigant to delay or harass the other litigant, and they should determine that the extension is being sought in good faith. The granting or denial of an extension is ordinarily not the kind of matter that may be taken to a sage or a Review Beth Din.

5. Even if the plaintiff produces the witnesses who signed the instrument and they verify that the signatures are indeed theirs, since the defendant has raised the defense of forgery, the clause barring extensions of time would not apply.

6. There are many authorities who hold that when a claim is based on a written instrument, no extension beyond thirty days should ever be given. The reason is probably that if the parties have gone to the trouble and expense of preparing a written instrument, then it can be assumed that they wanted the instrument to speak for itself and be immediately enforceable.

Extensions of time during the trial

Motions may be made by either party during the trial for extensions of time. If the plaintiff believes that he is losing the case, he may request additional time to amend his complaint and/or to produce additional proof and additional witnesses. The defendant, if he believes that he is losing the case, or that he may win the case only if he takes an oath denying liability, may request additional time to amend his answer and/or to produce additional proof and additional witnesses.[7]

The beth din will ordinarily grant the party making the application a thirty-day extension.[8,9,10] The beth din may reduce this period if it feels that the pleas can be amended and/or the additional evidence and witnesses can be produced in a shorter period. The beth din may also grant a longer period of time if it feels that it is necessary. In granting extensions to one party, the beth din may, of course, grant appropriate extensions to the other party.

At the end of the extended period, the trial will resume and a judgment will be entered, whether or not the party making the application was able to produce the additional witnesses and evidence. If the defendant loses the case, he may still make application for additional time to produce witnesses or documents if he pays the

---

7. There are times when the defendant may take an oath, whether of biblical or Rabbinic origin, and obtain a judgment dismissing the defendant's complaint. (See Chapter 75.) In spite of this, the defendant may seek to win the case on the basis of witnesses and/or documents and thus avoid the necessity of taking any oath. It should be noted that many people are loathe to take oaths since they may unknowingly be violating the oath even when they have taken it in good faith. Some people would rather lose a case than take an oath, even when they are right.

8. The beth din does not actually have to believe that everything that the party says is true, since then it would find in that party's favor. The beth din has to believe only that there is a probability of the party's producing the evidence or witnesses.

9. The thirty days begins from the time when the evidence or witnesses were produced to the beth din. If that were not the case, then the defendant could wait a long period of time and then make his application for the thirty-day extension, which would ordinarily be granted, unless the beth din believes that the application is not made in good faith.

10. There is a general principle that when the beth din grants times for the performance of acts (to pay money to the plaintiff), it is for thirty days. Of course, the beth din has tremendous latitude and may grant extensions for any length of time or not grant any extension.

judgment awarded against him. However, if the defendant demonstrates to the beth din that the plaintiff will be unable to repay the moneys that the defendant is paying to him and that the defendant has a good chance of having the decision reversed and obtaining a judgment dismissing the complaint, then the beth din may order the money paid to itself. Otherwise, the defendant does not have the option of paying the money to the beth din pending his bringing additional witnesses and evidence.

If the beth din is about to find in the defendant's favor if he will take an oath denying liability, then the plaintiff may request an additional indefinite period in which to produce his witnesses and evidence. This application will be granted to the plaintiff only if the defendant is not prejudiced thereby. If the defendant can show any prejudice, such as a negative effect on his credit or reputation as a result of the lawsuit, then the plaintiff's application for the indefinite extension will not be granted. In such a case the plaintiff is entitled to one thirty-day extension.

Subpoenaing evidence

If a litigant does not know who has evidence that he requires or who may act as a witness on his behalf, he may apply to the beth din to proclaim a general ban[11] on all those who have evidence or testimony to aid his claim or defense.[12] The bans were usually proclaimed in the synagogue, or in any other place of general assembly, on Mondays and Thursdays. (The topic of bans is discussed in Chapter 71.) A ban

---

11. The general ban also applies to the other litigant and also to relatives or other persons who might be ineligible to testify. The ban is only to obtain evidence. Even the other party and relatives or others who are ineligible to testify may produce evidence to the party seeking it. Of course, the beth din will have to decide upon the admissibility of the evidence.

12. The beth din proclaims a ban in accordance with the provisions of Chapter 71. It is assumed that a person will not want to risk being placed under the ban by not coming forward with evidence or testimony. There is a rule of law that if a person knows testimony on behalf of a party and refuses to come forward to testify, then although he has no monetary liability to the party, he has liability to Heaven, and that obligation can be removed only if he makes financial restitution to the party on whose behalf he did not testify. The ban in this case is in the nature of a broad-based subpoena to all those who know of testimony or evidence to come forward.

may not be used to discover evidence in a criminal proceeding nor even in a civil suit if it will turn up criminal evidence.

Either party may demand of the other party or of a third party a specific document which he thinks may contain something to help his case. The following are other cases where documents may be demanded:

1. If the other party or the third party admits that he has such a document and that it contains something that may help the demanding party, a copy of such document will be provided to him and the beth din.

2. If the other party or the third party denies that he has such a document, the demanding party may ask the beth din to proclaim a ban against anyone having the document, if such ban has not theretofore been proclaimed. If the demanding party states that he is certain that the other party or the third party has such a document, then he may ask the beth din to impose an oath upon them to deny that they have the document. But if the demanding party cannot convince the beth din that the other party or the third party has the document, then the party need not take the oath.

3. (a) If the other party admits that he has the document but denies that it contains any material that would benefit the demanding party, then he must show the document to the beth din and they will decide whether it would be beneficial. (b) If a third party admits that he has the document but makes such a denial, then he need not show the document to the demanding party unless he is ordered to do so on application to the beth din.

4. If the other party or a third party admits having the document but denies knowing whether it will help the demanding party, then the document must be shown to the beth din.

If either party states in his pleadings that he will introduce a document in evidence, and the other party alleges that it is a forgery, then the latter may obtain a copy prior to the trial. If the other party does not allege that the document is a forgery but alleges that there are defenses against the document, there are those who say that the other party may not obtain a copy prior to the trial.[13]

---

13. The theory of those who would deny the turning over of a copy of the document to the other side is that given time, the other party may devise some

Subpoenaing witnesses

If the party knows the name of a witness who refuses to come to beth din to testify, the party will give the name to the beth din and they will send the beth din officer to serve the witness with an order to testify.[14] Should the witness fail to appear, he will be placed under a ban.[15]

---

scheme to offset the effect of the document. This author prefers the view that holds that the other party may obtain a copy of the document prior to trial.

14. The topic of subpoenaing witnesses is dealt with in the *Shulhan Aruch* in Chapter 28. That topic is here included in this chapter because this chapter deals with the obtaining of evidence and the two topics are closely related.

15. In Chapter 11 the beth din proclaims the ban against a known individual—namely, the defendant who has refused to answer the summons. This ban is effective because all of society knows that the named person has been placed under the ban.

In this chapter, the ban, together with its accompanying curse, is known only to the transgressor. No one else knows that the transgressor has evidence or information regarding the litigant's case. What does the ban or curse achieve if no one else knows that this person is under a ban?

Furthermore, in Chapter 28 there is a statement that if one who has facts refuses to testify, he owes a judgment to Heaven. That means, of course, that he is liable to the judgments of Heaven for transgressing a Torah command to testify. What more does the ban instituted by the Sages achieve against the reluctant witness? The ban and the accompanying curse, whether issued by the judge or by the litigant, can be effective only if Heaven joins in the curse. But Heaven is already playing a role if the witness is liable to its judgment. Why, then, the extra curse?

Both questions—what does the ban achieve, and why the need for the extra ban—have one answer. The ban places psychological pressure on the witness to come forward. A person may pay little heed to a person who curses him, but when the curse is in furtherance of the authority of the Sages, then it may have more effect on the reluctant witness. The litigant who curses him does so knowing that the Sages have instituted the curse. The person who is being cursed also feels additional pressure to comply with the ban.

This author discussed this question with the great gaon Rav Adin Steinsaltz, and he agreed with the foregoing position and provided an insightful example. During the twelfth century, there was a Sage called Yehuda he-Hasid. His students attributed many ethical and mystical teachings to him. Upon his death, many of these teachings were published under the title *Zavva' at Rabbi Yehuda he-Hasid* (The Will of Rabbi Yehuda the Pious). Many later halachic works contain some of these non-halachic teachings as part of the halachah, and they are treated with great reverence. Rav Steinsaltz stated that if the will of Yehuda he-Hasid had contained the admonition against stealing, it might possibly be taken more seriously than the admonition against stealing contained in the Torah.

A litigant who does not know whether there are any witnesses to his claim may apply to the beth din to proclaim a general ban that all those who have information regarding his case should come forward to testify.[16] The ban was usually proclaimed in the synagogue, or in any other place of general assembly, on Mondays and Thursdays. The litigant cannot, however, adjure persons to come forward to swear that they have no knowledge on which to testify. Some authorities hold that the general call for witnesses must be answered, even by relatives and other persons who would be ineligible to testify, and even by adversaries. There are those who disagree. This author believes that the views of those who disagree should be followed. The ban will usually not be repeated even if it failed to turn up witnesses.

If one of the parties is physically or politically powerful and witnesses for the adversary are reluctant to testify against him, then the adversary may make a motion to the beth din to order the powerful party to produce the reluctant witnesses. If after a hearing the beth din determines that the claim is correct, it will issue an order requiring the powerful party to produce the reluctant witnesses.[17]

A witness cannot avoid testifying on the basis of a privilege; for example, he cannot claim he was sworn to secrecy regarding the matter.[18]

Thus the ban, although known only to the witness himself, might prove effective in compelling him to come forward.

16. The call is in the nature of a fishing expedition. The party throws out the ban in the hope of catching some witnesses. It must be remembered that each person knows his responsibility to testify in a matter of which he has some knowledge.

17. The theory is that a person may be afraid of the powerful person and therefore will not come to beth din, but once he comes to beth din there is no apprehensiveness that he will testify falsely.

18. Authorities differ on the question of whether a vow to keep information confidential must be annulled before the person who made the vow may testify. The majority view seems to be that the vow is not effective, which obviates the need to have the vow annulled. In *Shulhan Aruch, Yoreh De'ah*, Chapter 228, para. 33, Karo states that if a person swears that he will not be bound by the regulations of the community it is a vain oath, and the community's regulations are imposed on the person against his will. Ramo adds that if a person swore that he would not reveal certain information and the community subsequently decrees that he must reveal the information, he is bound to do so. Even according to the view that the vow requires annulment, the proceeding is taking place in a beth din, where the vow can be annulled.

Chapter 17

EQUALITY OF TREATMENT IN THE BETH DIN AND OTHER CONDUCT OF THE BETH DIN

INTRODUCTION

This author would have commenced the *Hoshen haMishpat* with this chapter and the second section of Chapter 8. Although Tur does not start with this chapter, his introductory remarks to Chapter 1, which deals with the jurisdiction of the beth din, contain an insight into the function of the judiciary in conformity with the aforesaid chapters. In essence, the judiciary is the agent of the Almighty in meting out earthly justice in disputes between men. It is an enormous responsibility. The Creator of the billions of galaxies and the Sustainer of the Universe has delegated one of His functions to man—namely, the meting out of justice. How very seriously one should take this task! The notes to many of the concepts in this chapter contain Torah prohibitions cited by some of the great authorities to show the seriousness of the laws herein contained.

This chapter is only a beginning. Each judge must acquaint himself with the ethical literature of the Sages. As a start, *Aboth*, together with some of the classical commentaries, should be compulsory reading for every judge.

TEXT

There is a Torah requirement that the parties to a litigation be treated equally in all respects

"Ye shall do no unrighteousness in judgment; thou shalt not respect the person of the poor, nor favor the person of the mighty; but in righteousness shalt thou judge thy neighbor" (Leviticus 19:15).[1,2] The Bible is replete with admonitions to act fairly in meting out justice.

Meting out justice commences with treating the parties to the litigation equally in all respects. If the parties are not treated equally, then the one who feels that he is not being treated fairly will feel intimidated or helpless and will, either consciously or perhaps unconsciously, fail to put his best case forward.

The names in the summons should be formulated in the same manner. That is, honorary titles should not be used in describing one of the parties while the other party's name appears without a title.

When the litigants appear in beth din, one should not be welcomed in a more friendly manner than the other. One party should not be afforded more honor than the other party.[3] One should not be given a more prominent place to sit. There should be equal numbers and types of chairs available for both parties. Although originally the rule was that the judges sat and the litigants and witnesses stood, the custom nowadays is for both litigants and witnesses to sit during the trial.[4] Even if the judges do not sit during the trial, the proceedings are valid.

---

1. Rambam, in *Laws of Sanhedrin,* Chapter 21, law 6, states: "It is essential that both litigants be alike in the judge's estimation and affection. The judge who does not know either litigant and the life he leads is in the best available position to render a righteous judgment."

2. A word commonly used in the Bible for *justice* is *zedek*. Mandelkern's *Concordance on the Bible* lists over 260 verses that contain a reference to *zedek* or one of its derivatives. It also lists over 400 references to *mishpat,* or judgment.

3. There was a time when the parties were asked to dress in the same style of clothing so that one would not feel inferior to the other. If one could not afford to dress in the same manner as the other, then the wealthier party was told to provide the poorer with clothing similar to his own.

4. Even in those times when litigants stood, if a sage who was a litigant came to beth din he was afforded the honor of being seated. Some of the codes also instructed that in such a case the beth din should advise the other litigant, if he was not a sage, that he too could be seated.

Each litigant, or his counsel, should be permitted equal opportunity to be heard. If a time limit to present pleas is set, it should be equal for both parties, and the parties and their counsel should be so advised before the start of the trial.[5] If there are several litigants on one side and fewer litigants on the other side, the beth din should make arrangements so that the side with fewer litigants does not feel intimidated. This could be done, for example, by restricting the number of litigants who can recite their pleas, or perhaps by having them state their pleas and then leave the seats reserved for the litigants.[6] When the verdict of the beth din is to be announced, both litigants should stand.

The beth din should not hear the pleas of one of the litigants before the other litigant has been brought into the lawsuit.[7,8] If a person who

---

5. Some authorities say that the beth din may limit the time that is allocated for witnesses to testify. This author disagrees. Whereas the presentation of pleas may lend itself to a time limit, testimony is for the purpose of proving a cause of action or a defense; the witnesses should be allowed to testify in full because the judges can learn the facts of the case only through the witnesses. Unless the beth din believes that the witness is not being responsive and is giving answers that are more detailed than that which the beth din requires to ascertain the facts, the witness should be allowed to testify in full.

6. The beth din should use its discretion in all of these situations. The rules that are stated here are to be used only as a guide and are based on the traditional rules that appear in the codes and commentaries.

7. The authorities cite many Torah prohibitions against hearing one litigant before the other has been brought into the lawsuit: "Keep thee far from a false matter" (Exodus 23:7); "nor put a stumbling block before the blind" (Leviticus 19:14); "Hear the causes between your brethren, and judge righteously" (Deuteronomy 1:16).

8. It is noted in Chapter 11 that there should be some provision for default judgment, as where a defendant fails to respond to a summons. Such should also be the case when, after both parties have appeared before the beth din, one of the parties fails to continue to appear in the trial. In order to render a judgment in those situations, the beth din will have to hear the pleas of the litigants and the testimony of the witnesses in the absence of the other litigant. This chapter does not deal with those kinds of situations. We are dealing here with a situation in which both of the parties do eventually appear before the beth din but one of the parties discussed the case with the judge before the trial, either because he came to beth din before his adversary did or because he had unknowingly discussed the case with a judge who would eventually try the case. This prohibition also does not apply to the situation discussed in Chapter 13, wherein each litigant selects his own judge. Part of the selection process is for the litigant to explain the proposed case to the judge whom he has selected.

serves as a judge of the beth din or is the sole judge selected by the community to judge cases did discuss the case with one of the litigants or with someone else familiar with the case prior to the case's having come to trial,[9] then (1) if he knew of the pending or threatened litigation, he should excuse himself from the trial; (2) if he advised the litigant on how to act in the trial, he should recuse himself even if he did not know of the pending or threatened litigation; (3) if he did not know of the pending or threatened litigation and he did not advise the litigant who sought his advice in the matter, he should advise the other litigant of the fact that he had already discussed the case with the first litigant or with someone else and allow the second litigant to decide whether he wants the judge to excuse himself from the case.

Great authorities refrained from writing answers to legal questions unless the questions were from leading authorities or from a recognized beth din seeking guidance.

The prohibitions herein contained have no application in the procedure whereby each litigant selects one of the judges and the two judges select the third judge, as outlined in Chapter 13.[10]

Some trial procedures to ensure equal treatment to all litigants

Where possible, the litigants and witnesses should testify in the language that is being used by the beth din.[11] If a party or a witness has difficulty with that language, then such party or witness may

---

9. Some authorities make a distinction between the litigant himself discussing the case with the judge and someone else discussing it with the judge. They would say that the prohibition does not apply in the latter situation. It seems to this author that it makes no difference. Once the judge has heard the facts of a case, regardless of the source of those facts, and has made a mental decision, it is very difficult to overcome this decision.

10. There is also authority to the contrary, but procedure stated in Chapter 13 for the selection of judges cannot function properly unless each party is able to advise the judge he selects of the facts of the case. The judge may not want to serve unless he has this information.

11. If the beth din is trying a case between a Jew and a non-Jew, then the judges should not speak to the Jew in a language that the non-Jew does not understand; otherwise, he may suspect that the judge and the other party are conspiring against him because he is a Gentile. Such action will desecrate the Name of Heaven.

testify in a language with which he feels comfortable.[12] Wherever possible, the judges should hear the witnesses' pleas and testimony in the language in which they are spoken. If the judges do not understand the language spoken by a litigant or witness, then a beth din–appointed interpreter[13] should be used to translate the pleas and testimony.[14]

After the beth din hears the pleas, one of the judges of the beth din must repeat them so that there can be no mistaking their meaning.[15] Nowadays the pleas are usually in writing, and if the judges have any difficulty understanding the nature of the written pleas, they may ask for written clarification.

The judges should not help any litigant in presenting his case. The judges should not tell the litigants before the close of their case that they have failed to make a *prima facie* case or defense. There is also strong contrary authority, however. If the judge sees that the litigant is struggling to present his views, then the judge may, with great discretion, offer some help to the litigant in expressing himself. This should be done only in rare cases and only after much deliberation! The judge is not to intrude himself into the case to help either side.

In rendering its decision, the beth din shall not favor the poor

---

12. The beth din, on oral examination, can determine whether the party or the witness is truly not able to testify in the language of the beth din. If they find that the claim is valid, then they should appoint an interpreter to translate the testimony and the pleas.

13. If an interpreter is used, each side reserves the right to question his credentials to act as such. Each side may also question the adequacy and accuracy of the translation. Chazon Ish suggests that one of the reasons that a trial becomes difficult when interpreters are used is that the questions and answers are then given in choppy sequences while waiting for the interpreter's translation.

14. When the judge hears the words directly from the litigant or witness, he has a better grasp of what is being said. He can also better determine the person's demeanor. Certain nuances may be lost even in a good translation.

15. Some authorities hold that this applies only to a single judge, but that if there are three judges, then the judges can review the pleas among themselves. This author believes that it does not matter how many judges are trying the case. The procedure should be uniform: The beth din or the single judge should review the pleas so that there can be no misunderstanding. It makes no difference that the pleas are in writing; they may still be ambiguous or poorly articulated. The pleadings limit the scope of the trial and should therefore be understood by the beth din in the manner in which the litigants intend them to be understood. Some authorities say that it is not necessary to repeat the pleas in the rules outlined in Chapter 13 regarding the selection of judges. This author disagrees and contends that this should be done in all cases.

person with mercy by saying that the other party is so rich that he will not even miss the small amount of money being awarded to the poor person. In rendering its decision, the beth din shall not favor the mighty or important person by rendering a decision in his favor and later privately telling him to pay the other party the amount that they really believe should have been awarded him. The same holds true in all comparable situations, as where one of the litigants is a wicked person, or a scholar, or an unlearned person. Each litigant's claims should be thought of as equally false until he proves them to the satisfaction of the beth din. If a litigant or his attorney makes a false statement of the law in an attempt to intimidate the other litigant, the judge is permitted to state that the law is otherwise.

Rambam[16] states that the verse that appears at the beginning of this chapter, "Ye shall do no unrighteousness in judgment" (Leviticus 19:15), teaches that the beth din may not pervert justice by acquitting the guilty or by condemning the innocent. It also refers to the beth din that delays judgment.

The beth din may not render a judgment in an amount exceeding the amount sought by the party.[17] If the beth din believes that the party should have sought a greater judgment but failed to do so out of ignorance of the law, then the beth din may ask the party why he failed to request a greater judgment, but the admonition previously stated should be observed.

If a beth din or a judge has second thoughts about a decision after it has been rendered, they should not attempt to rationalize the decision. Rather, the beth din should consult a leading authority as to what to do.[18] If the greater authority advises that the original decision was not correct, or if the beth din itself believes that it made a mistake, then the beth din must retract the decision.

---

16. *Laws of Sanhedrin*, Chapter 20, para. 6.

17. The beth din should take into account that perhaps the party intentionally omitted his additional claims out of fear that they might provoke a counterclaim, or perhaps because the balance of the claim was previously forgiven, or for some other good reason.

18. See Chapter 13 regarding consultation with a sage or more learned beth din for advice on how to decide a case.

Chapter 18

DELIBERATIONS
OF THE BETH DIN

INTRODUCTION

The actual procedure for trial is described in the chapters dealing with evidence, commencing with Chapter 28. The purpose of bringing the litigation and of defending the litigation is to achieve a judgment in favor of either the plaintiff or the defendant. The beth din does not entertain moot questions. (Often a sage will entertain moot questions so as to strengthen the knowledge of Torah, but this is not the task of the beth din.)

The beth din must decide the issues of fact and law that are presented to it, commencing with the pleas and the opening statements, and proceeding to the witnesses' testimony, the evidence, and closing statements, if any. The beth din must then weigh all of the foregoing and arrive at a just decision. The process begins with the deliberations of the members of the beth din.

TEXT

Deliberations of the judges

After the trial has been completed as set forth in Chapter 28, the judges retire to deliberate on the case. The judges should be alone when they are deliberating.[1] Some authorities hold that the junior judge should express his opinion first.[2]

The vote

After the judges have finished deliberating, they take a vote on the outcome. The vote may be unanimous in favor of one party.[3] If unanimity is not reached, the opinion of the majority is followed.[4] If one or more of the judges say that they cannot arrive at a decision,[5] then the procedure set forth in the footnote is to be followed.[6]

---

1. There are several reasons that the judges should be alone when they are deliberating the case. The most important is that the litigants should not know or be told by others who were present which judge sided with which litigant. Also, the litigants should not know the detailed thoughts of the judges and thus be able to fabricate evidence or obtain perjured testimony either on a retrial or on a motion to reopen the trial on the grounds of newly found witnesses or evidence. Furthermore, the judges may be reluctant to disclose their thoughts if others will overhear them. Also, the judges may wish to gain favor with one of the litigants and may say things in his favor that they do not truly mean and would not say if they were alone.

2. There are conflicting opinions on the issue of which judge should express himself first during the deliberations. Some hold that the senior judge should speak first, since he is the most experienced and may be a guide to the less experienced judges. However, the majority view now seems to be that the junior judges may be intimidated by the opinion of the senior judge and thus may be reluctant to express their own true opinions after the senior judge has expressed his views.

3. See Rambam, *Laws of Sanhedrin*, Chapter 9, para. 1, that if all the twenty-three judges of the Lesser Sanhedrin vote for conviction in a capital case, then the accused is acquitted. Only if there are some judges who cast arguments in his favor and they are outvoted by at least two judges for conviction is the defendant put to death.

4. The decision of the majority is followed even if there are more than three judges on the beth din. The same procedure will probably be applicable if the beth din was originally composed of three judges and then two or more judges were added.

5. If a judge does not know how he wants to vote, he should not go along with the other judges simply because he respects them. If he were to do so, then the beth din could have consisted of just those individuals.

6. Rambam, *Laws of Sanhedrin*, Chapter 8, para. 2, sets forth a procedure to be followed if one or more of the judges cannot come to a decision. If one votes for the plaintiff and the other for the defendant and one has formed no opinion, or even if two find for either the plaintiff or the defendant and one has no opinion, two more judges are added. Then all five judges deliberate the case. If three (or more) find for the plaintiff and two (or fewer) for the defendant, or three (or more) find for the

If a judge becomes incapacitated or dies or resigns during the trial[7] or before the deliberations have been completed, and if the parties do not agree to have the decision rendered by the remaining judges, then the procedure outlined in note 6 should be followed.[8]

If any of the events just described should occur, the litigants should be advised at the earliest possible moment. The litigants may then agree that the remaining judges can decide the case, or they may decide that the remaining judges need add only one more judge and that the judge who cannot form an opinion should be discharged from the panel of judges. If the litigants cannot agree that the remaining judges should decide the case, then all of the evidence and testimony will have to be produced before the judges who have been added.[9]

---

defendant and two (or fewer) find for the plaintiff, then the decision of the majority is followed. If, of the five judges, at least three find for either the plaintiff or the defendant, then the decision will follow this view even if the other judge or judges have not formed an opinion. If, of the five judges, two vote for the plaintiff and two vote for the defendant and one has no opinion, then two more judges are added. This is so whether the judge who is unable to decide is one of the original three judges or one of the judges who has been added. This process of adding two judges continues as long as there is no majority opinion, until there are seventy-one judges on the beth din. When this maximum number is reached and there are an equal number who find for the plaintiff and defendant, and if the judge who is undecided cannot make up his mind, then the case is found in favor of the defendant, since the plaintiff has failed to prove his case. A judge who does not have an opinion on how to vote need not provide a reason for his indecision.

7. "During the trial" does not mean that the trial actually had to commence, but this procedure will be followed as soon as the panel has been named and is binding on the litigants, or consists of a permanent beth din. In those communities where a beth din system has been instituted, rules will be made for handling just such situations.

8. There will now be an even number of judges, and judges will be added until such time as a majority will hold for either the plaintiff or the defendant, until there are seventy-one judges on the beth din. While the procedure outlined in this note and in note 6 is theoretically possible, if there is no majority finding after the first two judges are added, the litigants should be encouraged to permit the judges who are present to adopt some other way of deciding the case. Otherwise, the best alternative might be to declare a mistrial and leave each party to bring and to defend another action.

9. The thought of having to retry the case will ordinarily convince the litigants that they should waive their rights to have three judges decide the case. Of course, there may be times when the defendant will want the case to drag on so that the plaintiff will tire of the procedure and drop the case rather than start it afresh. The judges on the panel should take this possibility into account and devise a way to decide the case so that all three judges have a part in the decision.

In the following cases, the decision of the judges must be unanimous:

1. Where the parties have so stipulated.
2. Where the community has chosen a panel of more than three judges to adjudicate its cases.[10]
3. In cases of arbitration.[11]
4. In cases to be decided according to the law merchant.

In all of the foregoing cases, the litigants may, at any time prior to the rendering of the decision, waive the unanimity requirement and agree that a decision of a majority or any number will suffice.

If the panel cannot reach a unanimous decision in those cases where it is required, the complaint will be dismissed with prejudice.[12]

If the judges do not know how to decide a case, they may seek advice from a more learned beth din or from sages, as stated in Chapter 13.

The decision may be rendered even if one or both litigants are not at the beth din (see Chapter 13).

---

10. Where the community appoints a council of seven elders to decide its affairs, all members of the council must be present for all decisions, and their decisions must be unanimous. Most communities have rules that relax these requirements.

11. See Chapter 12.

12. The burden of proof is with the plaintiff, and since he did not receive a decision in his favor, the case will be dismissed without prejudice to the plaintiff's bringing another action.

Chapter 19

THE DECISION

INTRODUCTION

At the conclusion of the deliberations described in Chapter 18, the decision of the beth din is announced. Actually, part of the subject matter of this chapter appears in Chapter 18 of the *Shulhan Aruch*, where it is stated that it is not necessary for the litigants to be present when the decision is announced. This chapter also deals with another topic that appeared earlier in *Shulhan Aruch*, in Chapter 14: the writing of the decision. Finally, the situation in which the losing party does not abide by the decision of the beth din is dealt with. There are, of course, other chapters that will deal with methods of collecting judgments. In this chapter, the topic deals with placing a recalcitrant loser under a ban or under excommunication. Under an established beth din system, all of the remedies can be pursued simultaneously.

TEXT

Delivering the decision

After the judges have arrived at a decision, the litigants and their counsel are asked to enter the beth din to hear it. (It is not necessary that the litigants or their counsel be present in the beth din when the judges announce their decision.)[1]

The senior judge announces the decision.[2] It is concise and states who won the case. If the decision is unanimous, it states, "Plaintiff, P, and defendant, d, appeared for trial. We find in favor of P (or d)." If the decision is not unanimous, it states, "Plaintiff, P, and defendant, d, appeared for trial, and after the decision it is found that P (or d) has won the case." Perhaps the better practice would be for a beth din to adopt one or the other of the statements in all cases. It is prohibited for any person to divulge which judge voted in favor of the plaintiff and which judge voted in favor of the defendant. This prohibition continues after the trial. A person who divulges such information has transgressed the prohibition of "he that goeth as a talebearer revealeth secrets" (Proverbs 11:13).[3]

A third person may not criticize the decision of the beth din. This prohibition against criticism does not extend to refraining from advising the losing party that the mistake is so obvious that it will probably be reversed on appeal. The line between what is prohibited and what is permitted is so fine that it really depends upon the intent of the person who is advising the losing party.

The written decision

Some authorities hold that the decision need not be reduced to writing unless one of the parties requests it. The better view seems to be that the decision should be reduced to writing in all events, especially in an established beth din system.

There may be two types of written decisions: (1) a short-form

---

1. See Chapter 13, where the question of the litigants not being present for the beth din proceedings is discussed. In this case the litigants were before the beth din and presented their cases with all of their witnesses and evidence. The case has been properly tried. It is just the ministerial act of the reading of the decision from which one or both of the litigants are missing.

2. One of the reasons given for having the senior judge announce the decision is to show him respect. A more cogent reason is that if another judge were to read the decision, it might be assumed that the one reading the decision voted in favor of the winning party.

3. Some of the authorities state that he may also be violating the prohibition "Keep thee far from a false matter" (Exodus 23:7).

decision stating the names of the parties and the winner of the case, similar to the oral statements just described, and (2) a long-form decision, which, in addition to naming the parties and the winner of the case, also states the issues, the decision on the issues, and the reasons for the decisions. A decision must be very specific in its operative decrees so that there can be no mistake as to what each party must do.[4] A long-form decision must be written if either party demands it.[5]

The decision must be signed by all of the members of the beth din. However, the failure or refusal of a judge to sign the decision does not affect its validity. All of the prohibitions against divulging or indicating in the decision who voted for whom apply to written decisions. A beth din may keep in its confidential records a copy of the decision that states which judge voted with the majority and which judge dissented. This record is necessary if the judgment is reversed on appeal, because the judges who voted for the decision that was overturned may be liable in certain situations. The topic of appeals is covered in Chapter 25.

If the case is settled by the beth din, then the parties may enter into a stipulation embodying the terms of the settlement, and the stipulation should be signed by the judges.[6]

Acceptance of the Decision

The decision of the beth din is binding on the parties without any further action on anyone's part.

---

4. There is an opinion that the decision should also name any witnesses who were disqualified or who have committed perjury during the trial. Most authorities disagree with this opinion.

5. The plaintiff may want the decision, if he won, to be able to pursue his remedies with a decision which vindicates those remedies. A full decision may make it easier to impose whatever levies and examinations are necessary, since it will prevent the defendant from denying the nature of the original claim during supplemental proceedings. It may also enable the plaintiff to obtain injunctive relief against recurrence of the conduct on which the lawsuit was based. If the defendant won the case, then he will want a full decision to raise the defense of *res judicata* if the plaintiff once again sues on the same grounds. He may also want to enjoin the plaintiff from certain kinds of conduct. Either party may want the full decision so that he can show others that he was vindicated. Of course, the losing party will want a full decision so that he can determine whether he wants to appeal and so that he can use it to explain to the Review Beth Din the grounds on which he is appealing.

6. The judges should sign the stipulation so that neither party may then claim that it is spurious or is not to be used as a defense of *res judicata*.

If the losing party does not fulfill the terms within the time specified in the decision, or within any beth din–granted extensions thereof, then one of the remedies available to the winning party is to apply to the beth din to put the loser under a ban. The winning party must make a motion to the beth din on motion papers in conformity with Chapter 14. If the beth din is convinced that the losing party does not intend to carry out the decision, then he is served by the beth din officer with a written warning to appear in beth din on the following Thursday and the next Monday and the next Thursday. On each of these days the losing party is warned that if he does not carry out the terms of the decision, he will be put under a ban. If he does not carry out the terms of the decision while he is under the ban for at least thirty days,[7] then, again on motion, the losing party is ordered to appear in beth din and he is warned that if he does not carry out the terms of the decision within a specified time, he will be excommunicated. If he still fails to carry out the decision of the beth din within the specified time, he is to be excommunicated by the beth din.

If the losing party at any time after the decision is rendered states that he will not abide by the decision, or does not appear in beth din pursuant to its order to appear, then it may excommunicate him at once. If the losing party appears in beth din and is able to prove that he is not now able to abide by its decision, then he is released from the entire procedure.

The pursuing of the remedies stated in this chapter does not preclude the winning party from simultaneously pursuing any other remedies that may be available to him.[8]

---

7. There is also an opinion that the first time period is sixty days.

8. There are authorities who would permit the beth din to order the losing party beaten if they had the authority to do so, and if not, to apply to the secular authorities to do so. There are other authorities who authorize the beth din to instruct the losing party's employer to discharge him from his employment.

Chapter 20

VACATING A JUDGMENT

INTRODUCTION

There is a Mishnah in *Sanhedrin* that discusses the vacating of judgments.[1] Should a person who has lost a case and then discovered new proof be prevented from asking for a new trial based on this new proof? The answer seems to depend upon the availability of the proof during the original trial. If it was available, why was it not presented? What effort was made by the party to obtain all the necessary proof? This chapter attempts to answer some of these questions. In the final analysis, however, each beth din must decide

---

1. See *Sanhedrin* 31a and the discussion in the Talmud. There is a difference of opinion between the Sages and Rabban Simeon b. Gamliel. The majority view is that if the beth din ordered a party to present all his proofs within a certain time and he fails to do so, then he is forever precluded from vacating the judgment on the ground of newly available proof. Rabban Simeon b. Gamliel asked, "What is he to do if he does not have the proof available within this time?" The dispute between them also involves the situation in which the beth din asks the party whether he has any additional proof and he replies in the negative. The Sages hold that he is thereafter precluded from bringing additional proof, while Rabban Simeon again asks, "What is he to do if he did not know that witnesses were available but he did not discover them until afterwards; or that there was proof but he did not discover it until later?" The codes follow the view of Rabban Simeon.

the issue on the facts before it. In some aspects the laws of this chapter also apply to new claims or defenses. In this respect, some of the questions to be answered in a motion to dismiss a new complaint based on new causes of action are similar. Were these claims available during the first trial, and if so, why were they not brought? This presupposes that a motion was not brought under Chapter 28 to present all claims or defenses. Or it may apply when the party who was ordered to present all his claims stated that he had no others and now claims that he had others but had forgotten about them.

This chapter does not deal with the amending of pleadings during the trial, which is covered in Chapter 80.

TEXT

When a judgment may be vacated

The preferred practice is that a motion to vacate a judgment and permit a new trial on the basis of newly discovered matters be made before the same beth din[2] or judge who rendered the original judgment.[3] As used in this chapter, "newly discovered matters" includes witnesses, documents, and other evidence that was not introduced at the original trial. The making of the motion does not act as a stay to stop the enforcement of the judgment unless a stay is obtained from the beth din that rendered the judgment or from the Review Beth Din. If it is determined on the motion to vacate that the moving party knew of the newly discovered matters, then the motion to vacate the judgment will be denied.

The motion to vacate may be made at any time,[4] even if the

---

2. The beth din that rendered the original judgment is more apt to be familiar with the witnesses, testimony, and evidence that was presented at the trial and is thus more able to evaluate whether the alleged newly found matters are really new.

3. See Chapter 25 regarding review of a beth din's decisions by another beth din.

4. The beth din hearing the motion shall determine whether the time is reasonable, taking into account the diligence with which the moving party proceeded after he discovered such new matters. The beth din shall also take into account any prejudice there might be against the adversary. Some of his witnesses may have died or left the jurisdiction, or he may have acted in such a manner pursuant to the original judgment

judgment has been paid. If the motion is granted and the judgment had been paid, then the amount paid will be refunded and paid into beth din pending the outcome of the new trial.

In considering whether to grant the motion, the beth din shall determine whether the newly presented matter is admissible at a trial. The beth din shall also consider whether, assuming that the evidence is admissible and uncontroverted, it would have made any difference in the original decision.[5] The beth din shall also consider whether the newly discovered matters were available[6] to the moving party at the trial.[7]

If, at the trial, the moving party had been asked by the beth din or his adversary whether he knew of any other witnesses or evidence and he had replied that there were none,[8] then his current motion to vacate should be denied.[9] If, however, there was no way for him to have known of such new matters at that time then his answer at the original trial shall not be the basis of denying his motion. If at the trial, and in response to his request, the beth din granted the moving party

---

that it may be impossible to vacate the judgment without harming him. The beth din may make any order that it believes will be equitable on the motion to vacate.

5. There must be a showing that there would probably have been a different result at the trial had these matters been before the beth din. It is not all newly discovered matters that form the basis for granting the motion.

6. If the evidence was in the hands of a hostile person, then it is deemed not available.

7. The moving party must show that he had made diligent effort to obtain such matters but was not able to do so. He must show, for example, that the matters were in the hands of a third party who was out of the country.

8. The reason for denying the motion is that the moving party may introduce perjured testimony or false evidence; otherwise, why would he have stated that he had no additional witnesses or evidence available? If he was not asked this question at the trial and then rested his case without having gone on record that he did not have any additional matters to present, then he may be granted a new trial on the basis of newly discovered matters if he meets all the other criteria for having such a motion granted.

9. To permit a party to present only part of his case, with the hope that he had presented enough to win the case, but to hold back some other matters to be presented in case he lost the trial, would cause most judgments to be worthless and would make a mockery of the trial system because it would allow a party to present his case piecemeal and then if he lost, present a little more of his case, and if he still lost, present more of his case. If he presented all of his case in the first trial and lost, he would not have any other opportunity to have the matter retried. The harrassment of continual new trials based on new matters might well coerce the adversary into settling where he would ordinarily not have done so.

additional time[10] to present certain witnesses and evidence, and he did not produce them within that time, and a decision was rendered without such matters, then the moving party's motion shall not be denied solely on that basis. If, at the trial, the moving party stated that he knew of other matters but they were not then in the jurisdiction of the beth din (as, for example, if the witness or evidence was in another country and could not be brought back before the conclusion of the trial), then the unavailability shall be considered in the moving party's favor in considering his motion.

If the moving party was a party in the trial as the heir of an estate, the purchaser of a business, or similar situation in which he could not have known all the witnesses or facts at the time of the trial, then his failure to produce them at the trial should not in and of itself be the basis for denying the motion.

New claims or defenses

If a motion has not been made pursuant to Chapter 14 to present all pleas and defenses, then a party may start a new case with new pleadings. If, however, a party was ordered during the original trial to present all his claims or defenses and he stated that he had no others, and he now wishes to present new claims or defenses, then a motion will have to be made pursuant to this chapter on the grounds that he had forgotten about such claims or defenses. On such motion, the beth din shall consider whether to grant the motion; in so doing, they may employ any of the aforestated rules.

---

10. In computing the additional time, the Sabbath and Holy Days are included. (See Chapter 5 regarding days on which beth din does not meet.) It is assumed that the trial beth din granted the requesting party a reasonable period of time, taking into account the reasons for his request.

Chapter 21

STIPULATIONS REGARDING THE TRIAL

INTRODUCTION

Generally, any stipulation made between parties regarding monetary matters is binding on the parties. In this chapter the laws deal with two topics: (1) the binding nature of the stipulation and (2) under what circumstances the terms of the stipulation are rescinded because of impossibility of performance. Both topics appear frequently in halachah. This chapter deals only with the laws as stated in *Shulhan Aruch*, *Hoshen haMishpat*, Chapter 21, and they will be discussed again whenever they arise. This chapter seems to be used by Tur and *Shulhan Aruch* to introduce the next chapter, which deals with stipulations between the parties regarding waiving the strict laws of who may not be a judge in their litigation.

TEXT

Stipulations made by the parties regarding the outcome of the trial

The parties may make any stipulation regarding the outcome of or conduct of the trial. For example, if the plaintiff can take an oath[1] and

---

1. The topic of oaths is discussed in Chapter 87.

win his case, but the plaintiff is now loath to take the oath,[2] then the parties may stipulate that unless the plaintiff takes the oath within thirty days the decision will be in favor of the defendant. For another example, if the defendant can win the case by taking an oath but he is loathe to take the oath, then the parties may stipulate that if he does not take the oath within thirty days, judgment should be granted to the plaintiff. In both of these situations if the party failed to take the oath within the thirty-day period, judgment will be entered in favor of the other party. In the first example, the plaintiff's stipulation seems to be in the nature of forgiveness of debt. Although forgiveness of debt ordinarily does not require a *kinyan*,[3] in this case a *kinyan* is required,[4] since it borders on forgiveness in error, which is not binding without a *kinyan*.[5]

Although the judgment will be entered at once at the end of the stipulated time period, the losing party will still have the same time period to pay as if it had been a decision rendered after trial.[6]

Failure to comply with stipulation by reason of *onness*

Onness is defined for the purposes of this chapter to be any *force majeure* or unexpected and disruptive event operating to excuse performance by the party. The *onness* must have been entirely unforeseeable.

In the event of nonperformance due to *onness*, the entire stipula-

---

2. There are many reasons that a person may be loath to take an oath. Some people will not take an oath or swear as a matter of principle and would rather lose a case than take an oath. Or perhaps the person is not sure that the oath will be absolutely true and fears that he may be taking the oath falsely or in vain. The party may have asked for a time in which to take the oath because he thought that in the time allowed to him he might be able to find witnesses or evidence to win the case without having to resort to the oath. Or, he may have thought that his adversary might reach some arrangement with him on the dispute. Or he might have wanted more time to examine his position both as to the litigation and the taking of an oath.

3. See Chapter 12.

4. The topic of *kinyan* is fully discussed in Chapters 195, 203, and 205. See also the discussion in the notes to Chapter 12.

5. See Chapter 207.

6. This is the opinion of Shach, Chapter 21, para. 1.

tion will be rescinded. The trial will then proceed as if the stipulation had never been entered into. The burden of proof of *onness* and of the fact that it prevented performance is on the party alleging that *onness* prevented performance. *Onness* will also apply if the party's stipulation depended upon the performance of the adverse party. For example, if the plaintiff stipulates that he will forgive his claim if the defendant takes an oath within thirty days, then the defendant is prevented by *onness* from taking the oath. Here, too, the stipulation will be rescinded and the trial will proceed as if the stipulation was never entered into.

The *onness* may have occurred at any time during the period, rendering performance impossible, even at the very last moment. The beth din will determine whether *onness* prevented performance.

The stipulation does not become reinstituted after the *onness* is no longer present.

Chapter 22

STIPULATIONS REGARDING INELIGIBLE JUDGES, INELIGIBLE WITNESSES, AND OATHS

INTRODUCTION

Continuing the topic discussed in Chapter 21, this chapter also deals with stipulations. Earlier chapters dealt with the ineligibilty of judges,[1] and later chapters will deal with ineligible witnesses and with the topic of oaths.[2] In this chapter, some of the requirements and ineligibilities are waived by stipulation between the litigants. Although some of the matters discussed in this chapter may not be applicable in the beth din system as proposed in this book, most of the matters do have application.

TEXT

Stipulations regarding acceptance of ineligible judges and witnesses

The parties may accept as judges or witnesses persons related to one

---

1. See Chapter 7.
2. See Chapters 33, 34, and 35.

or both of the parties and/or related to each other.[3,4] Any witness, including an ineligible witness, may be given the credibility of two witnesses.[5] An otherwise ineligible judge in this case may be given the authority to sit together with other judges or to be the sole judge in the case.[6] These stipulations may be made at any time until the rendering of the decision of the beth din.[7]

The stipulations[8] require a *kinyan*.[9] If no *kinyan* was made, then either party may withdraw from the stipulation at any time until the decision of the beth din has been rendered.[10] If the stipulation regards witnesses[11] and no *kinyan* was made, then either party may withdraw

---

3. It has been suggested that the guardian of an infant may not accept a relative of an adversary to be a judge in a case involving the infant because it is not in the best interest of the infant.

4. A person may not be a witness if he is related to either party or to any judge in this case or to any to any other witness in this case. A person may not be a judge in this case if he is related to any party or any other judge or any witness in this case.

5. Generally, the uncontroverted testimony of two witnesses proves a fact. The parties are now stipulating that one witness, even if he would not be eligible to testify because of some general ineligibility or because he is ineligible in this case, will be able to testify, either as one of two witnesses or by himself, and be given the weight of two witnesses.

6. The parties may stipulate that all three judges who would be ineligible may judge the case.

7. If a party alleges that he did not know that the judge was related to the other party, he may take a *hesset* oath that he was not aware of the fact and that if he had been aware of it he would not have accepted him as a judge; if he does so, the judgment is vacated. If he raises the claim before judgment has been rendered, then he need not take an oath. If it was a widely known fact that the judge was related to his adversary, then he is not believed unless he can show that he was not part of the community that knew this fact. *Hesset* oaths are discussed in Chapter 87.

8. There is general agreement among the authorities that the stipulation must be accepted by both parties. It is not sufficient that one party agrees to accept the relative of the other party as a judge. If the judge rules against his relative, then his relative will be able to raise a claim of an ineligible judge having judged the case.

9. See Chapters 12, 195, 203, and 205.

10. See Chapter 19 that a decision is rendered when the judge states "We find in favor of plaintiff (or defendant)."

11. Similar to the stipulation regarding witnesses or judges is the stipulation regarding appraisers. There is a general requirement that three experts appraise a thing. If the parties agreed that they will rely on fewer than three appraisers, then there should be a *kinyan*, and if not, then either party will be able to change his mind before the final decision of the appraisers.

from the stipulation until such time as the witness named in the stipulation begins to testify.[12]

The best practice would be to have the stipulation and *kinyan* made in beth din. The stipulation can also be made before three members of the seven selectmen[13] of the city.[14] There are some authorities who permit the stipulation to be made before any three persons.[15] The stipulation must be specific[16] and unambiguous.[17]

---

12. Once the witness begins to testify, the parties are bound by stipulation whether or not the stipulation was entered into by *kinyan;* otherwise, the parties would have an option. If they liked the testimony, then they would seek to abide by the stipulation; if not, then they would seek to set aside the stipulation. Some authorities hold that if there was no *kinyan,* then either party may vacate the stipulation up until the judgment was rendered. The judgment is considered rendered when the judges say "We find in favor of plaintiff (or defendant)." There is still a third opinion, which says that as soon as the parties tell the beth din that they have agreed that a certain person may testify, they may no longer change their minds, since the beth din's acceptance of their stipulation qualifies as the rendering of a decision on that point. It is in the nature of an interlocutory decision.

13. The seven selectmen of the city have wide legislative and administrative power. There are some authorities who maintain that they occupy a place in their community similar to that of the Great Sanhedrin in earlier times. See *Ramo, Hoshen haMishpat,* Chapter 2, and also see note 2 to Chapter 2.

14. Some authorities hold that if at the time of the transaction that is the basis of the lawsuit the parties agreed on the judges in the event of a dispute and named a person or persons who were related to one of the parties, then the agreement is binding even without a separate *kinyan,* since it is included in the original transaction.

15. There are reasons on both sides of the issue of whether to permit the stipulation and *kinyan* to be made before any three persons. Three persons are required because the stipulation is a judicial matter and three persons are required to constitute a beth din. (Of course, if the parties have agreed to have their case heard by fewer than three judges, then the stipulation may be entered and the *kinyan* made before the fewer number of judges trying the case.) In some instances the beth din may not be in session when the parties agree to the stipulation, and they may change their minds before the beth din meets to have the *kinyan* made there. On the other hand, the beth din will have to pass upon the regularity and validity of the stipulation and will be in a better position to do so if it was entered into in the beth din and the *kinyan* made there. This author prefers the view that it should be made before any three persons and that they should also state that the *kinyan* was made in their presence.

16. For example, if the stipulation states that the parties accept a witness who is related, does it also mean that they accept him with the same credence that they would have attributed to two witnesses? In cases of doubt, the most restricted view against the acceptance of ineligible persons will be favored.

Some of the authorities permit the parties to stipulate accepting a Gentile as a witness. Some authorities permit the parties to stipulate that a Gentile judge their case if he states that he will judge according to his own sense of justice and not in accordance with the Gentile secular law.[18] This author believes that such permission sets a dangerous precedent and should not be followed. It may be used to nullify the effect of Chapter 26.

Stipulations regarding oaths

In a case in which a party must take a stringent oath[19] to win the case, whether as a plaintiff or as a defendant, his adversary may stipulate that he may take a less stingent oath and achieve the same result. A party who takes a Rabbinic oath to win a case may stipulate that his adversary take the same type of oath and win the case. The parties may stipulate that a party who was not required to take an oath may take an oath and win the case.

The stipulation becomes binding as soon as a *kinyan* is made. Any stipulation regarding oaths may be withdrawn, if there was no *kinyan* until the oath was actually taken. Once the stipulated oath was taken, the stipulation is binding.[20] Some authorities hold that if the stipulation was made in beth din then it is binding, even without a *kinyan* and even before the oath was taken. This seems to be the accepted law.[21]

If a person who was under an obligation to take an oath declared in beth din that he would not take the oath, then he may not change his mind and thereafter take the oath. This holds true only if the beth din

---

17. A stipulation to escrow money or documents or personalty pending a decision of the beth din does not confer any judicial authority upon the escrowee to make any decisions regarding the escrowed items. This last statement applies even if the escrowee is the community judge and even if he is eligible to be a judge in this case.

18. See *Aruch haShulhan*, Chapter 22, para. 8.

19. See Chapter 87, where the topic of oaths is discussed.

20. There is an opinion that if the oath was not taken when the agreement was made and if the agreement is unreasonably delayed, then the parties are no longer bound to the stipulation.

21. If there was a *kinyan*, then it is, of course, binding on the parties. For the case in which there was no *kinyan*, Shach, Chapter 22, para. 16, gives three views on the matter: (1) the view of Rambam that the party may change his mind until the oath is taken; (2) the view of Asheri that the party may change his mind until the trial is completed; (3) the view of Ramban that a party may no longer change his mind once the discussion in the beth din is completed even if the oath was not yet taken.

completed its discussion on this phase of the case and adjourned for a time and if the party who made the statement left the beth din even temporarily. If the party stated that he would not take the oath and added the words that he would pay, then he may no longer produce any proof in order for a decision to be rendered in his favor.

Chapter 23

LOST DECISION OF THE BETH DIN

INTRODUCTION

Many courtrooms have overloaded dockets. In some judicial systems, a landlord–tenant court may have all the trappings of a crowded market. A judge may have many cases to decide in one morning. Some of the cases are settled; some are dismissed because the plaintiff did not show up; some are granted default judgment (as was advocated in Chapter 11); some are adjourned; some are put on a waiting list; and some are tried. It is no wonder that a judge may not remember his disposition of every case. This is especially likely to occur in the beth din system that has been suggested here. Reliance on a written decision made by the judge may also not be a solution, since if a docket is lost among the many files in a clerk's office, it may never be located.

Therefore, there must be recourse to the judge to ascertain if he remembers the case and in whose favor he found. Such recourse may sometimes be necessary even if the written docket is available but the decision is not clear. It may occur if the judge announced his decision orally and later issues a written decision which one of the parties then claims is not consistent with the oral decision. These are just some of the potential pitfalls when it becomes necessary to rely on the judge's memory of his decisions.

This chapter deals with a situation in which there is no written decision available and the parties disagree on what the decision was, or for that matter that there ever was a decision in the case. The word *believed* as used in this chapter does not question the judge's integrity but rather his ability to recall the facts of the case or the decision.

TEXT

When the judge's statement of his decision is believed

A written decision of the beth din or judge or arbitrator cannot be impeached. If there is no written decision before the beth din or the judge or the arbitrator, then the following statements apply:

1. As long as the litigants are still before him in the beth din, the judge is believed when he states in whose favor he found.[1]
2. If the litigants have already left the beth din and the litigants are now litigants in a new action brought by one of the parties to enforce the judgment, then the following apply:
   a. At any time after the litigants have left the beth din, the judge has the credibility of one witness in stating his decision.
   b. If the judge is related to one of the litigants or else is otherwise disqualified to testify in the matter, then he has no standing in the matter even as a single witness.
   c. His testimony as to his decision assists the one in whose favor he testified to shift the burden of proof to the other party to take an oath to win the case.[2]
   d. If both parties admit that they do not remember the decision, then the judge's memory of the decision is believed.

---

1. The judge has the same credibility as two witnesses while the litigants are still before him, either because he is the judge appointed by the community or by the beth din system or because the litigants have accepted him as their judge. Others say that the reason is that the Sages said that the judge is likely to be scrupulous about the case as long as the litigants are still before him.
2. See Chapter 75 regarding shifting the burden of proof based on the testimony of one witness.

If the case consisted of undisputed testimony which can lend itself to only one decision, then the judge is believed that such was his decision even after the parties have left the beth din.[3] If the case was not an undisputed one, then the judge is not accepted as the equivalent of two witnesses after the parties have left the beth din, and the rules just stated apply.[4] The same holds true if the litigant alleges that his pleas and proofs were of one kind and the judge says that they were of another kind; the judge is not believed as two witnesses, and the rules just stated apply.

If the judge is not available to testify, or if he has died, then the parties will be left in the position in which they find themselves and will have to rely, if they can, on other proof to recall the beth din's decision. If the case involves money or a chattel, the party who has possession will remain in possession until the other party proves his case. If neither party is in possession, then the one who takes possession first will be deemed to be the possessor, or the parties will be asked to arbitrate. If both are in possession, then they will divide the property.[5]

If one party states that the case was not yet completed and the other party claims that it was completed and that a decision was rendered in his favor, and the judge concurs that the trial was not yet completed, then he is believed. He is believed if it is not disputed that

---

3. It is assumed that under any given state of undisputed facts the same decision would result. However, if even an agreed-upon statement of facts might lend itself to at least two different decisions, then the judge does not have any more credibility than one witness if the litigants have left the beth din.

4. The reason is that even with the same judge, the same pleas, and the same proofs, the case might be decided differently. This wide discretion given to the judge is known as *shoodah dedaini.* There is a dispute between Rashi and Tosafoth about what *shoodah dedaini* means. Rashi holds that there is some logical basis for the judge to decide the case the way he did, whereas Tosafoth contends that the judge could have made any decision in the case because there was no compelling reason to decide one way or the other. In a trial that is not *shooda dedaini,* the beth din retains continuous jurisdiction even after the trial has terminated and the decision has been rendered, as we can see in cases of appeals, or reversals for mistake, or the the ability to bring in newly discovered evidence. In case of *shoodah dedaini,* however, the right to decide comes under the power of *hefker beth din hefker,* or a limited jurisdiction that ceases as soon as the decision is rendered. In the other cases, however, the jurisdiction based on the nonlimited power of beth din continues uninterrupted.

5. These laws are fully discussed in Chapter 133.

he was the judge or if it can be proved independently that he was the judge.

If there are two or more judges on the beth din, then all of the foregoing does not apply and the two or more judges have full credibility to state what the beth din's decision was. This holds true even after the litigants have left the beth din. This also holds true even if there are two witnesses who dispute them.

All that which has been said regarding a judge of the beth din holds equally true for an arbitrator.

Questions regarding the written decision

If the parties have a question regarding the meaning of all or part of the decision, then the judge may explain his decision, so long as the explanation is tenable under the written decision. Even many judges sitting on the same beth din are not believed when they give an explanation that is untenable under the written decision.

An arbitrator's opinion of the meaning of his written decision is believed, so long as the explanation is tenable under the written decision.

Chapter 24

PLAINTIFF TO OPEN THE CASE

The matters discussed in this chapter of the *Shulhan Aruch* have been included in Chapter 28 of this book, which deals with all facets of the trial, including priorities in presenting cases.

Chapter 25

FINALITY OF JUDGMENTS, BETH DIN ERRORS, AND APPEALS

INTRODUCTION

The first topic discussed in this chapter is that of finality of judgments. In some codes and commentaries, this topic appears in Chapter 19 and others in Chapter 20 of *Shulhan Aruch, Hoshen haMishpat.* The most surprising thing is that the topic was not often discussed, although the Talmud states, "A beth din does not minutely examine the decisions of another beth din."[1] But as stated by Rashbam in his commentary, it applies to the topic discussed there—namely, the laws of *halizah* and *mi'un.*[2] It was not until the sixteenth century, nearly a thousand years after the Talmud discussion, that Ramo, in his *Darkai Moshe* commentary on Tur in Chapters 20 and 25,[3] reintroduced the topic of one beth din not second-guessing another beth din. He is quoted by Sefer Meiroth Anayim,[4] who is in turn quoted by Shach.[5]

This concept is not a readily acceptable one where the judicial system has not been universally recognized for nearly two thousand

---

1. See *Baba Bathra* 138b.
2. See Chapter 1 for definitions of the terms *halizah* and *mi'un.*
3. Actually it did appear in a responsum by Asher in the fourteenth century which is cited by R. Ramo, but it was not much followed.
4. Chapter 19, para. 2.
5. Chapter 19, para. 3.

years. It also did not have an organized appeals system. Thus one of the ways in which a litigant who had lost a case could obtain relief if he believed that the first beth din had erred in his opponent's favor was to have the original decision reviewed by a sage or by another beth din, sometimes more learned than the original beth din. The finality of the decision of the beth din is the first topic discussed in the section titled "Finality of Judgments."

Ramban, in his commentary on Deuteronomy 16:18, states that there was a superior Sanhedrin and superior beth din in each tribe, and if there was a doubt in the law, these Sanhedrins and beth dins would interpret it. Although this does not indicate that they necessarily had appellate jurisdiction, the entire history of halachah shows that there were always more learned and authoritative bodies that would review the decisions of the trial beth din or trial judge and suggest, or in some cases order, a reversal of the trial judgment. In fact, the Talmudic discussion that deals with reversal of a judgment cites several views regarding the liability of the judges who erred and also cites a decision that was reversed on appeal.[6]

The case cited dealt with a decision of Rabbi Tarfon, who declared a certain animal not fit for human consumption, which resulted in a monetary loss for the owner of the animal. When the case was reviewed by the sages in Yabne, they reversed and found that the animal was indeed fit for consumption.

As part of the discussion, the Talmud gives several explanations of what appear to be contradictory statements in different Mishnayoth dealing with judges who had erred in their decisions. One is Rabbi Nahman's, who said that the differences in the Mishnayoth can be reconciled by showing that one Mishnah dealt with a situation in which the community had a superior beth din to reverse the decision of the trial beth din, while the other Mishnah dealt with a situation in which no such superior beth din existed in the community. Rabbinic literature is replete with decisions contained in the Talmud and responsa throughout the ages wherein great Rabbis were asked to review decisions and then affirmed, modified, or reversed them. But despite this, there does not seem to be an accepted forum for direct appeals in the beth din system. Professor Menachem Elon,[7] in his

---

6. See *Sanhedrin* 33a.
7. Professor Menachem Elon of the Hebrew University School of Law is also a

article in the *Encyclopedia Judaica*, describes the process whereby the Rabbinic courts were established in 1921 in Palestine under Chief Rabbi Abraham Kook.

> An important *takkanah*, enacted immediately in 1921, established the Rabbinical Supreme Court of Appeal, thus introducing a regular appellate tribunal which had not previously existed in Jewish law. That this *takkanah* rendered the appellate court an integral part of the Jewish legal system was made clear in a judgment of the Rabbinic High Court of Appeal of Jerusalem which rejected the contention that no right of appeal existed in Jewish law, holding that "the right of appeal has been enacted by a rabbinical *takkanah*, the force of which is as that of a rule of our Holy Torah."[8]

Chapter 15 of the *Rules of the Israel Beth Din* contains twenty rules regarding appellate procedure in the beth din system. This author has therefore in Chapter 1 suggested a Review Beth Din for each city and for each district.

Appeals are discussed in the second section of this chapter. The third through fifth sections deal with the reversal of erroneous decisions and the liability of the judges, if any, for such decisions. *Shulhan Aruch, Hoshen haMishpat,* Chapter 25, deals with errors made by the beth din or by judges. The review would often be by the beth din itself, based on decisions called to its attention by the losing litigants who may have consulted a Sage on the matter. Sometimes the losing party would actually ask the Sage for a review of the decision. Often the beth din itself, feeling somewhat uncomfortable with its decision, might seek guidance from a beth din superior in knowledge even after it had made its decision, or as in the Israel Beth Din system, or in the situation which I have suggested, the judgment of the beth din is reversed on appeal. In all events, decisions of the beth din would sometimes be reversed. Decisions could be reversed because the judge or beth din erred in a matter that was so obvious that it lacked any semblance of a valid decision. This was known as

---

judge of the High Court of Justice of the State of Israel. He has written extensively on Jewish law, including many excellent articles in the *Encyclopedia Judaica*.

8. *Encyclopedia Judaica*, Vol. 12, p. 143.

erring in a law of the Mishnah. It was assumed that even a schoolchild would know what was stated in a Mishnah. Sometimes the beth din or judge would err in a matter known as weighing of precedents (*shikul hadath*). Somewhat more precise definitions of these terms are provided in the notes to this chapter. It must be understood, however, that this topic has been a controversial one among the commentators and respondents of the last few centuries. Rather than choose the preferable views among the hundreds of responsa and commentaries dealing with this subject, this author has followed the views of Rabbi Yehiel Epstein in Chapter 25 of his *Aruch haShulhan, Hoshen haMishpat*.

The halachah must provide a system of justice while at the same time taking into account that many communities are not equipped for such a system. Moreover, the Jews are living in so many countries that learned judges are not always available to adjudicate the local disputes. The first impulse is to have judges be absolutely immune from liability for erroneous decisions. Why would a person agree to judge a case if his decision might subject him to personal liability? On the other hand, judges might tend to become reckless if they were not held liable for patently erroneous decisions. The halachah provides for situations in which a judge or beth din is immune from liability even if their decisions are reversed. However, there are some situations in which they are liable even if their decisions are not reversed, and there are other situations in which their decisions are reversed and they are liable. As previously noted, there are many, many opinions in this area of the halachah. What is reversible error? Is it an error in a matter of a Mishnah? Is the judge liable in this case because of an error? Who is capable of reviewing the decision? It must be remembered that there must be a finality to litigation. Thus, how much forum-shopping for a reversal on appeal is available to a losing litigant?

In the appeals procedure suggested here, much of the differences of opinion are ameliorated. One method of encouraging capable judges while not making them vulnerable to liability might be for the seven selectmen of the city to declare that all judges be exempt from liability except in the most blatant cases of disregard of the halachah. Of course, if the city could find the most capable persons to judge in the first place, it would avoid many reversals on obvious grounds.

The procedure whereby judges are held liable for their obvious mistakes has been maintained here for two reasons. First and foremost, it has traditionally been part of the halachah. Second, the unified beth din system which has been suggested in this book does not seem to be an imminent probability, except for the limited jurisdiction of the beth din system in Israel. And even a unified beth din system may still require some sanction to ensure that judges do not disregard halachah and depend on a Review Beth Din to rectify their errors.

TEXT

Finality of judgments

The decision of the beth din is final.[9] Unless a community has an appeals procedure,[10] as suggested in Chapter 1 or as adopted by the Israel Beth Din system, there is no opportunity to appeal that decision. The litigant need not even appear in the second beth din that wishes to review the decision of the first beth din.[11] If the first beth din stated in its decision that it may be reviewed by another beth din, then the litigants may ask a second beth din to review the decision. Some authorities hold that finality of a judgment applies only if the decision was rendered by a beth din of three judges. There are those who disagree; however, this author believes that the latter view should be followed.

A beth din may, but is not required to, reopen its own decision if it can be shown that there was an error in the decision. This error may even be pointed out by another beth din or by a sage. Some authorities hold that a second beth din may retry the case on the basis

---

9. This topic is not to be confused with the topic discussed in Chapter 20, wherein a party may move to vacate a judgment on the basis of newly discovered or newly available evidence or witnesses or both.

10. See Responsum 42, *Hoshen haEphod*, which describes the review beth din set up in Sofia by the leaders of several communities.

11. This is not the same as *res judicata*, wherein a party defends an action on the basis that the issues were once tried; that defense may be brought even in the same beth din. The discussion of this topic centers on the second beth din's wanting to review the case and sometimes even wanting to retry it to determine whether the decision of the first beth din is valid.

of newly discovered evidence or witnesses. Other authorities disagree. This author suggests that the latter view is preferable.[12] The
second beth din may review the decision of the first beth din if it was
not in proper form—as, for example, if it was not signed by the judges.

Appeal procedure

After the judgment has been rendered by the beth din or by a judge,
any party may file a notice of appeal. The notice of appeal must be
filed with the original judge or beth din within thirty days after the
judgment was rendered.

If a party has filed a motion under Chapter 20 to be allowed time to
produce testimony or evidence to rescind the judgment, and if such
motion is granted, then the time for filing the notice of appeal shall be
extended until there is a disposition of the motion to rescind. The
appellant must file with the notice of appeal a copy of the pleadings,
a copy of the judgment, a halachic brief, and any other papers he
wishes. A copy of the notice of appeal and all accompanying papers
must be served on the appellee prior to filing the notice of motion. An
affidavit of service on the appellee must be filed together with the
notice of appeal.

The appellee's answering papers and halachic briefs shall be served
on the appellant and then filed with the clerk of the trial beth din
together with an affidavit of service on the appellant. The appellee's
papers shall be served and filed within thirty days after receipt of the
appellant's notice of appeal and accompanying papers. If the appellee
fails to serve and file his papers within the prescribed time, the clerk
shall notify the beth din and the judgment of the beth din or judge shall
be vacated.

If the appellee files his answering papers in a timely manner the
clerk of the beth din shall forward the appellant's papers together with
the appellee's papers to the Review Beth Din. The Review Beth Din
shall provide such rules as it deems necessary for the hearing and

---

12. The author thinks that it is a matter for the first beth din to examine the alleged
newly discovered evidence or witnesses. They would be more likely to know
whether the evidence is genuinely newly discovered than would the second beth din,
which would have to determine from conflicting statements which evidence was
presented to the first beth din and which was not.

determining of appeals. The Review Beth Din shall provide procedures enabling an appellant to obtain a stay of enforcement of the judgment pending the appeal. On appeal, the Review Beth Din may review only questions of law.

A mistake in Mishnah law

If a mistake is made in the category known as Mishnah law, then the judgment is void and a new trial must be held.[13,14] It is void even if the beth din consisted of three experts[15] and the litigants voluntarily accepted them to be their beth din. For the purposes of this chapter, a judge appointed by the community is deemed to be an expert, unless it is obvious that the appointee is not knowledgeable. For the

---

13. The mistake may be discovered by the Review Beth Din, as described in Chapter 1, or it may be discovered by a Sage or a superior beth din. Or, of course, the beth din that issued the decision may have discovered its own obvious mistake.

14. As stated in the introduction to this chapter, there are many differing opinions on what constitutes a mistake in Mishnah law. All agree that it is an obvious error in interpretation of elementary halachah that even a student would be expected to know. A few examples of what the commentators on Hoshen haMishpat, Chapter 25, have determined to be a mistake in Mishnah law follow. Shach, in Chapter 25, para. 9, states: "If a judge erred in a matter which is not explicitly stated, but yet over which there is no controversy—as, for example, if he decided the law to be such and so, while all the authorities decide the case the other way—this is a mistake in a matter of Mishnah law. A mistake in weighing precedents can occur only if there is a difference of opinion among the authorities and he decided against the weight of the deciding authorities." Tummin says that "if a judge were to decide any case against the opinion of R. Ramo, it would be an error of law in the category of erring in Mishnah law. Similarly, if one decided the law as stated by Sefer Meiroth Ainayim (Sma) against a holding of Shach, it would fall into this category." Pitkai Teshuva cites this with approval. Aruch haShulhan makes one simple statement: "If one errs in an explicit law stated in the Talmud or in the deciders of the law it is not a judgment at all." These are just a few of the many opinions offered on this subject. What emerges is that the reviewer of the decision must decide whether the error committed is so at variance with halachah that it must not stand.

15. The law determining who is an expert is applicable even in our times. There are certain laws that apply to experts that are not followed nowadays, because for those purposes we hold that such experts do not now exist. For the purposes of the laws in this chapter, however, the laws of experts do exist. An expert is a rabbi who is very well versed in the Talmud and codes, and whose logic has been substantiated by sages, and who is recognized by the community to be an expert.

purposes of this chapter, a judge is deemed to be voluntarily accepted by the litigant if he appeared there without coercion. It applies even if he appeared in response to a summons to appear. If he was coerced into appearing, then it is not a voluntary acceptance of the judge or the beth din.

If the judgment was executed, then there must be a return of the amount paid, even if the judges personally make the execution under the judgment. If it is not possible to undo the execution,[16] then, if the judges do not personally participate in the execution of the judgment, they have no personal liability[17] to the aggrieved losing party.[18] If the judges did actually participate in the execution of the judgment, then there may be equitable liability[19] on the judges to make restitution if it is impossible to undo the execution. Some authorities hold that, in this case, the judges will have to make restitution to the aggrieved party.

If the judges were not experts and/or the litigants did not voluntarily accept them as judges, and if the judge personally participated in the execution of the judgment, and it is now not possible to undo the judgment, then the judges must make restitution to the aggrieved party.

If the litigants accept the judges to judge either according to law or according to any standards that the judges will use, including mistaken principles, then there are some authorities who hold that the judgment is valid and the judges have no liability to the litigants no matter how serious the error.

---

16. It may not be possible to undo the execution, if the party who received the judgment was paid the amount of the judgment and then moved to another country, or if he quickly dissipated his assets, or if he is too powerful for the beth din to order a return of the judgment.

17. They do not even have equity liability to make restitution in this case.

18. The reason there is no liability is that there is no intent by the judges to cause damage to the party they wronged—this in spite of the fact that a person may be liable for his indirectly caused damage. (See Chapter 386.) As has been stated, there are many opinions in all of these matters. There are those who say that the judges are liable for their indirectly caused damage. This book, as previously stated, follows the views of Rabbi Yehiel Epstein in this chapter.

19. See the author's article on *Lifnim Mishurath Hadin* in *Annual Volume of Young Israel Rabbis in Israel*, Vol. 2 (1988).

A mistake in weighing the precedents[20]

If the judge was an expert or the beth din consisted of experts, and either the judges were appointed by the community or the litigants voluntarily appeared before them, then the judgment is valid if it has been executed. The judgment is valid if it has been executed even if there exists the possibility of undoing the execution. There is no liability on the judges to make restitution to the aggrieved party.[21]

A new trial will be ordered if there is a greater scholar in the community than the judges of the beth din, and he suggests to the beth din that they reverse their decision, and they agree to the reversal of their judgment, and if the execution can be undone.

If one of the following three factors is not present, then the judgment will not be reopened and a new trial will not be ordered: (1) the availability of a greater sage in the community to review the decision, (2) the acceptance by the original beth din or trial judge of the suggestion of the greater sage, and (3) the return to the original status before the execution of the judgment.

If no execution has been made on the judgment, the judgment will be reversed and a new trial ordered.

---

20. A mistake in the category of weighing the precedents is defined in the *Shulhan Aruch*, Chapter 25, essentially as follows: It is a case in which there is a dispute among the Tannaim or the Amoraim, and in which the halachah was not specifically stated to be in accordance with one of the views, and in which the world has accepted one of the views, and in which this judge or beth din decided in accord with the other view. *Sefer Meiroth Ainayim* gives three categories of cases that are considered to be in the category of weighing the precedents: (1) the explanation of Rambam and Semag that the custom has arisen to decide the case following one of the authorities in a discussion in the Talmud; (2) the explanation of Rashi that the majority of judges follow one precedent in an undecided discussion in the Talmud; (3) the explanation of Tur that the discussion in the Talmud from the type of questions being asked and the answers given therein that the law should probably follow one of the Talmudic opinions rather than the other. A mistake made in any of these three explanations would be a mistake in weighing the precedents.

21. There is no liability because there is not an actual mistake in the law. There is no liability even if the judge was personally involved in the execution of the judgment.

Cases in which the judge was not an expert or was not voluntarily accepted by the parties

If a nonexpert judge errs in weighing the precedents, then the judgment is reversed if execution has not been had thereon. The same rule applies even if he is an expert but is not voluntarily accepted by the litigants and has not been appointed by the community to be a judge. If execution has been had on the judgment, then the judgment will not be reversed; the judge will have to make restitution to the aggrieved party. If the mistake was in a Mishnah law, then the judgment will be reversed whether or not there has been an execution. If there has been an execution that cannot be undone, then the judges will have to make restitution to the aggrieved party. In all of these laws, if there has been partial execution, then the part executed will be separated from the part unexecuted. The executed part will be treated as executed, and the unexecuted part will be treated as unexecuted.

Reversal on appeal

If a decision is reversed on appeal in a beth din system that includes a formal appeal process, then the judgment will be reversed in all cases of mistake, whether the mistake was in a Mishnah law or in the weighing of precedents.

If the judgment is executed before the judgment is reversed, then the judges will not have to make restitution in any case unless (1) they personally participated in the execution process, (2) their mistake is blatantly erroneous, and (3) the losing party in the trial beth din is not able to avail himself of obtaining a stay of the execution.

Judgment of an invalid beth din

The judgment of an invalid beth din is a nullity.[22] If execution was had on such a judgment, then it will be undone. If it is not possible to undo

---

22. An example of an invalid beth din would be a beth din of fewer than three judges who were not appointed by the community to judge or who were not accepted by the litigants as judges.

the execution, then the judges of the invalid beth din must make restitution to the aggrieved party.

Errors in ordering oaths

If the beth din erroneously orders a party to take an oath,[23] and if the party instead of taking the oath compromises his claim or defense, or enters into arbitration, then the compromise or arbitration will be rescinded if the party who entered into the compromise or arbitration indicates at the time that he is following this path because he did not want to take the oath. The arbitration will be rescinded even if the parties agree to the arbitration with a *kinyan.*[24]

If the judgment following the arbitration or the compromise is executed and the mistake is in weighing precedents, the judgment will be allowed to remain.

Apportionment of restitution

If there was more than one judge on the beth din that unanimously decided a case in which the judges must make restitution, then they will share equally in the restitution. If any judge does not pay his share, then the aggrieved party may institute suit against him, but the other judges do not have to make up his payment.

If the decision is not unanimous, then the two judges who are in the majority must each pay one-third of the judgment, and the judge who voted against the reversed decision need not make any payment.[25] The aggrieved party will lose one-third of the restitution.

If there are five judges and there is a majority consisting of at least three judges, then the judges on the majority must pay the full amount of the judgment, each paying one-third or one-quarter, depending on how many judges constitute the majority.

---

23. See Chapter 87 regarding when a party must take an oath in beth din.

24. See Chapter 12.

25. This allocation of liability to two judges may be made only voluntarily among the judges, with the two judges whose majority decision is being reversed making the payment. If the judges do not admit which judges voted for the majority, however, then the third judge may disclose the identity of the judges who voted for the decision the first time; this would not be equivalent to tale-bearing, the admonition against which prohibits judges from disclosing the identity of the judges who voted for the majority.

Chapter 26

THE PROHIBITION AGAINST SETTLING DISPUTES IN GENTILE COURTS

INTRODUCTION

A beth din system assumes that all disputes will be adjudicated in the beth din. Even where there is no organized beth din system, the prohibition against adjudicating disputes in the non-Jewish courts applies.

Rambam stated the law as follows:

> Whoever submits his dispute to Gentiles and to their courts, even if their laws are similar to the laws of Israel, such a person is considered a wicked person. It is as if he had reviled and blasphemed and rebelled against the law of our teacher Moses, as it is written 'Now these are the ordinances which thou shalt set before them,'[1] before them, and not before Gentiles; before them, and not before laymen. If the hand of the Gentile is forceful and his adversary is powerful and the plaintiff is not able to recover from his adversary in a Jewish beth din, he must [nevertheless] institute suit in a Jewish beth din. If his adversary refuses to appear there, he must take permission from the beth

---

1. Exodus 21:1.

din and commence suit in the Gentile court against his adversary to recover what he claims.[2]

In Chapter 11, it was stated that one of the reasons that the beth din should have authority to enter default judgments would be to diminish the reliance on the Gentile courts to enforce claims against a recalcitrant defendant. In Chapter 22, it was noted that even if the parties stipulated a willingness to have their dispute adjudicated by a Gentile (as distinguished from a Gentile court), the best practice would be to avoid even this, because it approximated too closely the concept of permitting adjudication by the Gentile court.

The prohibition extends even to those situations in which Gentiles are operating their legal system pursuant to the Torah command for the Gentiles to observe the seven Noahide laws, one of which is to establish a system of courts.[3]

Scores of responsa were written during the hundreds of years when the Jews lived in the diaspora under many rulers who made many laws to compel the Jews to abide by the legal system of the city, state, duchy, or country of the ruler. Some permitted the beth din to operate but insisted that it follow the law of the land in topics for which it was not in keeping with halachah to follow the law of the land. In many lands the rulers permitted the beth din to function on a voluntary basis with no power to compel litigants to appear before it, and even if they did appear, with no power to enforce their judgments. Many of the rules in the text which follows come from these responsa. Because of persecution, the Jews were not always able to abide by the prohibitions discussed in this chapter. No one can fault the Jews in such situations. The fact that they were asking so many questions about the Gentile courts showed their great regard for halachah.

But in those lands where Jews were permitted to follow the Torah, there was a great rage on the part of the sages against those who invoked the jurisdiction of the Gentile courts. At the present time we are fortunate that there are many countries outside the State of Israel

---

2. Rambam, *Laws of Sanhedrin*, Chapter 26, para. 7.

3. See *Sheiltoth* 2. The command for Gentiles to establish a court and legal system is intended to enable them to mete out justice to Gentiles. The first six Noahide laws prohibit the following: (1) idolatry, (2) blasphemy, (3) murder, (4) adultery, (5) robbery, and (6) eating a limb taken from a living animal. The seventh Noahide law commands the establishment of a system of courts and laws.

where Jews can practice their religion openly and proudly. In such places, whether or not there is an organized beth din system, the prohibition of this chapter can certainly be followed.

TEXT

It is prohibited to invoke the jurisdiction of the Gentile courts to settle a dispute

The word *prohibited* is intentionally employed here, since this is a jurisdictional defect *per se*.[4] Employing Gentile courts rejects the entire Torah beth din system, organized or not. The prohibition extends to availing oneself of the Gentile courts in those situations in which one wishes to take the law into one's own hands, as described in Chapter 2 of *Hoshen haMishpat*.[5] The prohibition extends even to those places where the Gentile law is similar to, or even the same as, halachah. There are opinions that permit arbitration before Gentile arbitrators if they are appointed by the government to adjudicate certain types of disputes, such as landlord–tenant cases, and they do not follow the precedents of the Gentile courts but rather their own precedents. These same authorities would also permit such procedure in an industrywide practice. There are authorities who would prohibit both these exceptions.

The prohibition applies even if both parties agree to use the Gentile courts, and even if they agreed by *kinyan*.[6] The prohibition applies even if they swore to go to the Gentile courts. The prohibition applies even if it was included in an agreement between the parties, effected by *kinyan*, regarding other matters, such as going into a partnership together. The prohibition applies even if the agreement provided for penalties if either party refused to appear before the Gentile court. The penalties will not be enforced by the beth din. If, however, the money paid as the penalty was to be given to charity, the agreement

---

4. The prohibition applies even if one has excellent motives, as when one feels that one may bring about better relationships among people.

5. See Chapter 2 and the notes thereto.

6. The *kinyan* will be treated as a *kinyan* made in error, which can always be rescinded. See Chapter 195.

would not be enforced but the penalty to charity would be. The prohibition applies even if the judges of the Gentile courts are Jews. The prohibition applies to those who assist the party or both parties to invoke the jurisdiction of the Gentile courts.[7]

If possible, every effort must be made by the friends of the litigants and by the Jewish community at large to avoid the litigants' resorting to the Gentile courts.

If a person invokes the jurisdiction of the Gentile courts and loses his case there, he may no longer commence an action in a beth din.[8] If the litigation in the Gentile court is discontinued before a final decision is reached there, then the action may be recommenced in a beth din if the plaintiff reimburses all the defendant's expenses in the Gentile court, and upon such other terms and conditions as the beth din deems appropriate. There is an opinion that if the decision in the Gentile court is appealable and the time to appeal has not expired, the decision is not considered to be final and the action may still be brought to the beth din. The defendant is not precluded from instituting an action in the beth din even if he has appeared in the plaintiff's action in the Gentile court.[9]

If a party invokes the jurisdiction of the Gentile courts and obtains a judgment larger than the one he might have won in a beth din, then the overage must be returned to the defendant. He must also reimburse all the defendant's litigation expenses.

All that has just been said notwithstanding, if two Jews *do go* to the Gentile courts, then the decision of the court will be recognized. The winning party's penance for having gone to the Gentile courts should comply with the provisions of the previous paragraph. That which has been paid by the losing party to the winning party is not considered unlawfully acquired property in the hands of the winning party. There is also an opposing view which holds that if the winning party would

---

7. The prohibition extends to a person acting as a witness if he can avoid testifying. If he is subpoenaed and cannot avoid testifying, then he must testify.

8. There is also opinion to the contrary, which permits the beth din to hear his claims. Ramo's view, however, has been included in this text. See Ramo, *Hoshen haMishpat*, Chapter 26, end of para. 11.

9. If the defendant would fail to appear in the Gentile court, then the plaintiff would obtain a default judgment against him. Thus the defendant would be penalized for avoiding the Gentile court which had been invoked by the plaintiff. This would permit the transgressing plaintiff to benefit by his transgression.

not have won his case in a beth din, then that which he received is unlawfully acquired property.

If two Gentiles come before the beth din and request that their dispute be judged, then their request is granted.[10]

If a Jew and a Gentile bring their dispute before a beth din, then the beth din must treat them both fairly and, as was stated by Rabbi Akiva, it will enhance the sanctification of His Name.[11]

A great problem arises when the beth din or individual Jewish judges apply the precedents of the Gentile courts to cases before them in which both or one of the parties is Jewish. This is a practice to be prohibited because it negates the entire reason for the prohibition against using Gentile courts. Such a prohibition was to avoid enhancing the image of the Gentile court at the expense of the beth din.

The question of the courts in the State of Israel is discussed in Chapter 369. That chapter deals with a concept in halachah known as *dina d'malchuta dina* (the law of the land must be followed).

In Chapter 388 the liability as an informer of a party who invokes the Gentile courts is discussed.

Penalties for violating the prohibition

The beth din must first ascertain whether the transgressor was aware of the fact that he was transgressing. This can be ascertained by inviting him to discuss the entire matter as soon as the beth din becomes aware of the transgression or potential transgression. People are often not aware of the entire prohibition. There may be an emergency situation which compels the plaintiff to invoke the Gentile courts. Such an emergency might exist if the beth din is not in session, and the defendant is dissipating his assets, and the plaintiff needs a restraining order from the Gentile court to maintain the staus quo, pending the plaintiff's commencing his action in the beth din.

Only the penalties that a beth din may mete out are discussed here. The penalties of Heaven are left for Heaven to mete out.

---

10. See Rambam, *Laws of Kings and Their Wars*, Chapter 11, para. 12.
11. See *Baba Kamma* 113a. As Rambam stated in the paragraph cited in the previous note, the Rabbis bade us visit their sick and to bury their dead along with the dead of the Jews, and to maintain their poor together with the poor of Israel in the interests of peace.

If a person transgresses the prohibitions contained herein, the beth din may put such a person under a ban and may excommunicate him.[12] The transgressor may be prohibited from holding community positions and from officiating at prayer services. Where feasible, the beth din may impose a monetary fine. The beth din may deny the transgressor access to the beth din at any future time, either as a plaintiff[13] or as a witness if it serves his purpose to be a witness. The beth din may require the transgressor to pay all the defendant's expenses in defending the lawsuit in the Gentile court.

Exceptions to the prohibition

It was stated in Chapter 11 that the beth din should be able to grant plaintiff default judgment if the defendant fails to appear in beth din. All that follows is in addition to that suggestion, and in addition to placing the defendant under a ban and eventually excommunicating him for not appearing.

The plaintiff may be given permission by the beth din to invoke the jurisdiction of the Gentile courts. The plaintiff will not be given permission by the beth din to take his case to the Gentile court unless he has first commenced an action in the beth din. Some authorities hold that the summons to appear must be personally served upon the defendant by two persons who can testify that he was served. The current practice is for one person appointed by the beth din to serve the defendant one time before he is held in default if he does not appear. If the defendant appears and asks for additional time to plead, then this is certainly not a recalcitrant defendant. Similarly, if the defendant states that he wishes to avail himself of the opportunity to select another beth din as provided for in Chapter 13 or 14 (where

---

12. See notes to Chapter 1 regarding the use of the ban and the use of excommunication.

13. An example would be as follows: Mr. A. commenced to build onto his house an attic that blocked Mr. B.'s light. Mr. B. sued Mr. A. in beth din and obtained an injunction against Mr. A. to prohibit him from building his attic. Mr. A. refused to abide by the judgment of the beth din. Thereafter, Mr. C. commenced to build an attic onto his house on the other side of Mr. A.'s house, and Mr. A. wished to obtain an injunction in the beth din against Mr. C. to prevent him from building his attic. The beth din refused to take jurisdiction over Mr. A.'s claim.

there is no organized beth din system), then he is not a recalcitrant defendant.

The majority of authorities hold that if a community has appointed one person to be its judge, then his authority in granting permission to a plaintiff to invoke the Gentile courts is the same as that of a beth din of three judges.

If a plaintiff has a claim against a powerful person and the beth din is powerless to compel the defendant to appear before it, then the plaintiff must nevertheless commence an action before the beth din. If the defendant fails to appear and the beth din is convinced that he will not appear, then the beth din will give permission to the plaintiff to sue in the Gentile courts.

Some authorities hold that the permission will be granted only if the plaintiff is able to make a *prima facie* case before them and they are convinced that he is entitled to win the case.[14] If the beth din is not convinced that he is entitled to win the case, then they will refuse to grant him permission to use the Gentile courts. There is the fear that he may obtain a judgment in the Gentile court to which he is not entitled. If the beth din, after hearing the plaintiff's case, is convinced that he should surely win the case, they may assist him in his case in the Gentile court even to the extent of testifying there.[15] The beth din will also instruct witnesses to testify there on behalf of the plaintiff.

---

14. This is one of the proofs that was used in Chapter 11 to show that there are exceptions to not accepting any testimony or proofs in the absence of the other party. This is somewhat akin to the procedure for obtaining a default judgment that was suggested in the same chapter.

15. It has been asked whether the reason for not permitting invocation of the Gentile court is to avoid giving their system of law credence on a footing similar to that of halachah. Doesn't the appearance of the beth din judges before the Gentile court in this situation accomplish the same thing? One answer given is that the beth din judges are going to the Gentile court to testify, and this is not the same as invoking the jurisdiction of the Gentile court. It seems that the the better answer is that this is the lesser of the two evils. If the recalcitrant defendant knows that he can avoid defending himself by refusing to go to the beth din, then the entire judicial process would be open to abuse by flagrant violators. They would know that the beth din could do nothing to them, and that the plaintiff's religious beliefs would keep him from invoking the jurisdiction of the Gentile courts. People would act with impunity in all types of matters. Society would be left without remedies to protect itself. In addition, it is a safer practice to have the beth din appear in the Gentile court so that the general populace will realize that this is a special instance not to be emulated by them.

This author contends that the better practice is to give the plaintiff permission to invoke the Gentile courts without requiring him to show his case to the beth din.

If a party has obtained a judgment in the beth din and the other party refuses to abide by the terms of the judgment, then the winning party may apply to the beth din for permission to apply to the Gentile court to enforce the judgment or to commence his case anew there if that is the procedure that the Gentile courts follow. Many authorities permit the plaintiff to invoke the jurisdiction of the Gentile courts in this case without obtaining further permission from the beth din. This author believes that the better practice is always to obtain permission from the beth din before invoking the Gentile courts even to enforce the judgment obtained in the beth din.

In bygone days the community would invoke the jurisdiction of the Gentile courts to help it enforce tax collections against a member of the community who refused to pay his taxes.

Conflicts of law

If an agreement contained a term stipulating that in the event of a dispute the parties would invoke either the beth din or the Gentile courts, or only the Gentile courts, then, as was previously stated, this clause would not give rise to either party's invoking the Gentile courts. As previously stated, the same result would apply if the parties agreed by *kinyan*.

If, however, the party would be able to receive a more favorable decision in the Gentile courts than he could in the beth din, or, for that matter, a decision in the Gentile courts that could not be had in the beth din, and if it could be shown that this was the reason for including the term in the agreement, then the Gentile courts may be invoked. The agreement must have been made before the dispute arose and must be very specific and unambiguous; for example, if the indebtedness was cancelled by the year of *shemitah*,[16] and the plaintiff could still enforce the debt in the Gentile courts. Where a Jew has obtained

---

16. *Shemitah*, or Sabbatical year, is the seventh year in the Jewish calendar. Many agricultural activities must cease. In addition thereto, debts are generally cancelled. See Chapter 67 for those circumstances in which debts are not cancelled. Also see note 1 to Chapter 7.

a license from the secular authorities to sell goods, and another Jew from another community is unfairly competing without a license, then the beth din will give the licensee permission to invoke the Gentile courts since the beth din has no jurisdiction to stop the unfair competition quickly and the licensee will not be able to sue the other Jew because he is from a distant community. This is not a unanimous opinion. There are those who hold that even under such circumstances the Gentile courts may not be invoked.

If the same result can be achieved in the beth din as in the Gentile court, then the Gentile court may not be invoked.

If the beth din is able to decide the case according to Gentile law without transgressing Jewish law, then the beth din must take jurisdiction over the case and decide the case according to the Gentile law. This would be the case if, for example, a Jew purchased a promissory note from a Gentile that called for any dispute concerning the note to be brought to the Gentile court. Assuming that the Gentile court would give a more favorable result to the holder of the note than would a beth din, the holder of the note can insist that the beth din apply Gentile law to his case. Another example would be if the Gentile custom in the community permitted a holder of a note to seize property of the borrower without authorization of beth din. Such seizure is for the limited purpose of enabling the noteholder to levy upon the seized property at the conclusion of the case. Yet another example would be a case in which a woman would not inherit property under halachah but would inherit under Gentile law; if the property had been left to her by the deceased the beth din will instruct the heirs who would have inherited under halachah to effect a compromise with her.[17]

---

17. Laws of Inheritance commence with Chapter 276.

Chapter 27

NOT TO CURSE A JUDGE OR ANY JEW

INTRODUCTION

The title of this chapter as it appears in *Shulhan Aruch, Hoshen haMishpat* has intentionally been retained because it gives the tone and the essence of this chapter. People in modern times often tend to overlook the fact that the judge is fulfilling a most important function in society. In a society that attempts to treat all people as equals not only before the law but also in educational and business opportunities, the judge is not only given less respect than is due him, but is often relegated to an economic status that is exceeded by many who hold positions of less societal importance. In Chapter 8, reference was made to the respect to be shown to the judge and to his attendant in the beth din. As pertains to the judge, this chapter complements Chapter 8. The counterpart chapter in the *Shulhan Aruch* also discusses the respect that a person must have toward his fellow Jew. The text of the *Shulhan Aruch* has been provided in the note. This chapter sets forth a few small details dealing with the respect for the judge.

The rules of this chapter apply whether there is a beth din system or any other system of judges, either as it exists at present or as may from time to time be in effect.

This author has been asked why the laws against cursing a fellow

Jew appears in a jurisprudential code. The apparent reason is that the code was intended to enjoin the cursing of a judge and included the broader category of not cursing any Jew along with the particular prohibition against cursing a judge, lest by stating only the particular, the code might be mistakenly taken to imply that it is permitted to curse one who is not a judge. An additional reason is provided here. In Chapters 11 and 16 (and in *Shulhan Aruch* Chapter 28), reference is made to the ban that a party or a beth din may pronounce to obtain testimony or to punish one who does not answer a summons. If placing a person under a ban or curse was a very common procedure, it would soon lose its effect. Thus it is a jurisprudential injunction not to curse someone unless the halachah permits it.

TEXT

To respect the judge

Every person is obligated to give respect to the judge of the beth din, both within and without the beth din.[1] Anyone who shows disrespect

---

1. The following is a loose translation of the text of Chapter 27 of *Hoshen haMishpat*:

   1. If a person curses a Jew (gloss: even if he curses himself), using the Divine Name or by any similar one, or by any one of the names which the Gentiles call the Holy One, Blessed be He, and if this act took place in the presence of witnesses and with the requisite warning, he is flogged for transgressing the injunction "Thou shalt not curse the deaf" (Leviticus 19:14). And if he cursed a judge, he is additionally flogged for also transgressing the injunction "Thou shalt not revile the judge" (Exodus 22:27). The term *arrur* is considered to have the meaning of "cursed."

   2. If the requisite warning was not given, or if the curse was made without using the Divine Name or any similar name, or if the curse could be inferred from the statement which he made, as, for example, if he said "May he not be blessed unto the Lord," such person is not flogged. (Gloss: One who curses the dead is also exempt from flogging.) In these aforesaid cases, the prohibition against such action is nevertheless present. If one shamed a scholar, the beth din may put him under a ban. And if the judges wish to flog him they may do so and punish him as much as they see fit. And if he shamed an uneducated person, they punish him according to the demands of the times. (Gloss: Even if the one who was put to shame [another version,

to a judge in the beth din is in contempt of beth din and may be punished by the beth din. Similarly, anyone who shows disrespect for a permanent judge outside of the beth din is in contempt of the beth din and may be punished by the beth din.

Anyone who curses a judge in the beth din or a permanent judge outside of the beth din is in contempt of the beth din and may be punished by the beth din. The beth din may punish the person who is in contempt in such manner as the beth din may determine. A person may not be punished for contempt of a judge or a beth din until he has been warned to cease such conduct and unless it is determined that the affront was deliberate and premeditated. A hearing should be held before a person is punished for contempt of the beth din. The finding of a person in contempt of the beth din is reviewable on appeal.

A judge or a beth din may forego the honor to be paid to them unless it appears that to do so would demean the status of Torah in the community.

To respect a fellow Jew

A Jew must not curse his fellow Jew.

A Jew may not proclaim a ban against a fellow Jew. Examples of exceptions to proclaiming a ban or cursing a fellow Jew are the situations stated in Chapter 11, which deals with the case in which the defendant refuses to come to beth din in response to a summons, and in Chapter 16, which deals with the general ban against all those who have testimony or evidence but refuse to come forward to testify or to produce the evidence.

---

even if the one who was cursed] has waived the respect due him, he is nevertheless punished because he had already committed the sin and is thus guilty.) If one was to be placed under a ban because he acted contemptuously toward the beth din, and then the beth din wishes to waive its honor and not place him under a ban, they may do so, provided, however, that their foregoing the option to place him under a ban does not create a diminishing of the honor of the Creator. For example, if the people acted contemptuously toward the Torah and the judges, the beth din should act to fortify the law and mete out punishment as it deems necessary.

Part II

LAWS OF EVIDENCE

Chapter 28

TESTIFYING IN BETH DIN

INTRODUCTION

Chapter 28 commences the discussion of the laws of evidence, which continues through Chapter 38.

This chapter begins with a discussion of the obligation to testify. *Shulhan Aruch* also included in this chapter the procedure to be followed in getting witnesses to testify. This book includes the latter topic in Chapter 16, which deals with the subpoenaing of evidence. After that there is a section dealing with priorities in the presentation of cases, followed by the procedure for testifying in the beth din, including the requirement that the testimony be of a present recollection, even if recalled by some memorandum or by other persons. This chapter also deals with the subject of receiving testimony in the absence of the other litigant. A similar theme was dealt with in the discussion of receiving pleas of one of the litigants in the absence of the other litigant; see Chapters 11, 13, 14, and 19, and the notes to Chapter 13. The chapter concludes with a discussion of a Jew testifying in a Gentile court. The topic of dealing with lawyers is discussed by Tur and R. Karo in chapters commencing with Chapter 122.

Subsequent chapters deal with the prohibition against recanting of testimony, the examination of the witnesses; the contradictions between witnesses; admissions, and their admissibility; ineligiblity to testify; the possible tainting of the testimony of all the witnesses if an ineligible witness is part of the testifying group; and the laws of refuted witnesses.

In this entire section, it does not matter whether there is an organized beth din system or whether the beth din operates as it does today or under any other system. The laws governing witnesses and testimony are applicable.

The purpose of a trial is to arrive at a just solution of a dispute. The judges ordinarily do not have any independent knowledge of the facts of the case.[1] Once the facts have been proven to them, they will apply the law to the facts to arrive at a decision that is just according to halachah. They can determine the facts only by hearing the testimony that is presented to them by the witnesses and by examining the various forms of evidence presented. Thus there must be rules governing the types of persons who may or may not testify, the types of testimony they may give, and the types of evidence that are admissible at a trial.

TEXT

The obligation to testify

A person who knows evidence pertaining to a pending case has an obligation to testify[2] if the following conditions are met:

---

1. See Chapter 7 for those situations in which a judge or beth din may decide the case on matters of their own knowledge.

2. One of the 613 Torah commandments is for a person who has information regarding a pending litigation to testify in the case. "And if any one sin, in that he heareth the voice of adjuration, he being a witness, whether he hath seen or known, if he did not utter it, then he shall bear his iniquity" (Leviticus 5:1). During the time that the Holy Temple stood, a person who violated this commandment had to bring a special sacrifice to atone for the violation. There were ten requirements before the person would be liable for the sacrifice: (1) The litigant requested the witness to testify; (2) the suit was brought for a money judgment only; (3) the claim arose out of a transaction regarding personalty; (4) the other party would be found liable on the strength of these witnesses; (5) the witness, after being asked to testify, denied that he had any knowledge of the transaction; (6) the denial of knowledge was made in

1. He is an eligible witness.[3] If the witness knows that he is not eligible to testify (if, for example, he is an ineligible witness or a wicked person), then if he does not testify without stating what his reason is, he is not liable to the judgments of Heaven. The obligation does not apply if the two Jewish litigants are having their case tried in a Gentile court.

2. The testimony he is to give is admissible, and not hearsay testimony.[4] If the testimony will not result in a money judgment, then there is no obligation to testify. Thus if the witness were to testify that a certain person promised a second person a gift, assuming the truth of the statement, there is still no obligation to give the gift. Thus the failure to testify that the statement was made does not make the witness liable to the judgments of Heaven. If the testimony is not admissible, then there can be no benefit to the litigant who demanded that he testify and thus no liability to the judgments of Heaven.

3. He was asked by the beth din or by one of the litigants to come to the beth din to testify. There are opinions that if he knows that he has testimony but the litigants are not aware of this, then he must come forward to testify without being called, and failing to do so would subject him to the judgments of Heaven. The liability to the judgments of Heaven also applies if the witness knows that he is leaving the jurisdiction and that there will be a lawsuit started about which he has information that could be used as testimony. If he fails to go to beth din and to state his testimony there in anticipation of the lawsuit, then he too is liable to the judgments of Heaven. The liability to the judgments of Heaven is not present if the witness was asked to testify outside of the beth din.

---

beth din; (7) the denial was accompanied by an oath including the name of the Lord; (8) the knowledge was known to the witness before he took the oath; (9) the party asking him to testify separated him as his witness; and (10) the oath was taken in a language that the witness understood.

3. See Chapter 7 regarding who is ineligible to testify. If he is not eligible, then even if the ineligibilty is waived, there is no obligation to Heaven. There is also an opposing view which holds that if the parties waive the ineligibilty and the witness still refuses to testify, then there is liability to the judgments of Heaven. This author prefers the first opinion.

4. In those instances in which written interrogatories may be sent to the witness for answers, if he refuses to write the answers, the same rules apply to him as to a reluctant witness.

It does not matter whether he was originally designated to be a witness to the occurrence or he just happened to witness it. In either event he is obligated to testify.

The obligation applies whether he is the only witness on the side of the person who called him to testify or if there are other witnesses.[5] A witness may not absolve himself of the liability to Heaven by stating that he is waiting for the other witness to the transaction to testify first.

If a witness who has met the criteria specified in paragraph 1 does not testify, he has no monetary obligation to the party on whose behalf the testimony would have been useful.[6] He does, however,[7] have liability to the judgments[8] of Heaven[9] for not having testified![10]

---

5. In halachah there is a fundamental difference between the testimony of one witness or two witnesses. The testimony of the second witness is not merely cumulative and taken as additional credence to the testimony of the first witness. If two witnesses whose testimony is not contradicted or refuted testify in a money action, then the litigant on whose behalf they testify will be successful in the action. Thus if the plaintiff produces two witnesses who testify that the defendant owes him money, the judgment will be for the plaintiff. This is not so if there is only one witness. Generally speaking, a judgment will not be awarded a plaintiff in a money action based on the testimony of one witness, despite the fact that his testimony is neither contradicted nor refuted. The testimony of the one witness serves a distinct function: It shifts the burden of proof from the plaintiff to the defendant. When the plaintiff calls the one witness to testify, the plaintiff may rest his case after the witness has testified in his behalf, for the plaintiff has made a *prima facie* case. The burden of proof is then shifted to the defendant. The defendant may then admit or deny liability. His denial must be in the form of a Torah oath. If two witnesses testified on the plaintiff's behalf, then unless they are contradicted or refuted, the plaintiff will obtain a judgment. The defendant's oath will have no effect.

Oaths are discussed in Chapter 87. The difference between witnesses being contradicted or refuted is discussed in Chapter 38.

6. There is no monetary liability, since the failure to testify is only the indirect cause for the loss to the plaintiff.

7. There is an opinion that if the potential witness is liable to the judgments of Heaven, then he is not eligible to testify in any beth din. There is also a contrary view. This author believes that the second view is preferable. There is also the view that the potential witness may be publicly ridiculed and called a wicked person.

8. It might have been thought that there was no liability even to the judgments of Heaven, since the potential witness not only was not the direct cause of the damages, but did not even perform any act. Nevertheless, he is liable to the judgments of Heaven.

9. To be liable to the judgments of Heaven, the witness must be an eligible witness in that case. Thus while he may be eligible in other cases, he may be related to one

There is no monetary obligation even if there were two witnesses and they conspired not to testify. If the potential witness who refused to testify wishes to purge himself of his liability to the judgments of Heaven, he must make restitution to the person who lost the case because of his refusal to testify. The litigant who lost because of the refusal of the witness to testify may not sue the refusing witness and may not use self-help to recover his losses, even in places where self-help is permitted.[11]

A person may not appear in beth din with the purpose of intimidating one of the parties by causing him to think that his adversary has more witnesses than he really has.[12]

Priority in presenting the case, motions regarding production of claims, and motions for declaratory judgments

The general rule is that the plaintiff presents his case first.[13] Under the following circumstances, the defendant will present his case first

---

of the parties or to another witness who has testified or to one of the judges and thus be ineligible to testify in this case. Even if the litigants stipulate that the ineligible witness may testify in this case, and he still refuses to testify, he is not liable to the judgments of Heaven. The testimony must be admissible testimony; otherwise the witness will not be liable to the judgments of Heaven.

10. Some authorities hold that the reluctant witness can be coerced into testifying just as a person may under certain circumstances be coerced into performing a commandment.

11. See Chapter 4 regarding self-help.

12. As was stated in note 5 of this chapter, there is a substantive difference between one witness testifying on behalf of a party and two witnesses testifying. We are now dealing with a situation in which a person absolutely believes that the plaintiff is an honest person. The plaintiff tells this person that the defendant owes him money, but there is only one witness to the transaction. The plaintiff asks this person to come to the beth din and merely stand there as if he were going to testify on behalf of the plaintiff. The defendant, seeing that there are two people ready to testify, the real witness and this other person, may become intimidated into settling the case or admitting to something he might not have admitted to had he thought that there was only one witness. It is prohibited for this nonwitness to stand there as if he were going to testify. There is great danger in this type of intimidation. It may well be that the defendant is actually not liable to the plaintiff but because he sees two witnesses, he capitulates and agrees to a settlement that he might not otherwise have made.

13. The party who files his claim first with the beth din is the plaintiff, even if the counterclaim is the exact same claim.

whether it is his counterclaim or his defense:[14] If the defendant will suffer monetary damage[15] by the continuation of the lawsuit against him and the plaintiff is not prepared to proceed to trial on the complaint; if the defendant claims that the plaintiff is holding the defendant's security which is about to depreciate in value if the claim on the security is not heard immediately,[16] and the plaintiff is not prepared to proceed to trial on his complaint; and if the defendant's witnesses are ill or about to depart the jurisdiction and the defendant will not be able to present his defense or counterclaim without them. However, if the plaintiff's witnesses are also about to leave the jurisdiction, the priority will be given to plaintiff.

Even if the beth din hears the plaintiff's case first and renders a judgment in his favor, it may enjoin the enforcement of the judgment if the defendant will be prejudiced by the plaintiff's collecting the amount of the judgment. Prejudice might be shown where the defendant's counterclaim is equal to or larger than the amount of the judgment and there is danger that the plaintiff will divest himself of the moneys he will collect from the defendant.

If the defendant is not ready to proceed on his counterclaim, the beth din may grant the defendant an adjournment on the counterclaim and proceed to judge the plaintiff's case.

If both parties are ready to proceed to trial on their complaint and

---

14. Once the plaintiff has filed his complaint, the defendant cannot hasten to the beth din and admit part of the claim before filing his answer. The law is that if the defendant admits part of the claim before the plaintiff presents his claim, then the defendant does not have to take an oath of denial on the balance which must be taken by defendants who admit part of the plaintiff's claim. Once the plaintiff has filed his complaint, the admission made by the defendant, whether prior to or simultaneously with the filing of the answer, will not be deemed to relieve the defendant of the obligation to take the partial admission oath as to the balance.

15. The monetary damage may take many forms. It may be that the defendant's credit ratings are impaired while the suit is pending. It may be that he cannot dispose of merchandise or property because of the cloud on the ownership of the property stemming from the lawsuit. At any time that the defendant thinks that he will suffer a monetary loss if the plaintiff presents his case first, the defendant may make an application to the beth din to present his case first.

16. There are many variables that may affect the value of the defendant's security. The merchandise may be perishable, or perhaps he has out-of-town buyers who are about to leave the jurisdiction. Or, the merchandise may be going out of style, or it may be seasonal. In such situations, the defendant may always make application to the beth din to have his case heard first.

counterclaim respectively, then the beth din will hear the plaintiff's case first and then the counterclaim. The beth din may award one of the parties the difference between the two awards.

In a dispute between a borrower and a lender who is holding the borrower's collateral, even if the borrower instituted suit first to obtain the collateral, the lender will be deemed to be the plaintiff in the lawsuit.

There are times when a defendant may make a motion to the beth din that the plaintiff present any and all claims that he may have against the defendant in addition to the claim that is the basis of the pending lawsuit. The defendant may desire to obtain a general release from the plaintiff after all the plaintiff's claims have been adjudicated and the defendant has paid to the plaintiff all the moneys awarded by the beth din, including the award of the pending lawsuit.

This motion may be made as soon as the defendant is served with a summons in the first lawsuit or at any time during the trial. It may also be made by the defendant if he loses the lawsuit and would like to have all of the plaintiff's claims against him adjudicated before he pays the judgment amount, so that the defendant can obtain a general release of all claims. The beth din will decide whether the defendant's motion should be granted in full or in part or denied in full. In deciding the motion, the beth din may consider whether the trial of closely related claims will be equitable for both parties. For example, if there are still claims that are liens on the defendant's property and the defendant can show damages if these lawsuits are not all tried at this time, the motion should be granted. However, the motion should not be granted if the plaintiff is not ready to proceed to trial on the other claims and will be prejudiced if he has to wait with the claims with which he is ready. If the plaintiff is not aware of any other claims, he may state that he does not at the time know of any claims and should not be precluded when he learns of the claims.

If the plaintiff does not go to trial on all of his claims, then the plaintiff must give the defendant a partial release when the defendant pays to the plaintiff the amounts awarded to him by the beth din.

If the defendant makes a motion that the plaintiff present all of his claims against the defendant, then the plaintiff may crossmove that the defendant present any and all of his claims against the plaintiff. The beth din will decide who has priority for presentation of the cases if the beth din grants all or part of the parties' motions.

If the plaintiff puts forward a claim regarding the defendant's property, he may not thereafter discontinue his lawsuit because now there is a cloud over the defendant's property.[17]

If partner A in a business that is being terminated wishes to have a declaratory judgment initiated against partner B stating that all the assets that partner A took belong to A, the beth din should entertain such a suit, if partner B refuses to give a deed or some other instrument stating that the property that A took is A's.

A landlord may ask the beth din for a declaratory judgment that the tenant's lease terminates on a certain date, if the tenant has threatened not to vacate on that date because of some claim that he may have against the landlord.

A principal may ask the beth din to grant him a declaratory judgment that the power of attorney that his agent has is not valid, if the agent refuses to return it to the principal.

A maker of a promissory note may request that the note be returned to him from the holder if the maker disputes the validity of the note, and the holder refuses to return it.

In all of these cases there is a cloud hanging over the title of the plaintiff or over his property. The beth din should always consider whether justice will be served by granting the applications.

Procedure in beth din

The sitting of the beth din should be in the beth din and in no other place unless another place was so designated; otherwise the procedure may not be valid. There is also a contrary view. This author prefers the first view.

The proper procedure is for the judge or judges of the beth din to sit in their places during the judicial procedure.[18] If the judges stand it is also valid. The traditional procedure was for the witnesses to stand

---

17. No one will want to purchase the property from defendant or to lend money on the property, since there is now knowledge in the community that the plaintiff has some claim against the property.

18. The rules dealing with the position of the judges and the witnesses are no doubt intended to convey to the participants in the beth din drama the idea that the trial is solemn and serious and that the parties would not be before the beth din if they did not feel that their rights were involved. The dignity of the proceedings helps the litigants and witnesses to realize that the Ultimate Judge is also present in the beth din. (See also Chapter 17.)

while testifying. The requirement that the judges sit is derived from various Torah sources. Most authorities hold that this is only a first-instance requirement, and if they do not sit then the judgment is still valid. Similarly, the requirement that witnesses stand is also a first-instance requirement, but if they do not stand then their testimony is still valid. Similarly, if the judges or witnesses leaned on something, then the procedure is valid.

There is an opinion that when the witnesses stood while testifying, the litigants also stood.[19] The traditional procedure was that an exception was made in the case of a sage, who was permitted to sit while testifying. The current procedure is for all witnesses to sit while testifying.

There is a first-instance requirement that testimony be taken only during the daylight hours. This too is a first-instance requirement, and if the litigants do not object, then taking of testimony during evening hours is also valid. The proper procedure would be for the beth din to advise the litigants at the outset of the trial that it may be necessary to take testimony at night and for them to agree.

The judges should be capable of understanding the language spoken by the witnesses. (The use of translators is discussed in Chapter 17.) If a Jew and Gentile are before the beth din, the judges should speak to the Jew in a language that the Gentile understands so that he will not suspect that perhaps the Jews are conspiring against him.

The procedure is for the parties to present all of their witnesses to the beth din at the outset of the trial. It is at that point, after the parties have recited their pleas, that the beth din addresses the witnesses and tells them about the seriousness of their position as witnesses.

The witnesses are addressed by the judge or head of the beth din, and the importance of not committing perjury is explained to them.[20] They are told of the punishments that await a perjurer in this world[21]

---

19. The opinion holds that all those who are involved in the judicial process, except for the judges, must stand while the process is proceeding. This is reminiscent of the time when all the Jewish people stood at Mount Sinai to receive the Torah.

20. The procedure is also used when a sage is testifying, since failing to use it would cause the other witnesses to feel that they were under suspicion while the sage was not. In all events, the failure to attempt to impress the witnesses is not grounds for reversal of a judgment.

21. The witnesses are told that famine and pestilence are brought about by those who testify falsely, and then they are told of the other matters stated in the text.

and in the world to come;[22] of the shame that will come to them in this
world when their perjury is discovered; of the contempt that the
person who engaged them will feel for them; and of the fact that
corruption of the judicial system harms all of society, not only the
perjurer. The warnings are meant to discourage those who may be
more impressed by the harm to society and those who may feel that
they will be put to shame when they are discovered. Even if they are
not discovered, they still have to meet their Maker. In some communities in the Middle Ages, the witness would take an oath before
testifying to tell only the truth. Nowadays each community or each
beth din must make its own rules in this respect. If it believes that the
oath to tell the truth is a deterrent to testifying falsely, then it may
institute such an oath.[23] There is an opinion that if the witness refuses
to take such an oath but promises to testify truthfully, he is not
compelled to take the oath.

All witnesses are then removed from the beth din.[24] The senior
witness then testifies. Before he testifies, each witness should be

---

22. The litigants may suggest ways to convey to the witnesses the importance of
telling the truth. The beth din must use its discretion in determining just how much
fear to instill in the witnesses. Such efforts may have a counterproductive effect,
leaving the witnesses reluctant to testify to anything of probative value.

23. The oath that a witness takes not to testify falsely is not the oath of witnesses
mentioned in the Torah. The latter oath is that taken by the witness to swear that he
knows no testimony. This may very well be an illusory oath, since the Torah already
requires him to testify truthfully. However, some people may be more influenced by
this particular oath to testify truthfully than by the Torah injunction against testifying
falsely. (See note 15 to Chapter 16.) Whatever seems preferable to the beth din
should be employed.

24. The authorities differ in their opinions on the issue of whether all persons
except for the judges, the litigants, and their counsel are removed, or only the
remaining witnesses are removed. This author holds that only the witnesses need be
removed. The witnesses are removed because if they were to hear the prior
witnesses' testimony, they would be able to tailor their testimony to match it. Others
would be asked to leave the beth din room because witnesses may find it easier to
testify if there are fewer people present. Some feel that it is also easier to
cross-examine witnesses when fewer people are present. Now that counsel is often
used, this last reason is no longer applicable. It has been suggested that the reason to
remove all others from the room is that the witness may wish to confess that he came
with the idea of giving false testimony, and he may not make this confession in the
presence of many people. However, the litigants will still be in the beth din, and they
can just as easily tell the community what they heard.

asked by the beth din whether he is the plaintiff's or defendant's witness so that he understands that his testimony may help that side to win the case. He testifies as to the events as they occurred. The witness must not be asked leading questions; rather, he must describe the event in his own words. (The actual method of examination of the witnesses is discussed in Chapter 30.)

Hearsay testimony is not admitted.[25] The witness must state exactly what he saw; he may neither add nor subtract from what he saw. The witness is instructed not to offer his conclusions, but rather to state the facts as they occurred. The judges of the beth din should not attempt to cut short the testimony of the witness unless it is clearly not responsive or not relevant. He may not state that he saw something which he did not see,[26] even if he is absolutely certain that the event occurred, and even if there is no other possible explanation for the event. He may not even rely on statements made by two persons whom he knows to be absolutely trustworthy, reliable, and honest. Even two witnesses may not rely on statements made by two persons who witnessed the event, even if they know the original witnesses to be absolutely trustworthy, reliable, and honest. Admissions made in his presence may be admissible if they meet the criteria outlined in Chapter 81. Former testimony—that is, testimony given at a previous trial and accepted as evidence at that trial—may be the

---

25. The halachah usually classifies testimony into four categories: (1) The witness testifies as to what he actually saw. This is the best type of testimony. (2) The defendant, the plaintiff, and two other persons were present, and the defendant followed the procedures stated in Chapter 81 and admitted in full detail that he was indebted to the plaintiff. This type of statement, if it complies with the requirement of Chapter 81, may be admissible in the beth din. (3) The defendant admitted to two witnesses his indebtedness to the plaintiff. He failed to comply with the requirements of Chapter 81. The defendant may then explain away his admission as described in Chapter 81. This admission is not admissible. (4) The witness testifies as to what someone told him about the occurrence. This is pure hearsay and cannot be admitted as evidence.

26. The authorities now hold that if a witness saw something with a telescope or microscope then it is admissible, even though it is not seen directly with the naked eye. A similar question was originally considered if a witness saw something in a mirror. Nowadays, authorities hold that all such aids are permissible. Parenthetically, it was once questioned whether seeing the evidence with eyeglasses was considered seeing so as to permit a person to act as a judge, since a blind person may not act as a judge.

basis for receiving evidence in the pending case in the form of a written transcript or an oral report or a witness's previous testimony. A statement may be introduced not so much to show that what was said was true, but rather to show the frame of mind of the person making the statement. The admission exception is discussed in Chapter 81.

There is a difference of opinion as to whether a person may testify to what he heard—if, for example, he recognized the voice of a person making an admission as he was sitting in another part of a room and the face of the person making the admission was not visible. Those holding that he may not testify contend that many people sound like other people. Furthermore, even if a person has a distinctive voice, there are others who can imitate such a voice, especially in an effort to trick people into believing that the other person made an admission. The best procedure is for each beth din to judge the testimony on its own merits to determine whether it is admissible.

After the first witness has completed his testimony and has been examined by the judges and the other side, the witness is excused and the other witnesses on behalf of the plaintiff testify, one at a time. At the conclusion of the plaintiff's case, the defendant may make motions to dismiss the plaintiff's complaint for failure to prove a *prima facie* case. If the motion is granted, then the complaint is dismissed on the merits. A dismissal on the merits precludes the plaintiff from ever again suing the defendant on the same causes of action. If the motion is denied, the defendant presents his defense. The defendant may then present his witnesses in the manner just described.

If the testimony given by one of the witnesses seems to correspond too exactly with the other witnesses' testimony or seems well rehearsed, then the witnesses are subjected to intensive cross-examination as discussed in Chapter 30.

The testimony of the witnesses must be oral. A witness is not permitted to write his answers and forward them to the beth din. There is also a contrary opinion, but the law follows the first opinion. There are some exceptions to the foregoing:

1. In extraordinary circumstances a Sage may write the answers to questions that have been forwarded to him and return them to the beth din. This may be done only if the sage is clearly superior in Torah learning to the judges of the beth din. A sage who could take

advantage of this exception but waives the privilege is a true sage! He enhances the name of Heaven. There is a difference of opinion among the authorities as to who forwards the questions to the Sage. Does the beth din itself go to him, or may a messenger of the beth din represent the beth din? The majority seems to follow the view that either the beth din goes to the Sage or else they send three persons to him to watch him answer the questions. The litigants may be present when the Sage reads and answers the questions. The answers are to be given in the presence of either another group of three persons or the representative of the beth din. The former view is preferable. The sage must write that the answers are given as testimony in response to the questions asked in the litigation.

2. If the witness is in the beth din, he may also, under extraordinary circumstances, write his testimony and then declare that the deposition is his answer.

3. If the witness is outside the geographic jurisdiction of the beth din, the witness may testify before his local beth din by answering questions put to him by both parties. This testimony will be forwarded to the beth din where the trial is taking place. Deposition testimony must be taken down verbatim.

4. A community may decree that depositions may be given before a beth din of fewer than three persons.

5. If testimony is by deposition, it must be read in beth din in the presence of both parties.

6. Testimony of persons who are about to depart the jurisdiction may be written down to perpetuate the testimony. There are people whose business takes them from community to community. In their situation an exception is made, and testimony may be reduced to writing in one community and forwarded to the other community where the litigation is pending.

7. Documents of indebtedness are admitted if their authenticity has been established.[27] This exception was established so as not to stifle

---

27. There seem to be four opinions regarding such documents: (1) If the witnesses write the document with the consent of the obliger, then it is deemed to be testimony and not written testimony, which is excluded (Rashi and Baal haMoer). (2) If the document is written like a document of indebtedness, it is to be treated as such and is not a writing to be excluded as not being oral testimony (Ramban). (3) There is no exclusion for written testimony except if a person cannot speak. Otherwise written testimony is inadmissible (Rabbenu Tam). (4) The admissibility of documents of

commerce. No one would make loans or sell goods on credit if the witnesses to the transaction would have to come to beth din to testify in case of a dispute. The two witnesses sign the document and when it is introduced as evidence, their signatures are given the same credence as their testifying in beth din. Documents of indebtedness are defined in Chapter 39. Ordinarily, book entries are not included in this category. The document had to have been written as a note of indebtedness and not as an entry to remind a person of what transpired at the time.

8. In those situations in which written testimony is permitted, it acquires the quality of testimony when it is read into evidence at the beth din.[28]

A witness can testify only as to what he remembers at the time the testimony is being given. He must state that which he does not remember or about which he is not clear. The fact that something transpired many years before is no reason to preclude the testimony. There is an opinion that after sixty years a person probably will not remember an event. There are some opinions that a person is more apt to remember an event if at the time of the event he was *designated* to be a witness to it.

A witness may refresh his recollection by examining a document, but if after examining the document he still does not recall the event, then he may not testify as to the event. The witness is not testifying as to the accuracy of the document or as to its contents. He merely looks at the document to refresh his recollection. If he cannot recall the events after examining the document, but if the document meets the requirements as stated in Chapters 46 and 61, it may be introduced into evidence as an exception to the hearsay rule as a record of a past recollection.

Before testifying, a witness may have his recollection refreshed by another person, whether another witness or even a relative of one of the litigants. However, this may not be true if the recollection is refreshed by a litigant or by a member of the litigant's immediate

---

indebtedness is only of Rabbinic origin, but according to Torah law they are also to be excluded as written testimony (Rambam).

28. Thus, if the witness died or became incapacitated or otherwise disqualified between the time when he gave the deposition and the time when it is read into evidence at the beth din, the deposition is not to be admitted into testimony.

family. There is a fear in such cases that the litigant or the members of his family will talk the witness into thinking that he remembers instead of just refreshing his recollection. If the litigant is a sage, then he too may refresh the recollection of the witness because it is assumed that he will not try to influence him unduly. But his recollection may be refreshed by an attorney or agent of the litigant.[29]

The beth din should examine each case and determine whether each witness was inappropriately persuaded how to testify.

A witness may not testify in the absence of the litigants

In Chapter 17 the prohibition against talking about the case before litigation began was discussed. In this chapter we are discussing the prohibition during the trial.

A witness may not testify in the absence of the litigant (or his counsel) against whom he is testifying. Some authorities hold that only the testimony must be in the presence of the litigants; they need not be present for the cross-examination. This author believes that the better view is that they should be present for the testimony and the cross-examination because the cross-examination is just as important, and sometimes more important, to prove or disprove the testimony of the witness. If the litigant who was absent waived the prohibition, then the other party who called the witness may not insist that the testimony is not valid. The litigant who called a witness to testify in his favor and against the other witness may not thereafter state that the testimony is inadmissable because the other party was not there, when it turned out that the testimony helped the absent litigant more than it did him. The reason is that a witness will be more careful about his testimony if the litigant against whom he is testifying is there to hear it. Therefore, where there is no cause for concern, exceptions have been made.

After both parties have appeared in the litigation, if the beth din calls a witness, it must advise the other side when the witness is to testify and must give him ample opportunity to be present to hear the testimony. If he does not appear, then the testimony will be taken in

---

29. It is assumed that the agent of the litigant will not exert enough influence over the witness to have him falsely state that he recollects something that he does not recollect.

his absence. If the beth din believes that the witness will testify more truthfully in the absence of the litigants, then they may examine him privately and have him repeat his testimony in beth din in the presence of the litigants, where they can question him. If testimony was taken in the absence of a litigant, then the procedure is for the witness to retestify in the presence of the litigants. Some authorities hold that if the rule was violated and testimony was given in the absence of the opposing litigant, it is nevertheless admissible and need not be retestified. This author believes that the first view is preferable.

If the witness altered his testimony between the first version, in the absence of the litigant, and the second version, in the presence of the litigant, there are several views. The prevailing view is that his second testimony is to be given more credence, although the beth din may take into account that he has changed his earlier testimony. Another view holds that if he took an oath when he testified the first time, then only his earlier testimony is to be given credence, since a witness may not recant his testimony after he has completed it (see Chapter 29).

If one of the litigants is a powerful person and the beth din believes that the witness is apt to be intimidated by the litigant, then he may testify in the absence of the litigant. The beth din may even keep the identity of the litigant or witness secret, if necessary, to protect him.

If one of the litigants is a minor, then the testimony may be given in his absence, if his guardian is present (see Chapter 110).

The beth din in its discretion, in order to ameliorate the strife between the parties, may take the testimony of the witnesses privately without revealing the names of the witnesses to the litigants. This should not be done in a strict legal proceeding unless the litigants waive their rights in the matter.

If the witness is ill and there is a danger that he will not be able to testify if the beth din waits until the other litigant arrives, then they may hear his testimony in the absence of the other litigant. If the plaintiff is ill and there is the danger that he will not survive, then his witnesses may testify even if the defendant is not present.

If the witnesses are about to depart the city, then the plaintiff may have their testimony taken immediately. If the defendant is in the city, he will be notified of the taking of the testimony. If he does not appear, then the testimony will be taken in his absence. In cases in which the witnesses cannot wait, the requirement of notifying the defendant may be waived by the beth din.

If the witness is in another city, the beth din may ask a beth din in that other city to take the witness's testimony. The litigants will be advised of the time when such testimony will be taken in the other city, so that either or both litigants may be present when the witness testifies. If the litigants do not avail themselves of the opportunity, then the witness will testify in the absence of one or both of the litigants. With modern technology, there is no reason that the testimony should not be videotaped. Alternatively, or in addition, a telephonic hookup can be connected between the witness and the parties and judges in the beth din.[30]

A potential defendant may ask the beth din to hear and perpetuate testimony of witnesses who are about to leave the jurisdiction even if no lawsuit has yet been commenced, if the potential defendant can convince the beth din that he is in danger of being sued by a potential plaintiff.

Unless the testimony falls into one of the aforementioned exceptions, a judgment entered after the admission of such testimony will be overturned.[31]

It seems to this author that once both litigants have appeared in the case, and one of the litigants then walks out of the beth din, the case should continue.[32] With the now wide use of attorneys in the beth din,[33] many of these problems are not as acute as they were in former times.

During the preliminary hearings a litigant may be asked to name his witnesses. If during the trial one of his witnesses has no testimony to give, it does not disqualify the other witnesses from testifying.[34]

---

30. In all of these instances, of course, it must be ascertained that the person on the other end of the telephone line is really the one who is named as witness.

31. There are two opinions on the effect on the testimony given at a trial where the judgment was overturned. One holds that the testimony is null and void, and may later be recanted or changed. The other opinion is that the testimony of the witness remains so that he may no longer recant or change it. This author believes that the testimony should remain, for even if the verdict is overturned, the testimony is not affected.

32. There is also a contrary view which holds that if either litigant walks out of the trial it should not continue, since testimony may not generally be heard unless both litigants are present. However, such a rule gives either party the opportunity to frustrate the trial. If either party needs an adjournment or postponement once the trial has started, application should be made to the beth din as provided in Chapter 16.

33. See Chapters 122, 123, and 124 regarding the use of attorneys in beth din.

34. This rule is necessary so that the beth din should not be able to say that if one witness does not provide any testimony then the list of witnesses is false. Each witness must be viewed independently.

A Jew testifying in Gentile courts

Where the Gentile is the plaintiff and a Jew is the defendant, the following apply:

1. If the result of the testimony of the witness would be the same in the Gentile court as it would be in the beth din, then the Jew may testify.[35]

2. If the result would be worse for the Jewish defendant than it would have been in the beth din, then the Jew may not testify. Some authorities hold that he may not testify voluntarily but must testify if subpoenaed. This author prefers this view.

3. If the Jewish witness testified in case 2, he is placed under a ban unless the defendant admits that the testimony was truthful. This author would suggest that the Jewish witness not be placed under a ban if he can prove to the beth din that his testimony was truthful, even if the defendant did not admit it.

4. Even where the witness is placed under a ban, he need not make any monetary payment to the defendant. He will be required to make monetary payment to the defendant if he testified falsely, however.

5. If an individual was originally asked to witness a transaction so that he could later testify on behalf of the Gentile, and if the transaction came to litigation, then he must in all events testify. To do otherwise would create a desecration of the Holy Name.

If the Jew is the plaintiff and the Gentile is the defendant, then the Jew may testify on behalf of the defendant.[36]

In all of these situations there must be an awareness that by not testifying, the Jewish witness may be profaning the Holy Name. The witness should always consult a great Torah authority for advice in such a case, since his conduct may reflect on the entire Jewish community.

---

35. For example, two Jewish witnesses may testify, since their testimony would have resulted in a judgment in favor of the plaintiff in a beth din. Another example is where the Gentile court requires the defendant to take an oath if there is only one witness, the same as would be done in a beth din.

36. His testimony in this case would be the same as if he had testified in a beth din.

Chapter 29

A WITNESS MAY NOT RECANT HIS TESTIMONY

INTRODUCTION

This chapter focuses on a principle of law that is fundamental to the system: Once a witness has testified, he may not recant his testimony. If a witness could at any time recant his testimony and a new trial could be granted on such change in testimony, judgments would never be finalized. A trial could end, a decision could be rendered, and even after execution and even after appeal, the parties still would not be sure that the case had been concluded. When the trial and appeal procedure has been exhausted, the judgment must be final. This has nothing to do with the topic discussed in Chapter 20, where the focus is on newly discovered evidence and newly discovered witnesses. In this chapter it is the same witnesses who have already testified who wish to change their testimony.

The law against recanting testimony also applies to testimony within the same trial, before the trial is concluded. Once a witness has testified during the trial, he may not recant unless he does so within a moment of ending his testimony, or unless he does so within a moment of the subsequent witness's ending his testimony, provided that the subsequent witness started his testimony within a moment of the time that the recanting witness terminated his testimony. This rule is probably intended to prevent a witness from recanting his testimony based on a subsequent witness's testimony or because of pressure from one of the litigants.

The last law in Chapter 29 of *Shulhan Aruch* deals with two people who were standing next to each other when an alleged event took place. One of the two came to beth din to testify that he saw an event that is part of a lawsuit. The other person who was also there testifies that he did not see the event. The essence of the second witness's testimony is that the first person also did not see the event. In this book, this topic has been moved to Chapter 31, which deals with witnesses who contradict each other.

TEXT

A witness may not recant his testimony

Once a witness has testified in the beth din[1] and "a moment" has elapsed since the conclusion of his testimony, he may not recant it. Even if the witness gives a valid reason for wanting to recant the testimony that he provided in beth din,[2] he is not permitted to do so.[3]

A witness may not add a condition to his testimony.[4] There is also authority that the witness may add a condition to the events to which he testified. Even according to this opinion, the condition may be added only if there is still a possibility of the condition's being fulfilled. This author believes that the first opinion should be followed. Where

---

1. There appear to be no clear-cut decisions on the question of whether the witnesses may recant their testimony in a different case with different parties, or with at least one different party.

2. Anything that the witness may have stated outside of the beth din (except under a deposition taken outside of beth din) does not affect his ability to testify in beth din and contradict that which he stated outside of beth din. The rule against recanting applies only to testimony given in beth din (or under a deposition).

3. For example, if the witness stated that he was mistaken when he testified, or that he unwittingly so testified, or that he was intimidated into so testifying, he is not permitted to change his testimony.

4. For example, a witness might testify to an employment agreement and then want to add that the employment was based on certain precondition. Some authorities would permit such an addition, while others would not. This author contends that exceptions make the rule weak. In addition, if the parties are represented by counsel, the condition should be revealed in questioning the witness.

there is an obvious error, the witness may correct the error,[5] and this is not considered a recanting of testimony.[6]

If the original testimony is ambiguous, then the witness is permitted to clarify it, so long as the clarification does not contradict the original testimony.

If a ban is proclaimed in a synagogue for witnesses to testify, and a witness leaves without stating that he knows facts on which to base testimony, he may nevertheless thereafter testify. Even if the witness originally states in the synagogue that he knew no facts on which to base testimony, and he now gives a reason satisfactory to the beth din for so stating, he may now testify. But if he states in beth din that he knows no facts upon which to give testimony, he may not change his mind and state that he knows such facts.

A witness may recant or amend his testimony if he does so while he is still in the midst of testifying and for a moment thereafter.[7] If the testimony takes several days, then the entire testimony is deemed to be one continuous testimony, so that the witness may recant on the last day of testimony the testimony that he gave on any prior day. This time may be extended to a moment after any other subsequent witness has testified or during such subsequent witness's testimony. This holds true only if the subsequent witnesses testified within a moment[8] of each prior witness.[9] Cross-examination[10] is still consid-

---

5. The codes and commentaries provide this example: A litigant brings a friend to be his character witness, and the judge asks this character witness whether the party who brought him is a falsifier. The witness answers yes. He may then later explain that he misunderstood the question.

6. There is an opinion that if the witness alleges that he did not know that he had to tell the truth and then in the middle of the trial was told that he must tell the truth, then this is a mistake that permits recanting of testimony. This is probably a question that every judge and beth din should decide independently.

7. A moment is defined in halachah for this purpose as the amount of time it takes to state the three words "welcome my teacher." A few authorities hold that it is the time it takes to say the four words "welcome rabbi and teacher." The actual term used instead of moment is the time of an utterance. Taken literally, this is a very short time interval—perhaps a second or two. Therefore, the term should be expanded to include the time necessary for one witness to step down and the next witness to be called to testify.

8. Great scholars with whom this author has consulted explain that "within a moment" means that if the subsequent witness was called to testify without any undue delay almost immediately after the prior witness had testified. In such a situation, the prior witness may still testify. One great scholar even said that so long

ered part of testimony, and the witness may recant or amend his testimony during this time.[11]

If a witness in the middle of the trial is reminded by the judge that he must testify truthfully, and then the witness changes his testimony, it is within the permissible time. If the testimony of a witness was interrupted to permit another witness to testify in the meantime, then the resumption of the original witness's testimony is considered part of his earlier testimony.

The signing of a document by the witnesses is equivalent to their testifying in beth din,[12] and they may not recant and say that the document is not valid.[13] If the signatures of the witnesses are not independently authenticated, but the witnesses themselves are depended upon to authenticate them, then the witnesses may recant their testimony if they state that they were forced to sign under the threat of death.

Witnesses may state that the document may be terminated by a subsequent condition. They may not state that the effectiveness of the document was conditioned upon a condition precedent. The document is equivalent to testimony in the beth din as soon as it is delivered to the creditor, and its production in beth din is not required to make it effective as testimony that cannot be recanted.

Depositions may be recanted until such time as they are introduced as evidence in beth din.

---

as the beth din is still proceeding and discussing the testimony of the prior witness, it would be considered "within a moment"; otherwise the phrase "within a moment" would be almost meaningless, since it takes longer than the "moment" for the witness to leave the stand and for the next witness to be called and then for him to proceed to the stand and begin to testify.

9. One authority holds that the testimony of all the witnesses on one side is counted as one continuous testimony, and any witness on that side may recant his testimony. This isolated view is contrary to the position taken by most authorities, who restrict the right to recant testimony.

10. There are authorities who hold that the moment the witness concludes his direct testimony marks the end of his testimony for the purpose of recanting. They hold that cross-examination does not extend the time of his testimony.

11. Some authorities hold that as soon as one line of questioning has been concluded, the witness may no longer recant the testimony elicited during this line of questioning. This author does not agree with this opinion.

12. See Chapter 46 regarding the effect of witnesses signing a document of indebtedness.

13. Of course, other witnesses may testify as to the validity of the document and any other matters pertaining to the document.

Liability of recanting witnesses

If a witness states that he has previously testified falsely, then his current statement does not affect the outcome of the trial, but he is liable to the party who lost the case because of his false testimony. If one of the witnesses says that he testified falsely and the second witness states that he testified truthfully, then the first witness may not be sued by the party whom he admits having wronged.[14] If the first witness now states that both he and the second witness testified falsely, then the first witness must pay the full amount of the damage caused to the wronged party.[15] If the second witness also admits that he testified falsely, then each of the two false witnesses must pay half the damage. Even if a witness admits that he testified falsely but he has no information about whether the other witness testified falsely, then both are exonerated from making payment to the injured party.

---

14. The reason is that the damage is not certain in that the beth din found against the wronged party, since in essence the second witness states that the first witness did not cause any damage to the alleged wronged party.

15. This follows the general principle that if two parties jointly cause damage, and if the injured party cannot collect from both, then he may collect the entire amount from one party.

Chapter 30

INTERROGATION
OF WITNESSES

INTRODUCTION

Torah law requires all witnesses to undergo cross-examination.[1] The examination consists of three distinct types: *drishah, hakirah,* and *bedikah.* There is some difference of opinion regarding the first two types. Are they both the same, and the general category is *drishah* and *hakirah,* or are they two different types of examination? Most of the codes and commentaries treat *drishah* and *hakirah* as one category and *bedikah* (or *bedikoth* in the plural) as another category. *Drishah* and *hakirah* will be translated here into "inquiry," and *bedikoth* into "interrogation."

Inquiry consists of pinpointing the time and place of the event. Inquiry comprises seven questions, six of which deal with time, and the seventh with place. The seven questions inquire as to (1) the cycle of years;[2] (2) the year; (3) the month; (4) the date of the month; (5) the

---

1. The requirement for cross-examination is derived from the verse "Then shalt thou inquire, and make search, and ask diligently; and, behold, if it be truth, and the thing certain" (Deuteronomy 13:15). Rambam enumerates the commandment as number 179 of the positive commandments.

2. See notes to Chapter 1 where it is explained that the Jewish calendar was divided into fifty-year cycles, at the end of which was the jubilee year. The remaining

day of the week; (6) the hour; and (7) the place. Interrogation, on the other hand, deals with the event itself. What transpired? If a loan is at issue, who lent money to whom? How much was lent? What were the terms of repayment? What was the type of currency loaned?

There was one fundamental difference between inquiry and interrogation. If in the area of inquiry there were no two witnesses who agreed on all the answers, then their testimony was discarded.[3] If only two witnesses were brought by the plaintiff and they could not agree on all the answers to the inquiries, or even if one said that he did not know the answer, then the testimony was discarded. In the area of interrogation, on the other hand, if a witness said that he could not remember, his testimony was not discarded.[4]

Since failure to agree or even to know the answer to one of the inquiries would disqualify the witness, people would be loathe to extend credit or to enter into any type of commercial transaction. It was therefore decreed, that in commercial transactions, the witnesses would no longer be questioned as to the matters designated as

---

forty-nine years were divided into seven cycles of seven years each. It is this cycle that is spoken of here.

3. See Rambam, *Laws of Evidence*, Chapter 2, para. 3, where he states that in criminal cases even if there were many witnesses and even if only one contradicted the others, the testimony of all may be void.

4. Several opinions are given for discarding the testimony of a witness who does not testify accurately as to time and place. There is, as will be seen in Chapter 38, a topic in halachah called *zommemim*, which has been translated here as "refuted witnesses." This is as opposed to *hakchasha*, which has been taken here to mean "contradicted witnesses." Refuted witnesses are not contradicted regarding the occurrence. The second pair of witnesses who are produced in the beth din rather testify that the first pair of witnesses were with the second pair of witnesses at the time that they claimed to have witnessed the event in a place from which it was not possible to have witnessed the event. The second pair of witnesses attack the veracity of the first pair of witnesses and say nothing about the event except that the first witnesses could not possibly have seen it. Contradictory witnesses contradict each other regarding the event itself. A witness cannot be refuted unless he pinpoints the time and place where the alleged event took place. Hence the requirement for time and place.

Many authorities disagree, stating that the reason for pinpointing time and place is to enable the beth din to see determine whether the witnesses are testifying truthfully. The more detail the witnesses provide on these points, the more able the judges are to determine whether the witnesses are truthful.

inquiries.[5] In cases where the judges suspect that the truth is being disregarded, they may still subject the witness to full or partial inquiry examination.

This chapter deals with the extent to which witnesses may be questioned in cases in which a money judgment is being sought. There is also discussed the combining of the testimony of several witnesses to prove a point, the combining of witnesses who testified on different occasions, and finally the requirement that the testimony of the witnesses be complete. Since some of the rules are difficult to follow, *Shulhan Aruch* and subsequent codifiers and commentators have provided examples. The same has been done here, and the examples are interspersed between the text and the notes.

TEXT

Inquiries are generally not permitted in cases in which a money judgment is sought

Inquiries are generally not permitted[6] in any case over which the beth din has jurisdiction.[7] For example, if the witnesses testified that a loan for $100 was made in the year 5747, but they did not mention the month[8] or the place, their testimony stands.[9] If the beth din did permit

---

5. According to the explanation that it was so decreed to encourage lenders and creditors to extend credit, it was suggested that it is only for the benefit of creditors and not for the benefit of debtors that the decree was enacted. It is unanimous, however, that the decree applies to all parties in the litigation.

6. Some authorities hold that if the beth din did engage in inquiries without any reason, that the procedure is nevertheless valid, and if the testimony of the witnesses is thus disqualified, so be it. Many authoritites disagree with this view. This author is inclined to follow the view of the latter group, since this seems to be the intent of the enactment.

7. See Chapter 1 for the jurisdiction of the beth din.

8. This holds true if one witness testifies that the loan took place in January, and the second witness testifies that it took place in February, and the plaintiff alleges both loans. It also holds true if one witness testifies that the loan took place in January, and the second witness testifies that he does not know the date, and the plaintiff alleges only one loan.

9. This case seems to show that the decree effectively disposed of the possibility of refutation of witnesses in most cases, since the time and place are not pinpointed.

inquiries, the answers are to be stricken from the record, and if they are contradictory, the contradiction is of no effect. Some authorities differ on this last point. This author prefers the first view.

Inquiries may be resorted to in assault cases.[10] Inquiries are encouraged in cases in which the beth din is uncertain of the trustworthiness of the testimony. There are some opinions that the beth din should engage in inquiries if it suspects the complaint or the answer is not trustworthy. The inquiries need not be as detailed as they are in capital cases. If the inquiries show that the witnesses, the complaint, the answer, or all three are not trustworthy, the beth din may take appropriate action, such as dismissing the complaint or answer, with or without prejudice. In suspicious cases, the beth din may recall the witnesses to retestify, which is a departure from the rule that a witness may not recant or add to his testimony after he has completed it.[11]

In those cases in which inquiries are permitted, if any witness answers that he does not know the answer, then his entire testimony is discarded. Some opinions disagree. This author prefers the first opinion.

In those cases in which inquiries are permitted, if there are only two witnesses to the event and they contradict each other, then neither testimony remains standing. If there are more than two witnesses and there are not two witnesses who agree on the answers to all the inquiries, then their testimony is discarded.

If the plaintiff produces only one witness and the beth din believes that he should undergo inquiry, then if he does not know the answer to any of the inquiry questions, his testimony is discarded.

There is an opinion that the law stating that the year was mentioned but not the month means that nothing regarding time was mentioned. Other opinions hold that the year was mentioned so that it can be determined whether the parties were of age if that is in dispute. It seems to this author that if a dispute arose it would be because of a shorter period than a year. Another contention is that a year is mentioned so that the beth din will know whether it is the last year of the seven-year cycle, the *shemitah* year, in which case the indebtedness would be cancelled. See Chapter 67.

10. It is not clear why this is so. It means only that the perpetrator of the act will feel freer to assault, since it might be possible to have the case thrown out of beth din because of some contradiction by the witnesses. On the other hand, it will discourage flimsy lawsuits in a very serious area if the requirement for inquiries holds in assault cases.

11. See Chapter 29.

Interrogation is required in all cases

The beth din must interrogate each witness. Interrogation is of two types: (1) that which goes to the essence of the event and (2) that which is peripheral to the event. Take, for example, a case in which a loan was made for the sum of $100, and a promissory note was signed by borrower. Testimony regarding this goes to the essence of the transaction. However, if the witness cannot recall on which bank the check was drawn or what color the check was, this does not go to the essence of the transaction.

In an interrogation question that goes to the heart of the matter, if there are not two witnesses who agree on the answers, then their testimony will be deemed insufficient to prove a case.[12] This author believes that if a third witness's testimony contradicts two witnesses who agree, then his testimony is discarded. In interrogation questions that do not go to the heart of the matter, however, if there are some contradictions, or if a witness states that he does not know the answer, it is not critical to the testimony. It is vital that the judges of the beth din study the testimony to see whether the witnesses are contradicting each other and the litigants either explicitly or implicilty, and whether it is an essential or nonessential matter.

Examples of nonconflicting testimony, contradictory testimony, and combining witnesses

The beth din in each case must decide whether the decree that was made against inquiries in monetary cases applies to the case at hand, remembering that decrees cannot be taken lightly. The beth din must examine to see whether the plaintiff has proven his case and whether the defendant has proven his defense, and where there is one witness, whether he can be relied upon to obligate the defendant to take a Torah oath.

There are two guidelines for the beth din to follow. (1) Whenever

---

12. There is an opinion that one of the witnesses must be telling the truth and thus there is one witness who can obligate the defendant to take a Torah oath regarding the claim.

possible, the testimony of the witnesses should be given credence and (2) in monetary cases, even if the witnesses did not witness the event together, their witnessing may sometimes be combined, so long as they do not contradict each other in nonessential matters. For example, one witness testifies that the loan was made in his presence on January 1, or on that date the borrower admitted that he borrowed the money. The other witness testifies that the loan was made on February 1 in his presence, or on that date the borrower admitted the loan. Their testimony is combined.[13] Thus any combination of witnessing the loan or hearing the admission may be combined.[14] Another example would be a case in which two witnesses, each of whom testifies as to a different loan, have their testimony combined if the complaint states both as causes of action.

If the plaintiff claims a loan of $200, and the first witness testifies to a loan of $100, and the second witness testifies to a loan of $200 at the same time and place, then the testimony is combined to enable a judgment for the plaintiff for $100, since $100 is part of $200 and there are two witnesses for $100.[15] If the complaint had stated that $100 was lent, then the plaintiff would get nothing, since the complaint contra-

---

13. For example, if the first witness testifies that plaintiff lent the defendant $100 in January, and the second witness testifies that he heard from the defendant in February (in accordance with the rules of admissible admissions) that he owes the plaintiff $100, then a decision will be rendered in favor of the plaintiff, since the beth din assumes that both witnesses are testifying to the same loan. This is true even if the complaint states only one cause of action for $100.

Similarly, if they both testify to admissions that they heard, the first witness having heard an admission for $100 in February and the second witness testifying that he heard the admission for $100 in March, then both admissions are combined, and the plaintiff will receive a judgment for $100.

14. There is an opinion that if after the first witness testified to the loan, the defendant took a Torah oath denying the loan, and thereafter the second witness testified to the loan, the defendant may be able to take a Torah oath of denial. It is only if both witnesses testified about the loan before the defendant took the oath that their testimony is combined. While this appears in the commentaries on *Shulhan Aruch* in the section discussing the combining of witnesses, it would seem that this comment should be placed later, in the discussion of the combining of testimony that is not all given at one time.

15. In these situations the complaint must allege causes of action totaling $200. Thus if one witness testifies to a loan of $100 in January and the second witness testifies to a loan of $100 in February, their testimony is combined for a judgment of $100.

dicted the second witness. If the complaint alleges two loans, one for $100 and another for $200, and the first witness testifies to a loan of $100 in January and the second witness testifies to a loan of $200 in February, then the plaintiff will receive a judgment for $100. It is not necessary in monetary matters that the witnesses witness the event at the same time. If the complaint alleged only one loan for $100, then the plaintiff will lose the case because the witness is contradicted by the complaint.

If the first witness testifies to the type of merchandise sold and the second witness testifies to a different type of merchandise, but they are close enough in type that it might be difficult to distinguish between the two, then their testimony will be combined. The defendant will have to pay for the less expensive of the two items. If they testify to two obviously different items, then their testimony is considered contradicted. For example, a complaint alleges that $1,500 is due to the plaintiff from the defendant. Witness 1 testifies that he saw a loan of $100. Witness 2 testifies that he saw a loan of $200. Witness 3 testifies that he saw a loan of $300. Witness 4 testifies that he saw a loan of $400. Witness 5 testifies that he saw a loan of $500. If each testifies that he saw the loan at a different time, then the plaintiff will receive a judgment for $700 and the defendant will have to take a Torah oath[16] of denial regarding the $100 and a revolving oath[17] regarding the remaining $700.[18] But if all of the witnesses

---

16. See Chapter 87 regarding the different types of oaths that a party must take. Generally speaking, a defendant must take a Torah oath if the plaintiff produces one witness to support the complaint. The one witness shifts the burden of proof from the plaintiff. If the defendant takes the Torah oath denying the indebtedness, then the decision will be in favor of the defendant.

17. See Chapter 87 regarding the obligation to take a revolving oath.

18. Witness 5 and witness 4 agree that $400 is due. There is still a surplus of $100 from the testimony of witness 5. This $100 surplus combines with the testimony of witness 3 so that there are now witnesses for another $100. This leaves a surplus of $200 from witness 3. This surplus of $200 from witness 3 combines with the testimony of $200 from witness 2 to form an obligation for $200. The combined total is now $700 ($400 + $100 + $200). The testimony of witness 1 obligates the defendant to swear a Torah oath that he does not owe the $100 testified to by witness 1. Since the defendant must take a Torah oath, it revolves on him to take an oath regarding the remaining $700. The remaining $700 would not be the subject of an oath by the defendant if not for the testimony of witness 1. Since their testimony has already enabled the plaintiff to collect money, the testimony cannot be used for a

testified that they witnessed the loan at the same time, then they have contradicted one another and the decision will be for the plaintiff for $200.[19]

In those situations in which the date is crucial, if the witnesses differ in their reports of the date of the event by one day,[20] they are not considered to be contradictory witnesses.

If one witness testified that he witnessed the event and that the other witness also witnessed the event, then if the second witness states that he was not present and did not witness the event, their testimony is not contradictory.[21]

The plaintiff claims that the defendant is holding $200 of his as a deposit, and the defendant denies that he is holding anything. One witness testified that the defendant admitted to him that he is holding $50 for the plaintiff. A second witness testified that the defendant told him that he is holding $150 for the plaintiff. The defendant is presumed to be a liar and must pay the full $200. Actually, the defendant is obligated to pay only $50, which is what both witnesses agree is the

---

second function, namely that of requiring the defendant to take a Torah oath. The obligation to take a Torah oath is present only because the testimony of witness 1 was not used to obligate the defendant to pay any money. Once there devolved an oath on the defendant, there revolved upon him an oath for the balance.

The combinations could have produced different results. Witnesses 1 and 2 could be combined and there would be an obligation of $100. Witnesses 3 and 4 are combined for another $300, making a total of $400. Witness 5 obligates the defendant to take an oath for the $500. Or, witnesses 1 and 2 could be combined to obligate the payment of $100. Combine the remaining $100 of witness 2 with witness 3 to obligate an additional $100. Then combine the remaining $200 of witness 3 with witness 4 to obligate an additional $200. Finally, combine the remaining $200 of witness 4 with witness 5 to make a total of $600. The responsa all seem to favor giving the plaintiff the largest possible combination.

19. Witness 1 and witness 2 have in essence stated that the loan did not exceed $200. The fact that more witnesses, namely witnesses 3, 4, and 5, testified that the loan was for more than $200 does not alter the matter. In general, the testimony of two witnesses has the same effect as the testimony of many witnesses.

20. It is to be remembered that some of the rules dealing with dates refer to the dates of the Jewish calendar, which are not as definite as the dates of the secular calendar. (See Chapter 1 and notes thereto.)

21. A person is not always aware of others present when observing an event. Some opinions hold that if a witness was designated as such at the outset, then he would know the identity of other witnesses; but if a witness was not designated as such, then he may not know who the other witnesses were.

minimum amount due. The defendant is obligated to take a Torah oath regarding the other $150. Since he is presumed to be a liar in the case (because his denial is contradicted by two witnesses), the plaintiff may take an oath and collect the remaining $150.

The plaintiff alleges a cause of action for $200. The defendant alleges payment. The defendant produces two witnesses, one of whom testifies that in January the defendant repaid $100; the other witness testifies that in February the defendant repaid $100. Their testimony is combined. This assumes that the plaintiff does not assert that the payments were for another loan.[22]

All that has been said about loans holds true for any other type of transaction.[23]

Combining testimony

The previous section dealt with combining witnesses who did not witness the event at the same time. The following rules deal with the situation in which the witnesses testify separately.[24]

Witnesses need not testify at the same sitting of the beth din to have their testimony combined.[25] If one witness testified in one beth din and a second witness testified in a second beth din, and if all the members of the two beth din meet to decide the case,[26] then they

---

22. It is assumed that the plaintiff does not assert that the payments were for another loan not secured by a note of indebtedness, or for another loan that was secured by a note of indebtedness that was returned to the defendant when he paid this other loan.

23. Loans are most commonly used as examples in Rabbinic jurisprudence, since this was a form of transaction that often gave rise to litigation.

24. It does not matter when they saw the event, whether together or separately. We are now dealing with the testimony in the beth din. It is to remembered that the justice system was intended to be expedient. If the plaintiff instituted suit in the morning, the defendant would immediately be served with a summons to appear, and the trial would take place shortly thereafter; hence the necessity for detailing procedures to be followed if all of the testimony would not be received on the same day or at the same sitting of the beth din.

25. The reason that this law is necessary is that in capital cases the testimony must be taken without interruption. That is, there are no intervening days except for the Sabbath or a Holy Day.

26. There is an opinion that if two members of each beth din combined, then they may render a decision by combining the testimony given before each beth din. The better view appears in lthe next note.

may combine the testimony of both witnesses.[27] If two witnesses testified in one beth din, and then testified in a second beth din, and then testified in a third beth din, then one member of each beth din may join with the others to form a new beth din of three judges and decide the case on the basis of the testimony that they heard.

A witness in a new trial cannot combine with a judge of another beth din[28] who heard a second witness testify in the matter.

If one witness signed a document of loan that is introduced into evidence,[29] and the other witness testified in person that he witnessed the same loan, then the testimony is combined as if there were two witnesses[30] to the transaction.[31]

If the one witness who testified in person states that the defendant obligated himself by a *kinyan* to pay the note, but the plaintiff did not request that he reduce the obligation to writing, then the note signed by the witness and witnessed orally by another now has the force of a note signed by two witnesses, and the defendant cannot claim that he paid it.

There must be complete testimony from each witness

For example, if witness 1 testified that he saw the defendant use the field in question during 5745,[32] and witness 2 testified that he saw the

---

27. But if fewer than all the members of each beth din joined into the joint beth din, the testimony of both witnesses cannot be combined. Each beth din heard the testimony of only one witness. The testimony of the other witness repeated to the beth din is then only hearsay testimony.

28. Their testimony cannot be combined since there are two different kinds. One has first-hand information regarding the event, while the judge at a former trial is only relating hearsay.

29. The signature must have been authenticated.

30. There is a difference of opinion as to whether the note is now considered as having two signatures and thus may place a lien on the defendant's real property.

31. The note still is not considered a note with two witnesses, which in halachah has much more effect than a note that bears only one witness's signature.

32. See Chapter 140 dealing with how a person who possesses a field, but who alleges that he lost an unrecorded deed may defeat the prior owner's claim that the field still belongs to him. Generally, if the current occupant can show that he used the field for three consecutive years, the prior owner's cause of action to evict the current occupier will be dismissed. What the law shows in this paragraph is that the witnesses regarding the use for three years must each testify to some part or all of the full three-year period.

defendant use the field during 5746, and witness 3 testified that he saw the defendant use the field during 5747, then their testimony is combined with the same effect as if one of them was a witness for all three years since each did state a full testimony.[33]

33. Another example given is that in which a person claimed that he was the first-born of his father and was therefore entitled to a larger portion of his father's estate. (See Chapter 277.) He produced pairs of witnesses. The first pair testified that he was the firstborn of his mother, who had married only once. The second pair of witnesses testified that his father was married only once. There are differences of opinion on whether each pair has testified to a complete matter.

Chapter 31

THE ACCEPTABILITY OF TESTIMONY OF A WITNESS WHO MAY HAVE PERJURED HIMSELF IN A PRIOR TRIAL

INTRODUCTION

In this chapter, following the order of the *Shulhan Aruch*, the rules regarding witnesses who probably perjured themselves in a prior trial are set forth. The word *probably* is used because it is not known for sure which of the witnesses committed perjury. Thus in a prior trial there were two pairs of witnesses who testified. One pair, who shall be designated as pair A, consisted of witnesses WA1 and WA2; the second pair, pair B, consisted of witnesses WB1 and WB2. In the prior trial, pair A testified that a certain event occurred on January 1, which was a critical point. At the same trial, pair B testified that the event could not possibly have occurred on January 1. The discussion assumes that there was not present in the prior case an honest difference of opinion as to a date. Obviously, one pair of witnesses was lying. The prior beth din had no way of knowing which pair was lying. The result of the prior trial is not relevant in the case presently before the beth din. It may be assumed that the prior case ended in a judgment for the defendant, since the plaintiff was not able to sustain his burden of proof[1] because the testimony of pair B was

---

1. If the plaintiff's witnesses were contradicted on some point on which a judgment could still have been rendered in favor of the plaintiff, then all of the rules set forth still

enough to offset the testimony of pair A.[2]

The present case before the beth din involves a different plaintiff and different defendant. By coincidence, the same four witnesses are involved, sometimes individually and sometimes collectively, sometimes in the same alignment as in the prior trial and sometimes in a different alignment.

It is also to be remembered that the witnesses subscribing to a document are to be afforded the same credibility as witnesses who testified in a beth din. A document or documents are about to be introduced as evidence in beth din, and the subscribing witnesses are WA1, WA2, WB1, and WB2, or some combination thereof. They are the same witnesses, some of whom obviously perjured themselves at a prior trial. Also, the two documents may be held by one plaintiff against one defendant, by one plaintiff against two defendants, by two plaintiffs against one defendant, or by two plaintiffs against two defendants. The plaintiffs will be designated as P1 and P2; the defendants will designated as D1 and D2. The notes will be designated as note 1 and note 2.

In the *Shulhan Aruch*, after the laws regarding the foregoing are noted, two additional laws are stated, one of which deals with a plaintiff who produces succeeding pairs of witnesses, all of whom are discredited, until he finally produces one pair of witnesses who are not discredited. Should his prior attempts to bring discredited witnesses preclude the admission of the last pair of witnesses, who are not discredited? Finally, the second law deals with a similar situation in which a note of indebtedness is discussed. Since this last-mentioned topic will be dealt with in Chapter 63, it has been omitted in this chapter.

It should also be remembered that in this chapter, the witnesses

---

follow. Consider, for example, a situation in which it was not known that a woman was married, and such information is crucial to her case. She produces two witnesses who testify that she was married. One of the witnesses added that she was divorced, while the second witness testified that she was not divorced. Both witnesses fall into the category of being contradicting witnesses, one of whom is definitely lying. Yet the testimony of both proves that she was a married woman. Some authorities disagree and hold that since there are no two qualified witnesses to testify to her being married, there is no proof from these witnesses that she is married.

2. The defendant did not even have to take an oath to sustain his defense because he had produced two witnesses to support his contention.

have been contradicted by each other, and thus the order in which the witnesses testified is not important. As has been stated on several occasions, and as will be discussed in Chapter 38, in the case of refuted witnesses, as distinguished from contradictory witnesses, the sequence of testimony is critical.

TEXT

The acceptability of evidence of witnesses who may have committed perjury in a prior trial

If among witnesses WA1 and WA2, who testified as a pair to an event at a prior trial, and WB1 and WB2, who also testified as a pair at the same trial, one of these pairs perjured themselves at that prior trial but it cannot be shown which of the witnesses committed the perjury, all of them may testify at subsequent trials[3] and/or may sign documents as subscribing witnesses, and such documents will be admitted into evidence unless there is some other reason to exclude them.[4] An exception to the foregoing is if one of the witnesses[5] of the first pair combines with one of the witnesses of the second pair at the subsequent trial; then their testimony cannot be accepted,[6] since one of them obviously committed perjury at the prior trial.[7]

---

3. If all four testify on one side, then their testimony may possibly be dismissed if they fall into the scope of Chapter 36.

4. A judgment may be rendered on the basis of their testimony. The plaintiff has met his burden of proof on the basis of these witnesses. It cannot be said that there is a cloud on these witnesses. The fact that a pair of witnesses contradicted the first pair of witnesses is no reason to disqualify the first pair of witnesses. They can be disqualified only if they are refuted as discussed in Chapter 38 or for reasons stated in Chapter 34.

5. Beginning in the middle of the sixteenth century, many generations of scholars of Brisk discussed the issue of whether a similar result would follow if only two witnesses testified at the prior trial and each witness contradicted the other and one was an obvious liar and now both are paired on one side. The question revolves around the point that there were not two witnesses who contradicted either of them.

6. If the witnesses had contradicted themselves in a minor matter that did not affect the outcome of the prior trial, then one from each pair may combine to testify.

7. The defendant need not even take an oath against the witnesses, except a hesseth oath against the plaintiff's complaint. See Chapter 87.

The admissibility of notes signed by subscribing witnesses who may have perjured themselves at a prior trial

If one of the witnesses to a note is from pair A, and the second witness is from pair B, then the note is not admissible into evidence, since it obviously has one improper witness.

If note 1 is witnessed by pair A, and note 2 is witnessed by pair B, then the following rules apply:

1. If P1 and/or P2 bring consecutive lawsuits, each can maintain his lawsuit, even if brought before the same beth din.[8] There is a difference of opinion among the authorities in the case of one plaintiff, as to whether the defendant may make a motion that the plaintiff join both his lawsuits at once and thus fall into category 2 in the following paragraph, and if there are two defendants, if they may make a motion that the plaintiff join both lawsuits and thus fall into category 4 in the following paragraph.[9]

If the lawsuits on both notes are brought simultaneously, the following rules apply:

1. If P1 and P2 brought the lawsuit against D1 and D2, respectively, then each plaintiff may maintain his cause of action.
2. If there is only one plaintiff and one defendant, then the plaintiff may maintain his lawsuit on the smaller note,[10] and on the second note the defendant may take a Torah oath to have the cause of action dismissed.[11]

---

8. Some authorities say that one of the lawsuits must be brought before another beth din because the same beth din will take judicial notice that one note is obviously invalid.

9. According to the view that would permit the defendant or defendants to make such motion, the plaintiff is advised to destroy the smaller note so that he will be able to state that he has no other note. It might be preferable to advise the plaintiff to negotiate the note to another party and thus fall under category 3. This may be subject to a defense that the transferee takes subject to all of the defenses that the defendant had against the transferor.

10. The plaintiff stands in a weaker position because one note is obviously invalid.

11. The payment of the amount of the smaller note on the strength of the

3. If P1 and P2 brought the lawsuit against D1, then each plaintiff may take a Rabbinic oath to win his lawsuit.[12]

4. If P1 brings a lawsuit against D1 and D2, each defendant may defeat the lawsuit by taking a Rabbinic oath of denial.[13] Even if the defendant admits the validity of any of the notes, such an admission serves as a basis for a judgment that can be enforced against the property that the defendant owns at the time of the admission; however, such admission is not effective against property disposed of before the admission.[14] However, his admission does not have the effect of automatically invalidating the second note and disqualifying the witnesses to the note. If the plaintiff had sued only on the one note which the defendant admits is genuine, then the note effects a lien on the defendant's property retroactively to the date of the note. And the plaintiff may still sue on the second note, as described in paragraph 1 above.

Successive witnesses of the plaintiff who have been contradicted

If the plaintiff produces witnesses who are contradicted by the defendant's witnesses, and the plaintiff then produces other witnesses who are again contradicted by other witnesses of the defendant, this process can continue indefinitely until the plaintiff produces witnesses who are not contradicted.[15] He will then have met his burden of proof.[16]

---

witnesses to the note is equivalent to a partial admission, which obligates the defendant to take a Torah oath denying the balance; the defendant, upon taking such an oath, will obtain a judgment dismissing the complaint as to the balance. See Chapter 75.

12. There is a difference of opinion on the question of whether the plaintiff must take such an oath if the note specified that it could be collected without an oath on the part of the holder. In all events, if the defendant does not insist on such an oath, then the plaintiff need not take an oath.

13. The plaintiff cannot meet the burden of proof regarding either note.

14. See Chapter 39 regarding the lien created by a valid note of indebtedness.

15. In some of the codes, the term used is *refuted* rather than *contradicted*, since the former term implies that the first witnesses are not believed at all. Some codes use the word *contradicted*, but the witnesses are contradicted in such a way as to show that they were obviously lying.

16. The rule of law here teaches that the fact that the plaintiff produced so many false witnesses does not mean that he is dishonest. He could honestly have thought

This is the type of a case that may lend itself to cross-examination of the suspect witnesses, as described in Chapter 30. Some authorities hold that the same procedure is followed if instead of producing two witnesses each time, the plaintiff produced one witness each time who was shown to be lying.[17]

---

that his witnesses really knew of testimony to help his case. When the first pair of witnesses turned out to be false he sought other witnesses, until he finally found witnesses who could help his case. The presumption of his honesty is not rebutted by the fact that he produced false witnesses. There is no reason to believe that he is involved in a conspiracy.

17. The reason the plaintiff would bring one witness would be to shift the burden of proof to the defendant, who would then have to take a Torah oath of denial to defeat the plaintiff's claim.

Chapter 32

TESTIFYING ONLY TO FACTS REGARDING AN ADMISSION AND THE EXPLANATION GIVEN BY THE ADMITTING PARTY

INTRODUCTION

In Chapter 81 of *Shulhan Aruch, Hoshen haMishpat,* one of the many chapters devoted to the laws of pleadings, R. Yosef Karo discusses the situation in which Ruven admits that he owes money to Shimon. The admission was made in the presence of two persons, Levi and Yehuda. That chapter further discusses a difference of opinion between Tur and R. Karo. Tur follows the tradition that Levi and Yehuda can testify regarding the admission only if Ruven had designated them as witnesses. R. Karo holds that Levi and Yehuda can testify as to the admission even if Ruven had not designated them as witnesses.

In all events, Ruven will be given the opportunity to explain away his prior admission. The beth din then has the responsibility of weighing the testimony of Levi and Yehuda regarding the circumstances and the language of the admission and the explanation given by Ruven of his prior admission. All these rules are discussed by R. Karo in Chapter 81. In Chapter 32, which deals with evidence, R. Karo shows the importance of the testimony of the witnesses. Since the beth din will have to rely on their testimony, it must be precise. The testimony may not contain the witnesses' conclusions or opinions, nor can it contain legal conclusions. It can contain only the facts and, as nearly as possible, the exact words used by Ruven.

The second issue covered by R. Karo in this chapter is that of the person who hires false witnesses to testify on behalf of one of the litigants. This has already been covered by R. Karo in Chapter 29 and in this book in Chapter 29. Chapter 29 focuses on the topic of witnesses who admit that they testified falsely. It may be that the witnesses were not paid or even asked to testify falsely, and it is the liability of the witnesses that is discussed. This chapter discusses the liability of the person who hires the false witnesses. It should also be remembered that in Chapter 29 it was shown that a witness could not recant his testimony. In this chapter we are not dealing with a situation of reopening the trial, but rather with restitution to be made by the winning party, the false witnesses, or the hirer of the false witnesses.

TEXT

To relate the facts as they occurred

A witness may testify only to what he saw and what he heard. He may not state his conclusions, nor should he embellish or detract from that which was said. He should try as much as possible to use the exact words of a party if that party made an admission. He may not state opinions.

The defendant may explain the alleged admission to which the witnesses testified. He may explain that he was only jesting and did not think that his words would be taken seriously.[1] He may state that he wanted people to think that he was a debtor so that he could avoid lending money or making large contributions to charity.

Before rendering its decision, the beth din must weigh the statements, the circumstances under which they were made, and the defendant's explanations. This topic will be more fully discussed in Chapter 81.

---

1. If the admission was in writing, then the admitter's explanation that he was jesting is not available. It is also not available if the admitter admitted that he was holding a bailment for someone, or that he had stolen something from someone. It is also not available if he made a *kinyan* as to his liability. It is also not available if he admitted that he owed money to charity.

The liability of the hirer of false witnesses

If Levi hires false witnesses to testify on behalf of Shimon and against Ruven,[2] and Shimon, after the trial, admits the falsity of the testimony, Shimon must make restitution to the losing party. Ruven may sue Shimon if he does not make restitution. If Shimon is not available to make restitution or does not have the money to make restitution, then Levi is liable to the judgments of Heaven.

If Shimon does not admit the falsity of the testimony, but the witnesses admit the falsity of the testimony, then the witnesses must pay Ruven the damages that he suffered as a result of their false testimony.[3] Ruven may sue the witnesses if they do not make restitution.

If neither Shimon nor the witnesses admit the falsity of the testimony, but Levi later admits that he hired them to testify falsely, and if Ruven did not owe money to Shimon, then Levi is exempt from the judgment of the beth din[4] but is liable to the judgments of Heaven.[5] Levi can absolve himself from the liability to the judgment of Heaven by making restitution to Ruven.[6] If Ruven did owe the money to Shimon, then Levi is exempt also from the judgments of Heaven. He still carries the transgression of telling falsehoods, however.

---

2. It should be remembered that Shimon did not instruct or ask Levi to hire false witnesses. If he did, then Levi would be the agent of Shimon, and the acts of Levi would under all circumstances be imputed to Shimon.

3. The witnesses are not absolved from liability if they claim that they were coerced into testifying falsely.

4. The difference between the false witnesses and their hirer is that they are the direct cause of the damages to Ruven, while the hirer, Levi, is a remote cause.

5. Levi cannot absolve himself by stating that the witnesses should have known better than to listen to him. They should have known that the Torah prohibits false testimony. Nevertheless, Levi is still liable to the judgments of Heaven.

6. Until Levi makes restitution to Ruven, he may be disqualified from testifying in another case. Until he makes restitution, he is considered a thief. Once he makes restitution, he may testify in future matters; because a person may not incriminate himself, his confession does not disqualify him.

If Levi did not hire the false witnesses but rather just talked them into testifying falsely,[7] then he is even exempt from the judgments of Heaven.[8]

If Shimon hired the false witnesses on his own behalf, then he may be sued by Ruven.

If Levi hired the witnesses not to testify, then they would be liable to the judgments of Heaven as explained in Chapter 28, and he would be exempt even from the judgments of Heaven.

---

7. There are those who hold that even if a witness was talked into testifying falsely, the persuader would be liable to the judgments of Heaven if he felt certain that he was persuasive enough to have them follow his instructions.

8. There is also authority that Levi would be liable to the judgments of Heaven in such a case.

Chapter 33

THE STATUS OF KINSMEN AS WITNESSES

INTRODUCTION

In Chapter 33 of *Shulhan Aruch, Hoshen haMishpat*, R. Karo begins the discussion of the laws disqualifying certain persons as witnesses. In Chapter 33 he discusses kinsmen. In Chapter 34 he discusses transgressors of the law; in Chapter 35 he discusses the ineligibility of those who are deaf and mute, of limited intelligence, or underage; and in Chapter 37 he discusses those who have an interest in the outcome of the case. These topics are discussed in this book in corresponding chapters.

R. Karo begins Chapter 33 with an omnibus statement: "All those who are ineligible to judge are ineligible to testify, except those who are ineligible to judge because they are overly friendly or overly unfriendly to the litigants, who may testify although they may not judge."

This statement may refer us to Chapter 7, wherein is stated those who are eligible to judge and those who are not eligible to judge. There it was stated, "Those who are ineligible to testify on account of kinship or on account of sin are disqualified to sit on the beth din." The details regarding kinsmen are set forth in this chapter.

The various codes follow the language of a Mishnah which lists the classes of kinsmen ineligible to testify.[1] Rambam enumerates ineligible classes rather than ineligible individuals. Here, classes have been set forth following the text of Rambam; then, a comprehensive list of ineligible kinsmen has been set forth, with reference to the various codes and commentaries.

TEXT

Ineligible kinsmen

All those who are ineligible to judge are ineligible to testify, except those who are ineligible to judge because they are overly friendly or overly unfriendly to the litigants, who may nevertheless testify.[2] The Torah prohibits kinsmen to act as witnesses. Some of the kinsmen listed here are ineligible based on rabbinic rather than Torah law.[3] The prohibition applies whether the witness is a kinsman to another witness or to a judge or to a party to the litigation, and the term kinsman shall be used in this broad sense.

The law of disqualification on the ground of kinship does not apply to proselytes.[4]

A parent and child are considered kinsmen in the first degree.

---

1. Mishnah 4 in *Sanhedrin*, Chapter 3, states as follows: "The following are kinsmen: one's father, and his brother, and his father's brother, and his mother's brother, and his sister's brother, and the husband of his father's sister, and the husband of his mother's sister, and his step-father (his mother's husband), and his father-in-law, and his brother-in-law [the husband of his wife's sister]. Both they and their sons and their sons-in-law. [As for] a step-son, [it does not apply to his sons and sons-in-law]."

2. It is feared that the emotions of love or hate may unconsciously taint the judges' thinking and affect their ability to make just decisions. Witnesses, on the other hand, testify only to facts, and it is not feared that a person will misstate the facts because of love or hate.

3. The reason for not permitting kinsmen is simple: The Torah says so. It is not because it is expected that they will not testify truthfully; the prohibition applies whether they were to testify for or against their kinsmen. Even Moses and Aaron could not testify in the same case!

4. A person who becomes a proselyte has the status of a newborn, and thus all of his kinsmen prior to his conversion are no longer considered his kinsmen. Even if twin brothers have converted simultaneously, they may testify against each other.

Siblings, whether by the same father or by the same mother, are considered kinsmen in the first degree. Their children are relatives in the second degree. Their grandchildren are kinsmen in the third degree. Kinsmen in the first degree may not testify (for example, a father and a son, or a grandfather and a grandson, or two brothers). Kinsmen in the second degree may not testify (for example, first cousins). Persons in the first degree–second degree kinship may not testify (for example, an uncle and his nephew). There is a difference of opinion as to whether persons in first degree–third degree kinship may testify. Those who hold that it is prohibited state that this is only by rabbinic law (for example, a great-grandfather with his great-grandson).

Whoever is ineligible with respect to a man is also ineligible with respect to his wife; and anyone who is ineligible with respect to the wife is equally ineligible with respect to her husband. A divorce or death of a spouse breaks this kinship. For example, the son of a woman's previous husband from his previous marriage (therefore not her son) will not be a kinsman to her current husband. The husbands of two female first cousins may testify.

The following is a list of ineligible witnesses:

1. parent
2. child
3. grandparent
4. grandchild
5. sibling
6. nephew (brother's son)
7. niece's husband (brother's son-in-law)
8. uncle (father's brother)
9. uncle's son (first cousin)
10. female first cousin's husband (father's brother's son-in-law)
11. uncle (mother's brother)
12. uncle's son (first cousin, mother's brother's son)
13. female first cousin's husband (mother's brother's son-in-law)
14. brother-in-law (sister's husband)
15. nephew (sister's husband's son)
16. niece's husband (brother-in-law's son-in-law)
17. uncle (paternal aunt's husband)

18. first cousin (paternal aunt's husband's son)

19. female first cousin's husband (paternal aunt's husband's son-in-law)

20. uncle (maternal aunt's husband)

21. first cousin (maternal aunt's husband's son)

22. female first cousin's husband (maternal aunt's husband's son-in-law)

23. step-father

24. step-brother (step-father's son)

25. step-brother-in-law (step-father's son-in-law)

26. father-in-law

27. brother-in-law (wife's brother)

28. wife's sister's husband (father-in-law's son-in-law)

29. brother-in-law (wife's sister's husband)

30. nephew (wife's sister's husband's son)

31. niece's husband (wife's sister's husband's son-in-law)

32. wife's son

33. wife's son-in-law (wife's daughter's husband)

34. wife's father

35. wife's mother's husband

The father of the wife and the father of the husband are not considered kinsmen.[5]

If a witness to a gift *causa mortis*[6] was a kinsman of the donor but not of the beneficiary,[7] there are opinions on both sides.[8,9]

---

5. Although they are considered kinsmen for purposes of being judges, the reason is that they are very close to each other and are thus ineligible as persons who love each other. Just as persons who love each other are not prohibited from testifying, so are the father of the husband and the father of the wife not considered kinsmen and are not ineligible. See note 3.

6. Gifts *causa mortis* are made in contemplation of death. See Chapter 250.

7. Example: The witness was a first cousin to the donor. They stand in a second-degree relationship. The witness stands in a second-third-degree relationship to the donor's son.

8. Even according to the opinion that the witness to the gift is ineligible, if the donor was aware of the ineligibility, he will be permitted to testify since it was waived by the donor.

9. Those who hold that it is an ineligible kinship contend that the witness will have to testify to what he heard, and he heard the words of the donor, who is his

Kinsmen of a guarantor are ineligible regarding the creditor and the debtor of that transaction. The guarantor is, of course, ineligible.

In monetary cases it is not necessary that the witness be eligible both at the time of the transaction and at the time of testimony. If he was ineligible at the time of the transaction because of his status as an interested party, but he is eligible at the time of the trial because he no longer has an interest in the outcome of the trial, he may testify.[10]

If a community has appointed certain persons to witness all transactions within the community, then they are not ineligible because of kinship.

---

second-degree kinsman. Those who hold that he is eligible state that he is testifying regarding the donor's son, and the relationship with him is second/third degree.

10. At the time of the transaction he was an interested party and therefore was not in the category of being a witness. He was an interested party and now he is a witness.

Chapter 34

PERSONS INELIGIBLE TO TESTIFY BECAUSE OF TRANSGRESSIONS

INTRODUCTION

A system of law may prohibit a person from testifying if he is guilty of a crime against society. In halachah, the transgression is against the system of law, which encompasses all types of transgressions. It includes crimes that are ordinarily thought of as crimes against society, such as murder, robbery, larceny, and assault. It certainly includes crimes that are indicative of a lack of trustworthiness, such as having testified falsely at prior trials or having forged instruments.

Halachah also includes transgressions against other laws of the Torah, which are rules of God and are not the types of laws that man creates by himself to protect society. The punishments for transgressions differ depending on the transgression. Some are punishable by the death penalty, and some by flogging. Money crimes are usually atoned for by making restitution. For the purposes of declaring a person ineligible to be a witness, all transgressions are included, including transgressions that in many societies are thought of as against only religious or ritual laws.

It should also be remembered that in halachah, the Torah gave the Rabbis the authority to make decrees and injunctions and the penalties for violating them. Transgression of these laws may also render the violator ineligible to be a witness.

This chapter sets forth the types of transgressions that render a person ineligible to be a witness, how it is proved that he is a transgressor, and how he may reinstate his eligibility to be a witness. For the purpose of this chapter, the term *rasha* is translated to mean "wicked," and the term *avaira* is translated to mean "transgression."

TEXT

Not to testify with a wicked person

A wicked person may not testify.[1-5] If the beth din does not know that Ruven who testified is a wicked person, then the other witness, Shimon, who knows that Ruven is wicked, may not testify at the same

---

1. If the beth din knowingly accepted testimony from a wicked person, then it is guilty of a transgression.

2. As will be seen later in the text, a person is not considered a wicked person unless there were two witnesses who testified that he is wicked, as defined in this chapter. Thus, if the beth din knows that this person has been declared wicked on the strength of the testimony of two witnesses, then he may not testify unless he has been reclassified as eligible, as described in the text. The situation here is one in which the eligible witness, Shimon, knows that Ruven was declared wicked in a beth din, but he cannot prove it because he is the only witness before the current beth din with this information. The question presented here is: What is he to do?

3. Two of the reasons given for the prohibition are (1) if a person is wicked, then his trustworthiness is also in question, and (2) the Torah declared it to be prohibited. The second reason is given because the first reason may not suffice in a case where a person transgresses some area of law that does not necessarily reflect on his trustworthiness.

4. It is not permitted to proclaim a ban in the synagogue on all those who know that the witness is a wicked person but fail to come forward to testify against him. It is possible, however, to ask those who know that the witness was in a different place at the time at which he testified that he witnessed the event to come and place the witness at that place at that time.

5. There are different opinions if the wicked person is the only one who knows of his transgressions. Should he refuse to testify? As was noted in Chapter 28, all those who know facts on which to give testimony are obligated to come forward and testify. There are authorities on both sides, but this author agrees with those authorities who would permit him to testify. A person can remove himself from the category of wicked persons if he makes up his mind to repent. It is presumed that he intends to testify truthfully; otherwise the question would not arise.

trial.[6] This holds true even if Ruven testified truthfully.[7] Similarly, Shimon may not testify at a trial if he knows that Levi, the other witness testifying for the same side, is testifying falsely. In both situations, Shimon should ask to testify separately so that his testimony will not be combined with the testimony of either Ruven or Levi.[8]

Schach, one of the greatest of the commentators on the *Shulhan Aruch*, agonizes over the rules of this section.[9] Why should a defendant get away with not having to pay just because one of the witnesses is a wicked person? Why shouldn't the other witness or witnesses be permitted to testify so that the defendant will either have to pay if there are two eligible witnesses or at least have to take an oath of denial if there is only one eligible witness? One of the reasons Schach had to conclude as he did was that Chapter 36 states that if one of many testifying witnesses was proved to be ineligible, then the testimonies of all are invalid. Shaar Mishpat[10] quotes Schach and concludes that he apparently overlooked one of the great authorities, the Kol Bo,[11] who held that the eligible person is prohibited only from stating while he testifies that he and the wicked person were the witnesses. Rather, the witness must testify that he witnessed the matter (without any reference to the ineligible witness). Perhaps this is what Aruch haShulhan[12] meant when he stated, "What should he [the eligible witness] do? He should testify by himself in beth din

---

6. Since the testimony of the wicked person should not have been admitted and thus is really of no legal effect, although the beth din does not know it, the testimony of the eligible witness becomes crucial. If he is the sole eligible witness, then the beth din will decide the case under the misapprehension that there were two eligible witnesses. This, of course, will produce a miscarriage of justice.

7. If the other witness testifies falsely, then it does not matter whether he is wicked or not; it may still be illegal to testify together with him at the same trial. The law stated in this paragraph also applies if there are two eligible witnesses and one wicked person besides these two. They may not testify with him.

8. The rules have been formulated to answer many of the comments and questions of the great scholars. Only one of them is set forth here.

9. R. Shabtai Cohen who lived in Vilna and Germany, 1622–1663.

10. Written by R. Israel Isser b. Zev Wolf in nineteenth-century Russia.

11. The name of the title means "miscellany." The author is not known for certain, but it is attributed to R. Aaron b. Jacob haKohen of Lunel (southern France), 1330–1360.

12. Written by R. Yechiel Michel Epstein, who lived in Russia, 1829–1908. The quoted passage is from *Hoshen haMishpat*, Chapter 34, para. 1.

and beth din will decide the case on the basis of his testimony as a sole witness."

Who is a wicked person?

A wicked person is one who transgresses a law of the Torah for which the penalty is death at the decision of the Lesser Sanhedrin[13] or flogging[14] at the decision of the beth din.[15] The fact that at the present time there is no death sentence because there is no Great Sanhedrin sitting in the Chamber of Hewn Stone[16] and no Lesser Sanhedrin in existence is of no significance to this chapter. If the transgression is one for which the Lesser Sanhedrin would have been able to mete out the death penalty,[17] then the transgressor is ineligible to testify. Similarly, the fact that flogging[18] is not a punishment meted out by the beth din also does not affect this chapter. If the transgression is one for which a beth din could have decreed flogging, then the person is ineligible to testify. It does not matter whether he transgressed out of spite or for personal gratification.

If the transgression is not one that could have invoked the death penalty or flogging, then the ineligibility is of rabbinic origin. If the transgression is of a rabbinic decree, then the ineligibility is of rabbinic

---

13. If a person killed someone inadvertently, he is not ineligible.

14. There is a difference of opinion in the Mishnah (*Sanhedrin*, Chapter 1, Mishnah 2) as to whether flogging was meted out by the Lesser Sanhedrin of twenty-three judges (see notes to Chapter 1) or by the ordinary beth din of three judges. The halachah is that it was meted out by a beth din of three judges.

15. It would also include all those who, although not judged by a beth din, are judged by Heaven as being guilty of a major transgression.

16. Even when the Great Sanhedrin was still in existence, if they did not sit in the Chamber of Hewn Stone, then the Lesser Sanhedrins, which had jurisdiction to mete out the death penalty, could not exercise that jurisdiction. See notes to Chapter 1.

17. See notes to Chapter 1 for those transgressions for which the death penalty could be imposed.

18. Rambam, in Chapter 19 of *Laws of Sanhedrin*, lists three categories with 207 transgressions for which one is liable for flogging by the beth din. The three classes are: (1) 21 negative commandments involving excision but not execution by the Lesser Sanhedrin, (2) 18 commandments involving tangible action, the transgression of which is punishable by Divine intervention, (3) 168 negative commandments. There are 365 negative commandments, and the balance is not punishable by flogging.

origin. Some say that if the transgression is against a rabbinic decree, then the person is ineligible only if the transgression dealt with greed.

Transgressions that render a person ineligible

Any transgression that renders a person wicked makes him ineligible as a witness.[19]

The codes set forth some specific examples, and they are therefore set forth here, although the omnibus disqualification probably encompasses them all. They are set forth separately because of the accompanying remarks.

If someone swore falsely, then he is ineligible to be a witness.[20]

There are authorities who hold that the person is still eligible even if he violated his oath to perform an act or to refrain from performing an act.[21] There are also authorities who contend that he remains eligible if his oath violation resulted from failing to perform an act.[22]

---

19. Example: One who, out of laziness, fails to eat in a booth during the Holy Days of Succoth. But if he failed to do so out of contempt for the commandment, rather than out of laziness, then he becomes ineligible the first time he transgresses.

20. There are four classes of statements that rise to the status of oaths if they are uttered using the Divine Name: (1) the rashly uttered oath; (2) the vain oath; (3) judicial oaths; (4) testimony oaths.

(1) Rashly uttered oaths apply to things that are possible to perform and are false when made or will be false in the future. They may be divided into four subclasses: (i) I did do a certain act; (ii) I did not do a certain act; (iii) I shall do a certain act; and (iv) I shall not do a certain act.

(2) Vain oaths are also divided into four subclasses: (i) stating that a known fact is not a fact (such as stating that a man is a woman); (ii) stating a fact that all know to be a fact (a stone is a stone); (iii) an oath not to observe a commandment (not to eat unleavened bread [matzah] on the night of the first day of Passover); (iv) an oath to do something that is not within one's ability to do (to walk from New York to Los Angeles in one hour).

(3) Judicial oaths are of two types: (i) bailee's oaths (a bailee denying bailment or asserting nonliability to the bailor), and (ii) defendant's oaths (a defendant taking an oath of denial against the plaintiff's claim).

(4) Testimony oaths are taken by those who are called to testify and they deny having knowledge of the facts.

21. See previous note. The reason is that the oath was not false at the time.

22. Example: A person promises to eat fish tomorrow and then he fails to eat fish. He did not act.

If witnesses testify that the witness violated his oath, he may not reinstate his eligibility to be a witness by stating that he violated it inadvertently or was coerced into violating it.

A butcher or slaughterer who sells nonkosher meat as kosher is ineligible.[23,24] This author would add to that butchers who sell kosher meat at higher-than-warranted prices so that poor persons and others who are not strictly observant are induced to eat nonkosher meat.

A thief and a robber are ineligible from the time of the theft or robbery. One who falsely denies a bailment or the borrowing of money is also ineligible.

A refuted witness becomes ineligible from the time when he refutes testimony.[25,26] He remains ineligible even if he makes restitution.

A witness to a written instrument cannot be refuted[27] unless he testifies in beth din that he signed on the date written on the instrument and not on a later date.[28,29] If he does not so testify, then

---

23. This applies not only to butchers but to any person who sells nonkosher products as kosher.

24. Kosher meat is usually more expensive than nonkosher meat. (Why, this author does not know.) Thus the butcher or slaughterer who is knowingly passing off nonkosher meat as kosher meat is doing so only for greed. A person who causes unknowing others to transgress only for the sake of his own greed is not to be trusted to testify truthfully. This ineligibility has nothing to do with *his* eating nonkosher meat. The transgression lies in his "placing stumbling blocks before the blind."

25. It does not matter when he was refuted, even if it was after some time had passed. His ineligibility is retroactive to the time he gave the refuted testimony. A difference could arise if he testified at trial 1 and then testified at a nonrelated trial 2, and he was thereafter refuted at trial 1. His testimony at trial 2 is to be discarded.

26. See Chapter 38 regarding the difference between refuted and contradicted witnesses.

27. Some authorities hold that the law of refuted witnesses does not apply to written instruments.

28. As will be explained in Chapter 38, a witness is refuted if after he testifies, other witnesses testify that the first witness who testified could not possibly have witnessed the event. The second pair of witnesses testify that the first witness was with the second pair of witnesses at another place at the time when the first witness claims that he witnessed the event. Thus the witness on the instrument cannot be refuted unless he testifies that he was at that place at the time stated in the instrument.

29. A written instrument may be dated in one of three ways: on the date it was executed; and on a date after it was executed; and on a date prior to its execution. These topics are discussed in Chapter 43. Generally, if the date of the instrument is the

even if refuting witnesses testify that the signing witness was in another place on the date mentioned in the instrument, the instrument is still valid and the signing witness is not considered refuted.[30] If the witness testifies that he signed on the date written on the instrument, and he is refuted, then he is considered ineligible from the earliest date for which there are witnesses that he signed the instrument.[31] If there is no testimony that the instrument was seen with his signature prior to the date on which it was introduced in beth din, then the witness is deemed ineligible only from the date on which the instrument was introduced in beth din.

A witness who knowingly signs a predated instrument is ineligible as a witness.

One who hires witnesses (other than expert witnesses) to testify on his behalf is ineligible from the time at which they testify.[32]

Both the lender and the borrower who transact a loan that includes usury (interest) payments[33] are ineligible to testify.[34] If the interest is fixed, the ineligibility is of Torah origin. If the usury is Rabbinically prohibited, there is an opinion that only the lender, but not the

---

date on which it was executed or a later date, it is valid. If the date is a date prior to the instrument's execution, it is not valid. Thus the witnesses could have stated that they executed the instrument on a date prior to the date noted on the instrument.

30. The testimony of witnesses should be given credence whenever possible.

31. When witnesses sign a written instrument, their signatures acquire the same competence as testimony that has been given and examined in a beth din. Thus, signing the instrument is equivalent to the signatory's having testified in beth din; accordingly, when the second pair of witnesses testify that the witness on the instrument could not possibly have signed on the date on which he testified that he signed because on that date he was with the second pair of witnesses at another place, it is the same as his being refuted on the true date of the instrument.

32. He is not ineligible from the time at which they were paid, since they may return the money and not testify. This applies to all situations in which there is a time interval between the thought to transgress and the actual transgression: The ineligibility commences at the time of the transgression.

33. The charging of any amount of interest is usury and is prohibited by Torah law. The borrower and the lender are equally culpable, and thus both become ineligible to be witnesses. All those who took part in the transaction are also violators, such as the scribe who drew up the instrument, the witnesses, the surety, and the brokers; however, they are not ineligible.

34. It is to be noted that lending money at interest is not a transgression for which one is flogged.

borrower, is ineligible.[35] If a person who lent money at interest died and his signature appears on a written instrument, and if it is well known that he was a guardian on behalf of minors or a trustee of Gentiles, then his signature is not to be questioned, since it is presumed that he engaged in usurious transactions on their behalf. If it is not known that he was such a guardian or trustee, then his signature on the written instrument is ineligible. If a person who is presumed to be eligible is shown to have loaned money on interest, then the loan is to be attributed to a situation in which he would not become ineligible by the interest-bearing loan.[36]

One who intentionally and habitually transgresses a Rabbinic decree is ineligible to be a witness.[37]

Transgressions that render a person ineligible by rabbinic enactment

A person is guilty of a rabbinically prohibited class of theft if he steals the found objects of a minor, deaf and mute, or foolish person.[38]

Other examples include the following:

Strong-armed persons who buy things that the sellers do not wish to sell are ineligible.[39] Shepherds who graze their sheep on land belonging to other individuals are ineligible.[40]

---

35. There is also an opinion that even in the case of Torah-prohibited interest, the ineligibility against the borrower is only of Rabbinic origin.

36. As having been made on behalf of a minor or a heathen.

37. One who habitually and intentionally transgresses a Rabbinic decree is deemed a heretic, and thus his ineligibility is of Torah origin.

38. An example would be one who robbed that which was found by a deaf-mute, a fool, or a minor. Since legally they cannot acquire the lost object, they really do not have ownership, and one who would rob this found object from them would not be a real robber. However, the Rabbis have enacted a ruling that one may not rob or steal a found object from these persons, and anyone who does is guilty of a Rabbinically enacted class of robbery.

39. The Rabbis considered them robbers even though they paid for what they took. See Chapter 205.

40. This usually applies only to shepherds who are grazing their own flocks. If they graze the flocks of others, however, they will not want to violate a law against stealing to benefit others.

Tax collectors, but not revenue collectors, are ineligible.[41-42] If a revenue collector was found to overtax even one time, he loses his eligibility.[43]

Pigeon raisers[44] in a populated area are ineligible.[45,46]

Those who trade in produce of the seventh year are ineligible.

A gambler[47] who has no other means of support is ineligible.[48]

Whoever has no knowledge of Torah or Mishnah or of proper conduct is ineligible,[49] unless his life is full of religious and benevolent acts.[50]

---

41. The tax collectors referred to are those who are instructed by the king or ruling authority to bring in a certain amount of tax revenue. They then collect more and keep the surplus for themselves. This is a form of robbery. There is also the danger that the tax collector will collect less from those whom he favors at the expense of others.

42. The term designated for a tax collector is *moches*, and for a revenue collector, *gabbai*. The translations are this author's. The difference between the two is that in the former case, the king tells the collector how much revenue he wants. He does not care how much the tax collector taxes the people as long as he gets the amount he wants. The tax collector can overtax at his own discretion. The latter collector, the *gabbai*, is told by the king to fix a set sum on every individual. Thus the *gabbai* has no latitude to overtax.

43. If the beth din is certain that it happened only one time, there are those who hold that perhaps he should not lose his eligibility. Otherwise it is assumed that if he did it once, he did it more frequently.

44. The presumption is that they decoy pigeons that belong to others to join their flocks and thus steal from others.

45. In a nonpopulated area there is no ineligibility since the pigeons that accompany the raiser's own flock do not belong to anyone.

46. The people referred to are those who are usually idle but when the *shemitah* (Sabbatical) year commences they begin to trade in produce. It is presumed that they are trading in shemita crops, which is prohibited. If it was certain, then they would be ineligible according to Torah law. See notes to Chapter 1.

47. The term used in the codes is "a dice player." Gambling takes into account all types of games of chance, including racing birds or animals. The reason for the ineligibility is that the gains are considered ill gotten or a form of robbery, and thus the witness has benefited from a robbery, which is prohibited by rabbinic law. Another reason given is that they do nothing to better the world. See Chapter 207.

48. There are some who hold that even if he has other means of support but some of his support comes from gambling, then he is ineligible.

49. If a person is without basic knowledge of the laws to follow, then he has no standards to follow and is most likely a sinner.

50. It goes without saying that every scholar is eligible unless he is found to be

Self-abased persons are ineligible.[51]

Anyone other than an expert witness who accepts compensation to testify is ineligible.[52] An expert witness may receive compensation for testifying.[53]

If Ruven hates Shimon[54] and publicly stated that he, Ruven, would inform armed robbers of Shimon's wealth so that they could steal it, Ruven is ineligible to be a witness.[55]

Informers to armed robbers,[56] heretics, and informers to Gentiles are worse than heathens and are ineligible.

---

ineligible, while every ignorant person is deemed to be ineligible until it is shown that he performs righteous acts.

51. This category includes those who show no shame. They include those who eat in the street while in public view, or those who work almost naked in a repugnant occupation and show no sense of shame or embarrassment, or those who publicly accept charity from Gentiles when they could have found the funds privately. Such persons are not likely to find it demeaning to testify falsely.

52. This rule applies if the witness accepts compensation from both sides to testify. If he accepts from one side only, then he is ineligible for a different reason. He becomes a person interested in the result of the litigation. If he accepts from just one side, even if he returns the compensation, he is still ineligible. But if he accepts from both sides and gives back the compensation, then he becomes eligible to testify. One who is not being asked to testify falsely, just to tell the truth, still may not accept compensation. The reason is that all commandments, including the commandment to testify, must be performed without compensation. The ineligibility is only a penalty imposed by the Rabbis, however, since the witness has not technically transgressed any commandment. This is not the same situation as where a person accepts compensation to witness an event, such as a loan or a divorce, for in such a case one may accept compensation, since he could be earning money during that time. It is only if he accepts compensation to testify that he is ineligible.

53. See comments of *Turai Zahav* (Taz) on this paragraph in *Shulhan Aruch, Hoshen haMishpat,* Chapter 34, para. 18. The compensation is given for the expert witness's efforts in traveling to beth din and giving up time he could otherwise use to earn money.

54. See Chapter 33, where it is noted that hating someone does not render a person ineligible to testify. In this situation the hatred has resulted in antisocial behavior.

55. The mere public threat to inform by a person who hates another is sufficient to make the would-be informer ineligible even if it is not known whether he has actually informed. The reason given is that if a person is so arrogant that he can publicly make such statements, then he is a wicked person and is therefore ineligible.

56. This situation does not depend upon hatred, as in the previous case, nor does it depend upon a public threat to inform. The person does, in fact, inform.

All other transgressors of Torah law for which there is no penalty of capital punishment or flogging are ineligible.

Whoever transgresses a Rabbinic decree is ineligible.

Transgressions that do not render a person ineligible

Those who bury the dead on the first day of a Holy Day do not lose their eligibility.[57] The same would apply to any other transgression where the transgressor was certain that he was doing something that was permitted.[58] An example is one who lends with interest money belonging to minors.[59] Some say that this also applies to one who lends the money of widows, but most dispute this.

One who shares the gains of a robbery or of a theft does not lose his eligibility.[60]

A sharecropper who took a tiny amount of the crop for himself before the harvest was completed does not lose his eligibility.[61]

---

57. See Chapter 5. There it is stated that except for Rosh haShanah, Holy Days are celebrated for only one day in Israel and two days outside of Israel. The phrase "first Holy Day" is meant to apply to outside of Israel, where two days are celebrated, and also to the first day of Rosh haShanah, whether in Israel or outside of Israel. The dead may not be buried on the first Holy Day, whether two days are celebrated or only one. The dead should be buried on the second Holy Day. The reason for the law as stated in the text is that the persons who bury the dead do not realize that they are transgressing the law. They are certain that they are engaged in a most pious act, which they assuredly are. It is just the timing that is not permitted. They are not aware of the distinction between the first Holy Day and the second, and they are also aware of the fact that the dead should be buried as quickly as possible. Thus, taken together, these persons should be praised for the wonderful work that they do for the community. The transgression is not enough to make them ineligible, since the prohibition is only of Rabbinic origin and these persons are unaware of it.

58. Example: Borrowing books without permission of the owner to use them for studying Torah.

59. The lender who is attending to the affairs of the minor believes that he is enhancing the assets of the minor and that he is therefore permitted to lend the minor's money at interest.

60. If the person does so on more than one occcasion, he is ineligible. He is eligible only until he uses or alters the thing or money stolen or robbed.

61. The reason is that the beth din takes judicial notice of the fact that the owner of the field is not concerned with this small amount.

When does the ineligibility commence?

The person is deemed to be a transgressor if two witnesses testified that he committed the transgression, even if he was not warned not to do it.[62]

If a person's ineligibility derives from Torah law, his testimony is void even if his ineligibility has not been proclaimed in the synagogues and houses of study.[63] The ineligibility commences only when the proof of his having performed the wicked act prior to the testimony has been firmly established. If there is doubt about whether the performance of the wicked act preceded or was subsequent to the testimony he gave, then all testimony he gave prior to the wicked act remains valid.

If a person's ineligibility derives from Rabbinic law, his ineligibility commences after the proclamations have been made in the synagogues and houses of study. If the transgressor has been publicly punished for his transgressions, it is equivalent to a public proclamation of his ineligibility.

The commission of any readily recognized transgression[64] renders him a wicked person and therefore ineligible to be a witness.

If the transgression is not widely known to be prohibited,[65] and the person who does the act is not aware that it is prohibited, there must first be an admonition to the transgressor that his conduct is prohibited.

---

62. The purpose of the warning in halachah is to enable the transgressor to avoid the punishment due for the transgression. In this situation there is no penalty and therefore no necessity for the warning.

63. Any place where people assemble is also an appropriate place. The purpose is to publicize the ineligibility.

64. An example given by Rambam and repeated by R. Karo: swearing falsely, robbing or stealing, or eating nonkosher food.

65. Example given by Rambam and repeated by R. Karo: making a knot or untying it on the Sabbath. Many do not know that this is prohibited. The admonition should also remind the person that it is the Sabbath or Holy Day in case he forgot, although he knows what is forbidden on those days. The same applies to those who are affected by many of the Rabbinic ineligibilities, such as the gambler, the tax collector, and all those who may not be aware that their conduct will render them ineligible to be witnesses in a beth din. The beth din must examine the mores of the people to determine which of their acts are known to be prohibited and which are not known to them as such.

A person may not be deemed a wicked man on his own confession. It is a fundamental principle of halachah that a person's confession to illegal or wicked conduct is absolutely not admissible in beth din. A person may not incriminate himself. This law is absolute and may not be waived! For example, if a person testifies that he has robbed, although he has to make restitution on his own admission, he is not ineligible to be a witness.[66] Or, if Ruven testified that Shimon lent money to Levi usuriously, and Levi, testifying to the same loan, states that Shimon lent money to him at interest, Shimon becomes ineligible because of the testimony of both Ruven and Levi. Levi is not ineligible, however, since only Ruven has testified that Levi has transgressed the laws against usury. Levi's own statement is not admitted against himself, although it was admitted against Ruven. Levi's testimony was split.[67]

The sole witness on behalf of the plaintiff who obligates the defendant to take an oath of denial to win the lawsuit may join together with the plaintiff to show that the defendant is a transgressor. This may be done only in a new lawsuit and not in the lawsuit in which he testified. Similarly, two witnesses in two separate lawsuits, each of whom obligated the same person who was the defendant in both lawsuits, may join together to testify that the defendant was a transgressor. There are those who differ.

Reacquiring eligibility

A transgressor who repents of his actions is immediately eligible, no matter how serious his transgression.

If after two witnesses testify that the person was a transgressor two other witnesses testify that the person repented, he is immediately eligible. If the latter two witnesses testify that the person was punished for his transgression, the person is also immediately eligible. If, however, the latter two witnesses testify that the person was never

---

66. The testimony of the witness is divided. The "splitting of testimony" results in admitting into evidence that which deals with money and excluding from evidence that which deals with the witness's being a transgressor.

67. See previous note.

guilty of the alleged transgression in the first instance, the person is in a doubtful state until it becomes known that he is eligible.[68]

In the case of transgressions involving money, the general rule of repentance must be supported by evidence of repentance. The following are some examples:

1. A robber, after he has made restitution and the public has accepted him as being an honest person. If the robbery was an isolated incident on his part, then as soon as he voluntarily makes restitution, he regains his eligibility.[69]

2. A usurer, after he has torn up all the promissory notes that he holds and repents by not lending usuriously, even to a Gentile. He must also return all of the interest that he has collected; if he does not know to whom to return it, he must use the money for public good.

3. A gambler, after he destroys his gambling equipment and does not even gamble without money. Some say that he also has to make restitution.

4. Pigeon raisers, when they destroy the traps where they trapped pigeons belonging to others, and when they desist from such conduct.

5. Traders in Sabbatical-year produce, when another Sabbatical year comes and he does not indulge in this conduct. He must also confess in writing as to how much he gained by his illegal conduct and turn this sum over to charity.

6. A perjurer, when he comes to another beth din where he is not known and advises it that he is suspected of perjury; or if a beth din where he is not known imposes an oath upon him in a suit in which he could take the oath and save himself a large sum of money, and he pays rather than take the oath.

---

68. The defendant in a lawsuit is the holder of the money. The plaintiff asserts a claim against the defendant. The plaintiff has the burden of proof to obtain from the that which the defendant possesses. The plaintiff, who must prove his case, produced a witness whose eligibility is questioned. Therefore the witness may not testify to dispossess the defendant of that which he possesses, since the defendant is presumed to be the owner of that which is in lhis possession. What is taking place here is that a witness of doubtful eligibility is testifying to dispossess the defendant, who is certainly the possessor of his money or property. It is a general rule of law that a person cannot be dispossessed of the certainty of his possession by a doubtful witness or a doubtful fact. See Chapters 139, 175, 223, 390, and 410.

69. If the restitution was forced upon him by the beth din, then he is in the same category as a constant robber.

7. The butcher who sold nonkosher meat as kosher, when he has repented, which he evidences by the life he now leads. He should go to a place where he is not known and dress in modest (black) garments and look to voluntarily restoring something valuable to its owner or declaring nonkosher an expensive portion of meat in his possession.

8. A refuted witness. He should go to a place where he is not known and refuse an offer of a large bribe to perjure himself.

Chapter 35

WHO IS ELIGIBLE TO TESTIFY AND WHO IS NOT ELIGIBLE TO TESTIFY

INTRODUCTION

Chapter 7 delineated who is eligible to be a judge and who is not eligible to be a judge. This chapter, which parallels Chapter 7, deals with the personal status of the witness. In Chapter 33, ineligibility to be a witness was based on kinship. Thus a person might be ineligible to testify in the particular lawsuit in which a kinsman was a party, but such ineligibility might not extend to other lawsuits. Chapter 34 set forth the laws dealing with those who are ineligible because of having committed transgressions. A person could repent and become eligible. In Chapter 37 there are stated the laws of ineligibility based on the fact that the witness might stand to benefit or lose from the outcome of the lawsuit. This is similar to the ineligibility described in Chapter 33, since these same witnesses can be eligible in other lawsuits in which they have no interest in the outcome of the trial. The witnesses described in the present chapter, on the other hand, may not testify in any lawsuit. The appendix to this volume deals with the eligibility of women to be litigants, to judge, and to testify.

The following topics will be discussed in this chapter:

The proselyte as a witness
The bastard as a witness

253

TEXT

The proselyte as a witness

Proselytes may act as witnesses. A proselyte may not testify to an event that he witnessed before he became a proselyte.[1]

The bastard as a witness

A bastard may be a witness.

The blind person as a witness

A person who is totally blind may not testify. This is true even in a case in which beth din knows that he can recognize voices. A person who is blind in one eye is eligible as a witness.

The minimum age of a witness

Generally, a boy may act as a witness after he has attained the age of 13 years and a day. If younger, he may not testify, even if he is highly intelligent and educated.

There are those who hold that a person should not act as an

---

1. He may not testify even about those matters, which a mature person may testify, when he witnessed them as a minor.

appraiser of real estate until he has attained the age at which he can understand such matters.

A person may not testify after attaining maturity regarding things he witnessed when he was a minor. There are some exceptions. He may testify, together with a mature person, on the authenticity of his father's signature or that of his brother or his teacher. The boy and another (mature) person who witnessed the wedding of a previously unmarried woman may testify when he reaches maturity (together with the other witness) that it was indeed the woman's[2] first marriage.

All of the foregoing rules are only a guide to the beth din, which must decide each case as it sees fit.

Women as witnesses

Except as stated in section L, which follows, women may not testify at a trial. (See Appendix for the present-day status of women as witnesses.)

One whose sex is unknown may not testify.[3] A hermaphrodite may not testify.

Intoxicated persons as witnesses

One who is drunk may not be a witness. If a person has had some drink, he may testify if the beth din deems him fit to testify. He may not testify to a matter that he witnessed while he was drunk.

---

2. There is a difference between the amount the estate has to pay to the widow of the decedent, if the wife was previously married or if she was not previously married. Since the wedding took place many years before the death of the husband, there is no independent testimony, except for one person who witnessed the wedding as a child and another mature person who also witnessed the wedding. The case before the beth din places the widow against the other heirs of the estate. Of course, if the widow produces the marriage contract, then the question is moot, since the contract would have stipulated the amount.

3. A person of unknown sex or a hermaphrodite may not testify, since the person may be a woman and women are not permitted to testify. If the person is a woman, then her testimony will result in a verdict on behalf of a person who should not receive a judgment. It would amount to taking money from a person who was entitled to it on the basis of a doubt.

Gentiles as witnesses

A Gentile may not be a witness at a trial in beth din.

The mentally deficient person as a witness

The mentally deficient person may not be a witness. The beth din must decide in each case whether the person is so mentally deficient that his witnessing of the event and his testifying about the event are meaningless.

The inordinately foolish who are not able to distinguish between contradictory matters and do not understand things as persons of normal intelligence do may not testify.

Persons who are unduly impulsive and are quick to judge and who act like madmen are in the category of the mentally deficient.

The beth din must decide each situation as it deems appropriate.

The deaf-mute as a witness

A deaf-mute may not testify. A speaking deaf person may not testify.[4] A hearing mute may not testify.[5]

A person who lost his speech may not testify in writing.[6] However, he may testify to enable a woman to remarry.[7]

The epileptic as a witness

An epileptic may not testify while he is having a seizure. If the beth din is satisfied as to his incapacity, then he may testify while he is not having a seizure about a matter that he witnessed while he was not having a seizure.

The foregoing rules apply to any other type of illness that leaves a person capable at certain times and not at others.

---

4. He may not testify because he cannot hear the judges and their admonitions to testify truthfully.

5. He may not testify because he is required to give oral testimony.

6. He may not testify even if he was tested and found competent in a manner that would allow him to testify if he were to divorce his wife.

7. There are cases in which the only evidence that a woman may have to enable her to remarry is based on the testimony of a person who has lost his speech—as, for example, if he witnessed the death of her husband. The exception was made to prevent the woman from being perpetually unable to remarry.

Changes in circumstance

If a person was a deaf-mute or mentally deficient or totally blind when he acquired the evidence, then he may not testify, even after he regained his ability to hear and speak, or after he regained his mental ability, or after he regained his eyesight, respectively. If a person was able to hear and speak, or was able to see, or was mentally sufficient when he acquired the testimony, but was deaf or mute, or blind totally, or mentally deficient, respectively, when he came to testify, then he may not testify.

If a person was able to hear and speak and able to see and was mentally sufficient when he obtained the testimony and was also in such state when he came to testify, then he may testify even if in the interim he became a deaf-mute or blind or mentally deficient.

The general rule is, whenever his beginning (the time of observation) or his end (when he appears in beth din to testify) was under a disqualification, he is disqualified. But whenever his beginning and end find him in a suitable condition, he is eligible to testify.

Exceptions

1. All of the foregoing rules generally apply even if there are no other eligible persons there to testify.

2. There is an exception if the occurrence took place in a location frequented only by women, such as a women's section of a synagogue; in such a case, women can testify to the basic facts of the occurrence.

3. A minor may testify about events that took place in his classroom.[8]

4. A woman or a minor or a kinsman may testify that a Sage was assaulted or insulted,[9,10] or as to other spontaneous disputes or fights.[11]

---

8. Example: A case of student molestation by his teacher.

9. The reason is that otherwise people would assault or insult others with impunity, knowing that there were no witnesses present except for those ineligible to testify. Therefore, it is an ancient enactment to make exceptions in such situations.

10. They may only testify if called by the plaintiff to do so.

11. It is obvious that one cannot prepare eligible witnesses for a spontaneous event.

Chapter 36

IF SOME OF THE WITNESSES WERE KINSMEN OR INELIGIBLE TO TESTIFY

INTRODUCTION

The Torah combines the testimony of the witnesses in that if some of the witnesses who have testified are not eligible to testify for some of the reasons discussed in previous chapters or because they are kinsmen, then the testimony of all of the witnesses becomes disqualified. This chapter will discuss the general rule and the exceptions to the rule as developed by the commentaries and codes.

As has been stated several times, the witness can serve one of three roles.[1] (1) His presence as a witness may complete the act, such as a witness to a divorce decree or the witness who is present at the betrothal of the bride by the groom. The act cannot be valid without the two witnesses. In such a situation it is invariably possible to have two qualified witnesses present. The husband or the rabbi or other persons in the community will arrange to have two qualified witnesses present. Thus the question of mixing eligible and ineligible witnesses will ordinarily not arise in this context.

---

1. In the Appendix, there are only two roles since roles 2 and 3 there have similar laws regarding the eligibility of witnesses.

(2) Then there are those whose specific role is to witness an act so that if a question or dispute arises as to what took place, they can then testify in the beth din. Under this category, where the witnesses do not give effect to the act, but rather "look" at the act, there may or may not be time to prepare eligible witnesses. When a person wants to obtain a loan, he may go to his lawyer or to another qualified person to carry out the transaction, and the lawyer or other person will have eligible witnesses to "look" at the transaction and thus be able to testify later, in the event that a dispute or lawsuit arises. In such an instance the question of ineligible witnesses will seldom arise.

(3) The third role of the witness may come into play if there is a traffic accident in which two automobiles collide, and the plaintiff brings a lawsuit to collect for injuries and damages. He must locate persons who witnessed the occurrence. He certainly had no occasion to prepare witnesses. Even in a commercial transaction, when time does not permit the identification of eligible witnesses, the lender may believe that the persons who are "looking" at the transaction are all eligible witnesses, when in reality some of the witnesses may not be eligible. Certainly in most criminal cases the witnesses have not been standing by to witness the crime and were not asked prior to the crime whether they were eligible to witness it. In fact, many spontaneous occurrences are not witnessed by any eligible persons. What is the plaintiff, or sometimes the defendant, to do in such situations? There may be enough eligible witnesses to the occurrence to prove a cause of action or a defense, but there are also ineligible witnesses. As will be seen, the role of the witness is twofold. He sees the transaction, and he may later be called upon to testify regarding it.

A similar situation may arise regarding documents, such as deeds or notes of indebtedness. What if one of the witnesses is ineligible or is a kinsman of the other witness or of one of the parties to the transaction? Generally, the signatures of the witnesses on a document is equivalent to their having testified in beth din regarding what is written in the document.[2]

---

2. See Chapter 46.

TEXT

If any of the witnesses are ineligible, then all of the witnesses are not permitted to testify

The rule does not affect the testimony of eligible witnesses if the ineligible witness was a woman, a Gentile, or a minor.[3] If the ineligible witnesses were proven to be refuted witnesses,[4] then they are not regarded as ineligible witnesses to disqualify the testimony of the eligible witnesses. The rule is in effect only if the witnesses witnessed the event simultaneously.[5]

The rule is not in effect if a party to an event designated only certain eligible individuals to act as witnesses to the exclusion of all others.[6] The presence of ineligible persons at the event will not affect the eligibility of the designated witnesses.

The rule is in effect only if the ineligible witness intended to be a witness to the event.[7] If ineligible witnesses come to beth din to testify,[8] the beth din should examine them to ascertain whether they "looked" at the event with the intent of being witnesses or only as onlookers. The rule is in effect only if the ineligible witness testifies in

---

3. There are some authorities who hold that if the ineligibility arises from the witness's being a transgressor as stated in Chapter 34, then the otherwise eligible witnesses are ineligible only if the transgressions were of Torah laws, but not if they were of Rabbinic laws. In the latter case the eligible witnesses can testify.

4. See Chapter 38 for the definition of refuted witnesses. It will be seen there that their testimony is expunged from the trial and thus they cannot be considered to taint the eligible witnesses.

5. Thus if a person admitted an indebtedness in the presence of witness 1 in January and in the presence of witness 2 in February, and one of the witnesses was ineligible or a kinsman, then the testimony of the other witness is admissible. See Chapter 30 regarding the combining of testimony of witnesses who witnessed the event at different times.

6. This holds true even if a party sent out a call for all those who know testimony to come and testify; such a call means that he wants only eligible witnesses, and if ineligible witnesses show up, he may exclude them.

7. Witnesses need not intend to be witnesses. Their presence at an event is all that is required, unless all persons are excluded from being witnesses except those specifically designated to be witnesses. An example is at a wedding. There are many kinsmen present as the groom gives the ring to the bride. Therefore it is usual for the groom to designate two eligible persons to be the witnesses. The others are now only onlookers and not witnesses to the betrothal.

8. There are some authorities who hold that all of the witnesses must be examined to see whether they "looked" at the event to be witnesses or just as onlookers.

beth din.[9-11] The rule is in effect only if the eligible witnesses were aware of the fact that there was also an ineligible person or persons looking at the event as witnesses. The eligible witness is believed if he states that he was not aware of the other person's ineligibility, unless, of course, it is obvious that he knew of it.[12]

There are authorities who hold that the rule is in effect only if the ineligible witness testified immediately at the conclusion of or immediately prior to the eligible witness's testifying. In any of the situations in which two witnesses testified and one witness was ineligible or a kinsman, and the rule is not in effect, then the testimony of the eligible witness remains and is given the effect of a sole witness testifying.[13] If there were two eligible witnesses in addition to the ineligible witnesses or kinsmen and the rule was not in effect, then they are given the effect of two witnesses whose testimony is not disqualified.

Ineligible witnesses on written documents

The preferred opinion seems to be that as long as the document is not introduced into beth din as evidence, the eligible witness or wit-

---

9. According to this view two things are required to invalidate the testimony of the eligible witnesses. The ineligible witnesses must have been present at the event at the same time as the eligible witnesses and must have seen the event simultaneously. The ineligible witnesses must also have testified with the eligible witnesses. The other view holds that just seeing the event simultaneously (with the intent of testifying) disqualifies the eligible witnesses.

10. It seems to me that this holds true only if the witnesses were all called by the same side. Otherwise, the other party would introduce the testimony of ineligible witnesses to disqualify the eligible witnesses who testified against him. For example, the plaintiff brought two eligible witnesses to testify that he lent money to the defendant. The defendant, who cannot refute such testimony, produces a relative of the plaintiff to also testify that the loan was made. Since the relative of the plaintiff is ineligible, the testimony of the two eligible witnesses produced by the plaintiff would also be ineligible. This result would frustrate all trials. Thus a party has the right to select his own witnesses and to determine their eligibility before he produces them in beth din.

11. There are authorities who hold that as soon as ineligible persons saw the event and thought that they would go to the beth din to testify if the matter ever came before a beth din, then the mere presence of such ineligible persons at the event disqualifies even the eligible persons.

12. If the other person was his relative, he would be aware of it.

13. See Chapter 87 regarding the effect of one witness who testifies on behalf of a plaintiff.

nesses on the document may testify in beth din and the ineligible witnesses would be excluded. The fact that the ineligible and eligible witnesses witnessed the event simultaneously and signed the document as witnesses simultaneously will not affect the foregoing statement. Another view is that if one or more of the witnesses' signatures on a document is that of a person ineligible to be a witness, then the entire document is invalid. Under this view, the eligible witness may still testify to the event in beth din, if he has not already testified with the ineligible witness. The beth din may then write another document based on the testimony of two eligible witnesses. Another view is that once the witnesses signed the document, the eligible witness may not testify regarding the transaction since the document also contained the signature of an ineligible witness.

A document signed by the obligor is not deemed a document witnessed by an ineligible witness.[14]

A written decree whose signatories included community members is not invalid because the witnesses were ineligible as interested parties.[15]

---

14. The obligor did not consider himself to be a witness, but rather a party to the transaction. Even if he considered himself to be a witness, he is *not* a witness, but a party.

15. The community accepts the interested parties as being eligible just as a party may waive any other ineligibility. See also Chapter 37 regarding the rights of a community to waive all disabilities of witnesses as regards the community.

Chapter 37

WITNESSES INELIGIBLE ON ACCOUNT OF INTEREST IN THE LAWSUIT

INTRODUCTION

In this chapter we again deal with the subject of witnesses who are ineligible to testify. Now their ineligibility stems from an interest in the outcome of the lawsuit. It is logical that a witness's thinking will be tainted if he stands to gain as a result of a lawsuit. His testimony, whether consciously or unconsciously, will tend to seek the result that will be beneficial to him. The witness may honestly believe that he is telling the truth about the transaction or occurrence that he observed. In order to prevent the witness's being led into a situation in which he may not testify truthfully, whether intentionally or inadvertently, the halachah has disqualified him from testifying.

TEXT

A person may not testify in a matter in which he may benefit from the result

A person may not testify in any matter in which he may benefit[1] from

---

1. Two reasons have been suggested for the exclusion: Either the witness will falsify his testimony, or else he is deemed a principal, and the principal may not testify; he may only plead. A difference between the two reasons could arise if a person

the result. The ineligibility is present even if the benefit is minimal or remote. However, this does not apply if he testifies against his interest.[2]

There are two views regarding the situation in which the witness at one time had a beneficial interest in the occurrence, but by the time he came to testify he no longer had that beneficial interest. One view would allow him to testify, while the other view would not allow him to testify. I prefer the view that the time of testifying should be controlling.[3]

The beth din must examine each case to determine whether ineligibility exists

If a party alleges that a witness has a present interest[4] and should be ineligible to testify, then the beth din or judge judging the case must hold an independent inquiry regarding the allegation.

The witness may ask the beth din or judge to rule on his eligibility if the witness believes that he may have a present interest in the

---

signed a note of indebtedness as a witness and later became involved in the transaction as a principal. If the reason is on account of falsifying, there need be no fear in letting him testify. However, he is now a principal and may not testify; thus the entire note may be ineligible for admission into evidence. Also, if he testifies against his interest, he may testify if the fear is on account of falsifying.

2. In most other situations of ineligibility, the witness is ineligible even if he testifies against his interest.

3. The view of those who hold that if the witness was ineligible at the outset he may no longer become eligible may be based on the fact that a witness plays two roles. One is that of observing the transaction; the second is that of testifying before the beth din. This view holds that the witness must be eligible to play both roles. In this respect the position differs from that of the judge, who may adjudicate a lawsuit if he has no present interest in the outcome, even if he once might have had such an interest.

4. If the witness has no present interest, the fact that he may have an interest at some time in the future should not render him ineligible. An example is a person who, because of his poverty, is exempt from taxes. The city has a lawsuit with another individual regarding taxes. The poor person may testify, since the outcome of the lawsuit will not presently affect him. Whether the other individual pays or does not pay taxes will affect the tax rate only for other taxpayers, but the witness is exempt in any case. The beth din must not speculate that perhaps the poverty-stricken witness will falsify his testimony because he hopes to someday become wealthy and the result of the tax case may affect his tax rate if he becomes wealthy and thus becomes a taxpayer.

outcome of the case. The witness may advise the beth din that he believes that his beneficial interest in the outcome of the case will prejudice his testimony. In such a case, the beth din should prevent him from testifying. If the witness, after he has testified, tells the beth din that he has an interest in the outcome of the case, his admission is of no effect.[5]

Examples are given in the next section to serve as a guide to the beth din in determining the eligibility of the witnesses.

Examples

A servant or an employee may testify on behalf of his employer.[6] If the beth din believes that the employee or servant is afraid to testify against the employer, they may find him ineligible to testify on his behalf.

A partner (partner 1) as an owner of real estate may not testify against a plaintiff, Judah, who alleges that Ruven, the seller to the partnership, stole the property from the plaintiff. This also holds true if Judah alleges that he has a prior lien against Ruven, the seller of the property to the partnership;[7] the partners may not testify in favor of the seller against the plaintiff. This holds true even if the plaintiff is only suing other partners in the partnership that currently is the alleged owner of the property.[8] The witness, partner 1, may testify if

---

5. This follows the general rule that once a witness has testified he may not recant his testimony. See Chapter 29.

6. Assuming that the servant or employee loves the employer, there is no ineligibility to testify on behalf of someone whom the witness loves. But if there is fear that the servant or employee may lose his employment if he fails to testify in favor of the employer, the beth din or judge may find the servant or employee ineligible to testify.

7. See Chapter 39. In general, if Ruven borrowed money from Judah, and a note of indebtedness was written and signed by two witnesses, this note becomes a lien against the property of Ruven from the time of the writing of the note. If after that date Ruven sold his land to a purchaser and then Ruven could not pay the note to Judah, Judah can levy against the land that the purchaser holds. Thus the plaintiff, Judah, in the case against the partner, may be based on the grounds that the seller, Ruven, stole the land from the plaintiff or else that the seller, Ruven, sold the land subject to the prior lien of the plaintiff, Judah.

8. The result of the witnesses's testimony may cause the other partner to win his case against the plaintiff. The interest of the witness may be that if the other partner

he has relinquished his interest in the owning partnership to his partner, partner 2, before he testifies.[9,10] This may be done only if the relinquishing partner, partner 1, does not have any notes of indebtedness outstanding against him. If the relinquishing partner, partner 1, does have prior notes of indebtedness outstanding against him, he must give a warranty to partner 2, the remaining partner, against losses that partner 2 may suffer as a result of losing the land to the holder of the prior outstanding notes of indebtedness against Ruven.[11] But if the plaintiff does not allege that the partnership holds the property illegally against the plaintiff, but only that partner 2 holds his share of the property illegally against the plaintiff, then the witness, partner 1, may testify, even if he has not relinquished his interest in the partnership, since his testimony cannot affect his ownership in the property.

A tenant–farmer may not testify on behalf of his landlord against a plaintiff who claims the land. He may testify if he has not yet started to work the land, since even if his landlord loses the case without his testimony, the tenant is not affected.[12]

---

lost the case against the plaintiff and lost part of the land, the partner may now ask the witness to share the remaining land held by the witness in partnership with the losing partner.

9. This assumes that the relinquishing of his interest in the property was with a proper *kinyan*. See Chapter 205.

10. See Chapter 175, wherein it is shown that the witness cannot later allege that the division of the property was made in error and thus he was really an interested party when he testified.

11. Assume that Judah claims the interest of partner 2 in the land now held by the partnership consisting of partner 1 and partner 2. Assume further that the relinquishing partner, partner 1, does not give a warranty to the remaining partner, partner 2. Then if Levi, the holder of a prior note of indebtedness of partner 1, recovers the land from partner 2, partner 1 will thus have benefited from his testimony on behalf of partner 2, as the owner of the land deprived partner 2 of his land. But if partner 1 has given a warranty to partner 2 that if partner 2 will lose the land to a prior creditor of partner 1, then partner 1's testimony on behalf of partner 2 will not benefit partner 1, since in either event partner 1 will have to pay the amount of his indebtedness to Levi. If he pays Levi, then partner 1 has paid his indebtedness and partner 2 will retain the land. If partner 1 does not pay Levi and partner 2 loses the land to Levi, then partner 1 has to reimburse partner 2. Thus partner 1's testimony will not be of benefit to partner 1.

12. It is assumed that the tenant-farmer is able to find another place to farm. If he has already started to farm the land, however, and especially if the land has already

Ruven sues Shimon and Levi, alleging that he lent them money. Shimon admits the loan to both Levi and himself, but Levi denies the loan. If Shimon admits that the loan was made to them as partners, his admission is admitted into evidence and he must pay the entire judgment. No judgment may be entered against Levi on just this admission.[13]

A renter of a house is eligible to be called as a witness on behalf of the landlord against a plaintiff who alleges that *he* owns the house. This holds true only if the renter has not yet paid the rent to his landlord.[14]

Ruven owes money to Shimon. Levi claims that property in the hands of Ruven belongs to Levi. Shimon may not testify on behalf of Ruven unless it can be shown that Ruven has other property out of which Shimon can collect his indebtedness.[15]

A surety may not testify on behalf of the debtor in a lawsuit regarding ownership of the debtor's property, even if the debtor has other property upon which the surety may levy if he is called upon to pay the guaranteed debt.[16] A guarantor, however, stands in the same

---

borne produce, then he will be prejudiced if the plaintiff wins the case because he may lose the fruits of his labor. In such a case he may not testify on behalf of his landlord.

13. Shimon benefits from his testimony because if he is believed, Levi will have to pay half the loan. Thus his testimony is not admissible against Levi as being beneficial to Shimon.

14. Of course, if the renter has already prepaid the rent to his landlord, he has an interest in the case between the plaintiff and his landlord as to the ownership of the house. If the plaintiff wins and the landlord to whom he has paid the rent money does not have the money to repay him, then the renter may have to pay the rent again, this time to the plaintiff. Even if the landlord has the money, the renter may be relegated to a lawsuit to collect the prepaid rent from him. If the landlord has deposited the money in beth din or has returned the rent money to the renter pending the outcome of the lawsuit between the plaintiff and the landlord, there are two views. This author believes that the better view would be to let the renter testify. The other view holds that the renter will feel indebted to the landlord, who was nice enough to return the money to him pending the outcome of the lawsuit. This question will be discussed in Chapter 140.

15. If Ruven will lose this property to Levi, and if Ruven has no other property on which Shimon can levy if Ruven does not pay Shimon the indebtedness, then Shimon will be left without any property to make a levy. Thus it is in Shimon's interest to see that Ruven retains the property.

16. A surety is liable to the creditor whether or not the creditor has first proceeded against the debtor. Thus he would not like to see the creditor win his lawsuit against

relationship to the debtor as the creditor does in the previous paragraph.

Ruven sold land to Shimon in January and in February sold land to Levi. Judah claims that the land was stolen from him by Ruven's seller; or else Judah claims that he has a note of indebtedness against Ruven from the previous December and wants to make a levy against the land sold to Levi. Shimon cannot testify on behalf of Levi against Judah unless Ruven still has land to compensate Shimon if Shimon loses the land he bought from Ruven because of a preexisting note of indebtedness owed by Ruven or because there was a superior title to the land in the name of Judah.[17]

Ruven sold land to Shimon without a warranty. If Judah claims that the land was stolen from him by Ruven's seller, Ruven cannot testify on behalf of Shimon.[18] If Judah claims the land as a creditor of Shimon,

---

the debtor, since he may have to pay the creditor even if the debtor had money or property to pay the successful creditor. In the case of a guarantor, however, the creditor must first proceed against the debtor, and it is only if the debtor has no money or property to levy on that the creditor can proceed against the guarantor. Thus if the debtor has money or property to pay the debt, the guarantor is not prejudiced as to whether the debtor wins or loses his lawsuit against the other party.

17. In all of these situations, there is the exposure to Shimon. Either Shimon will not be able to place a levy on any land if he loses the land he purchased from Ruven on account of a preexisting note of indebtedness of Ruven; or else because a prior owner of the land that Shimon purchased can prove that the land still belongs to him, and thus Shimon will be dispossessed from the land he purchased. If Ruven has no money to compensate Shimon for the land he lost, then Shimon can look to Levi to recover the loss, since Levi purchased his land from Ruven after Shimon purchased the land he lost. Thus at the time of Shimon's purchase, the land that Levi would later purchase became encumbered to protect Shimon against any claims arising from the prior act of Ruven or because of the title that Ruven had when he sold the land to Shimon. Levi thus purchased the land from Ruven subject to such an encumberance in favor of Shimon. If Levi loses the land to Judah, the land now held by Judah is not subject to such encumberance. Thus Shimon would benefit if the land remained in the hands of Levi. That is why Shimon may not testify on Levi's behalf. Similarly, Levi may not testify on behalf of Shimon if the title held by Shimon is being attacked. Levi would be afraid that Shimon will make a levy on the land held by him if Shimon will lose the previously purchased land from Ruven.

18. Since the land was sold without a warranty, Ruven has no obligation to Shimon and would thus seem to be a disinterested witness. However, if a preexisting holder of a note of indebtedness of Ruven were to emerge and fail to find any other assets of Ruven on which to levy, he could levy on the land purchased by Shimon. Thus, there is benefit to Ruven if the land remains in the hands of Shimon. Furthermore,

Ruven may testify on behalf of Shimon.[19]

If a witness to a note of indebtedness purchases the note, the sale is valid.[20]

The officials in charge of the community's charity fund may testify in a lawsuit regarding the charity.[21]

Except as hereinafter stated, when a community has a dispute with an individual,[22] the members of the community are all counted as interested persons and thus may not testify. If some of the members of the community remove themselves, with a *kinyan*, from benefiting from the matter that is being disputed, they may testify.[23] Also, where the custom,[24] as it is in most communities, is to permit members of

---

Shimon still could not sue Ruven for the land lost to Ruven's preexisting creditor, since Ruven sold the land to Shimon without a warranty.

19. In this situation it makes no difference to Ruven whether the land is held by Shimon or by Shimon's creditor. In either event, Ruven's preexisting creditor will be able to make a levy on the land.

20. The witness of the note is now also the holder. If the note is contested, then the holder will then testify as to his signature. Thus the transaction is valid only if it took place. But in the first instance, this procedure should not be done.

21. The fact that the community wins a lawsuit against a person and there is thus more money in the charity fund does not make the officials or their relatives interested parties. The pleasure that the officials may derive from distributing the money at their discretion is not the type of interest in the litigation of which this chapter speaks. If the officials favor their own poor relatives in the distribution, then they are indeed interested parties and may not testify. However, if the officials have no discretion in the distribution and their relatives will receive the same sum allocated to the other poor of the community, then the officials may testify. The officials and all their relatives may testify, except the relatives who are poor and will be receiving money from the charity fund.

22. For example, in a dispute over ownership of the land on which the synagogue is built, all the members of the community use the synagogue and thus they are interested parties. If the individual wins the lawsuit, the synagogue will have to be rebuilt, and thus an additional tax may be placed on all of the community members.

23. In the example given in note 22, if there was another synagogue in the community, and two members of the synagogue in dispute renounce their membership from the synagogue, they will be able to testify. The renouncement must be made with a binding *kinyan*. Another example would be if a community is having a dispute with the heirs of a decedent who apparently left money for the poor of the community. If the persons who are to testify paid their poor tax for the year and the outcome of the litigation would thus not affect them, then they may testify. They may not testify, even if they have paid their assessment, if the outcome of the litigation might affect their rate for the coming year.

24. Since it is only a custom, the various rules of evidence are often waived.

the community to testify in matters affecting the community, although they may benefit from their testimony, members of the community may testify.

Arbitrators, judges, or guardians[25] of infants may testify in a matter in which they participated.

If Ruven sold personalty to Shimon without any warranty, then if Judah alleges that the personalty belongs to him, since Ruven purchased it from someone who stole it from Judah, then Ruven may testify.[26]

Furthermore, this is not like ordinary lawsuits, in which the testimony of two witnesses is given the same weight as the testimony of many more witnesses; rather, the preponderance of the testimony may decide the outcome of the trial. Hearsay evidence may be allowed. But the testimony must be given in the presence of the parties, unless it would be impractical to do so.

25. If the guardian stands to benefit personally in the matter, (for example, if his fees would be increased if the lawsuit was successful on behalf of his ward), then he may not testify.

26. Ruven cannot benefit from the outcome of the lawsuit. If Shimon loses, Ruven has no obligations to Shimon, since the sale was without any warranty. If Shimon wins, Ruven still does not benefit, since Ruven's prior creditors may not levy on the personalty because personalty is not encumbered by preexisting notes of indebtedness of the seller. The same law would apply even if there was a chattel mortgage placed on the personalty by one of Ruven's creditors. See Chapter 117. Nowadays this applies even if the chattel mortgage was part of a real estate mortgage.

Chapter 38

A FEW LAWS
OF REFUTED WITNESSES

INTRODUCTION

The title of this chapter is the title given by Karo in *Hoshen haMishpat*. In fact, R. Karo states just a few details, some of which appeared in previous chapters. R. Ramo, in his glosses, states:

> Author [R. Yosef Karo] was concise here when he should have been lengthy. Although the law of refuted witnesses is not practiced at the present time because it consists of penalties, nevertheless there is a difference. A refuted witness is disqualified to testify as was stated already Chapter 34, and a contradicted witness is eligible to testify as was stated in Chapter 31. That is why Tur wrote [in this chapter] many of the laws of refuted witnesses, and those who want to study them may study them there.

The difference between contradicting a witness (*hakhchashah*) and refuting a witness (*hazamah*) is the manner of the contradiction. In the case of contradictory witnesses, each pair contradicts the facts of the event. The two witnesses produced by the plaintiff testify that Ruven lent Shimon money on January 1. The defendant's two witnesses testify that no loan was made by Ruven to Shimon on January 1. The defendant's witnesses may state that Shimon was with them all day and no loan was made. The witnesses may say that it was Ruven who was with them all day and thus he could not have made the loan. The plaintiff's witnesses may testify that they saw Ruven assault Shimon at 10:00 A.M. on January 1. The defendant's witnesses testify that they were present and it was the plaintiff Shimon who assaulted Ruven. Thus the facts of the event are brought into question. What are the facts? Are they as stated by Ruven's witnesses or as stated by Shimon's witnesses? This process is called *hakhchashah*, which has been translated here to mean "contradicted." No one has attacked the integrity of either pair of witnesses. It is the facts that are in dispute. If the beth din has no reason to doubt the facts as testified to by the defendant's witnesses, then the verdict will be for the defendant, since the plaintiff has failed to prove his case. This is irrespective of how many witnesses the plaintiff produced to prove his claim. Ordinarily in a trial the testimony of two credible witnesses is tantamount to the testimony of a hundred witnesses. As was explained in Chapter 31, the witnesses are not disqualified to testify at future trials (except as stated in that chapter).

In the case of *hazamah*, however, the facts are not disputed. The plaintiff's two witnesses testify that the plaintiff lent defendant money at 10:00 A.M. on January 1 in New York City. The defendant's two witnesses testify that they do not know what took place in New York City at 10:00 A.M. on January 1.[1] They know that the event to which the plaintiff's witnesses testified could not have been witnessed by them. The defendant's witnesses testify that the plaintiff's two witnesses were actually with them in London at 10:00 A.M. New York time on January 1. Thus, as far as the defendant's witnesses know, the loan could very well have taken place in New York City at 10:00 A.M. on January 1. But the plaintiff's witnesses could not possibly have witnessed the event, since they were thousands of miles away at that time. The Torah teaches that the last pair of witnesses of refutation are to be believed. This cycle of refuting witnesses may go on indefinitely. Thus if the plaintiff produced other witnesses to refute the defendant's witnesses by stating that the defendant's witnesses were not in

---

1. Actually, the witnesses do not have to state that they do not know what took place. Their statement that the plaintiff's witnesses were with them in another place at the time that they say they witnessed the event is all that is required.

London on January 1 New York time, but rather were with them in Tokyo at that time, then the defendant's witnesses are refuted and the first witnesses produced by the plaintiff are reinstated. Alternatively, after the defendant's witnesses refuted the plaintiff's first pair of witnesses, the plaintiff might have produced a second pair of witnesses who testified that they were present in New York City at 10:00 A.M. on January 1. The defendant's same witnesses may once again testify that the plaintiff's second pair of witnesses were also with them in London at that time. This combination can be endless. The important thing that emeges from this is that the last witnesses are the ones who are believed, and the prior pair is refuted. Once witnesses are refuted, they may no longer be eligible to testify at any trial. There are thus meaningful differences between contradicted witnesses and refuted witnesses. In the case of contradictory witnesses, the plaintiff has failed to prove his case, since the beth din does not know which pair to believe. In the case of refuted witnesses, the last pair is believed. Contradictory witnesses are ordinarily not disqualified from testifying at other trials. Refuted witnesses, on the other hand, are not qualified to testify at future trials.[2]

The laws dealing with refuted witnesses are based on *Makkoth*, Chapter 1. See Rambam, *Laws of Evidence*, Chapters 18–21.

TEXT

Contradicted witnesses

If the plaintiff has produced two or more witnesses who testify on his behalf, and the defendant produces two or more witnesses who

---

2. There is another difference. A plaintiff produced two witnesses, and a judgment was rendered on the strength of their testimony. The defendant paid the judgment. Thereafter, the defendant had the trial reopened on the basis of newly discovered witnesses who contradicted the plaintiff's witnesses. On the strength of these two witnesses produced by the defendant, the beth din reversed the judgment and granted a judgment in favor of the defendant. The plaintiff does not have the money to repay the defendant. The defendant has no cause of action against the two witnesses who testified on behalf of the plaintiff. In the same case, except that the defendant's witnesses now refute the plaintiff's witnesses and the plaintiff cannot repay the defendant, the defendant may sue the refuted witnesses.

testify on the defendant's behalf and contradict the factual testimony of the plaintiff's witnesses, the beth din, if it believes the testimony of the defendant's witnesses or if it does not know which witnesses to believe, will render a judgment on behalf of the defendant.

Contradicted witnesses are not ineligible, because of the contradiction, to testify at other trials. However, see Chapter 31 for exceptions to this general statement.

If money has been paid on a judgment on the basis of testimony given by witnesses who are later contradicted, and the party who was paid the money does not return the money, then the party who paid the money may not sue the contradicted witnesses on whose testimony the original judgment was entered.

Refuted witnesses

If, after a witness or witnesses have testified in beth din, at least two other witnesses testify that the testimony of the prior witnesses cannot be believed because the prior witnesses were with the second pair of witnesses at some place other than where they state that the event occurred at the time that they state that the event occurred, then the first witnesses are refuted and their testimony is excluded. This procedure may go on indefinitely, and the immediately prior witnesses are always deemed refuted in this type of testimony. The second pair of witnesses does not testify to the event to which the prior witnesses testified. The later witnesses may well testify to the event as having taken place at another time than that testified to by the prior witnesses.

Refuted witnesses may be refuted only in their presence. If they are not present when the second pair of witnesses testifies, then the first pair is deemed contradicted.

Refuted witnesses are disqualified from testifying in other cases. They may have to compensate the party who paid a judgment based on their testimony. Refuted witnesses must pay the person against whom they testified for the damages he would have suffered if their testimony had not been refuted. In paying the aforesaid amounts, the refuted witnesses apportion the amount of the payments among themselves.

APPENDIX

THE ROLE OF WOMEN IN THE BETH DIN SYSTEM

This appendix discusses three aspects of the role of the Jewish woman in the beth din system: her role as a party to litigation; her role as a witness; and her role as a judge, and will provide a halachic background regarding these topical issues.

Regarding the role of the woman as a party in litigation, whether as a plaintiff or as a defendant, the Mishnah states[1] that women are included in the laws of torts. R. Israel Lifschitz,[2] in his commentary interprets this Mishnah as empowering a woman to be either a plaintiff or a defendant in a lawsuit. The Talmud[3] in its discussion cites the teaching of the school of R. Eleazar that stated that women and men are equal regarding all of the judgments of the Torah. Now these are the ordinances which thou shalt set before them.[4]

Maimonides discusses the role of the woman as a party in two different contexts. In *Laws Concerning Theft*, he states: "Whether the thief is a man or a woman" the penalty must be paid.[5] In *Laws*

---

1. Mishnah *Baba Kamma*, Chapter 1, Mishnah 3; *Baba Kamma*, 14b.
2. R. Israel Lifschitz, German Rabbinic scholar (1782–1860). See his commentary on Mishnah *Baba Kamma*, Chapter 1, comment 32.
3. See *Baba Kamma* 15a; *Kiddushin* 35a.
4. Exodus 21:1.
5. Maimonides (Rambam), R. Moses b. Maimon, lived in Spain and Egypt from 1135 to 1204. His comments are discussed in *Laws Concerning Theft*, Chapter 1, para. 7.

Concerning Hiring, he states: "A woman as well as a man, whether as bailor or as bailee, comes within the scope of the aforementioned rules of the 'Law of Bailment.'"[6]

R. Jacob Tur[7] writing in the fourteenth century, in discussing theft[8] and bailments[9] quotes Maimonides almost verbatim as does R. Joseph Karo[10] in the *Shulhan Aruch* in the sixteenth century. R. Mordecai Jaffe,[11] at the beginning of the seventeenth century, and R. Yehiel Epstein,[12] at the beginning of this century, in discussing the role of the woman in the laws of bailment, add that a woman is equal to a man in all the laws of the Torah.

It should be noted that exceptions are made for a modest woman. She does not have to appear in beth din; the beth din will send a stenographer to her home to take her testimony. Although this rule seems to be discussed only if she is being sued, I do not see why it should also not apply if she is a plaintiff.[13] From the foregoing it can be seen that a woman has the same status as a man in being able to sue and to be sued.

A far more restrictive approach is seen in the question whether a woman may act as a witness before a beth din. In Israel, the Rabbinic courts permit women to tell the court what they know. The courts treat the information related by the women as an appraisement, upon which they may base their decision. Appraisement procedure appears in halachah and is stated by Maimonides[14] as:

> A judge in monetary matters should act in accordance with what he is inclined to believe is the truth when he feels strongly that his belief is justified, although he has no actual proof of it. This in

---

6. Maimonides, *Laws Concerning Hiring*, Chapter 2, para. 6.

7. R. Jacob Tur, R. Jacob b. Asher, lived in Spain, 1270–1340.

8. R. Jacob Tur, *Hoshen haMishpat*, Chapter 349, para. 1.

9. R. Jacob Tur, *Hoshen haMishpat*, Chapter 302, para. 1.

10. R. Joseph Karo, author of *Shulhan Aruch*, lived in Bulgaria and Palestine, 1488–1575. See *Shulhan Aruch, Hoshen haMishpat*, Chapter 302, para. 1, and Chapter 349, para. 1.

11. R. Mordechai Jaffe lived in Poland, 1536–1612. See his *Eer Shushan*, Chapter 302, para. 1, and Chapter 349, para. 1.

12. R. Yehiel Epstein lived in Russia, 1829–1908. See his *Aruch haShulhan*, Chapter 302, para. 1, and Chapter 349, para. 1.

13. See Tur and *Shulhan Aruch*, Chapter 96 and Chapter 124.

14. Maimonides, *Laws of Sanhedrin*, Chapter 24, para. 1.

spite of the fact that there is no clear proof that the matter is so. It goes without saying that if the judge knows that he is certain that he is correct, he should so decide the case.

Maimonides asserts that a judge may decide by relying on persons he deems to be trustworthy. "This holds true even if the person who gave him the information is a woman." Thus this procedure seems to be limited to situations where there is no clear proof and only if the judge knows that the woman is trustworthy and reliable.

It should be remembered that witnesses serve two different functions. In some matters the act is given effect by the presence of the witnesses, such as at a marriage ceremony when a man betroths a woman or with a divorce document (get). The witnesses actually make the act effective, for without them the act would be a nullity. The witnesses are not there to testify as to the truth of the act; rather they affect the act. Thus, if the man and woman both agreed to a betrothal but the man betrothed the woman without witnesses, there would be no betrothal. The witnesses are there to accomplish the act, not only to testify that it happened. Thus, if a video camera showed us a man betrothed to a woman without witnesses, the act would still not be effective. Women may not act as witnesses here. This, however, is not a judicial function. There are other situations in which witnesses are used to prove that the act took place. For example, a loan is effective even without any witnesses being present. And if the borrower admits the making of the loan, then the borrower is bound to repay the loan. This is the kind of witnessing we are now discussing—to prove an act, not to effect the act.

Even in proving the act there are many different kinds of situations. A person can be planning to make a loan and will have witnesses prepared to testify to the act if the borrower denies liability. In many situations, the witnesses can be ready in advance, but this is not within the scope of our discussion, since in all these situations the law is almost clear that women cannot testify. I say "almost"clear, since it will be shown that the Talmud permits testimony in a situation where twins were born and the midwife can testify as to who was born first.

But there are situations in which one does not prepare witnesses in advance. One does not, before starting on a motor trip, line the route with qualified witnesses in case he should be involved in an automobile accident. Also, a pedestrian does not line his route with witnesses in case of a possible assault upon himself. Suppose the motorist is involved in an automobile accident, or the person walking down the street is assaulted or mugged? In these situations, suppose the only witnesses happened to be women? May they testify in a civil action where the victim of the automobile accident sues for injuries or if the mugging victim sues the assailant? (I used the example of a civil action, since in a criminal action it is clear that a woman may not testify.)

There are two Talmudic passages which seem to give conflicting inferences whether a woman may testify. In one passage, the Talmud[15] asks why a Mishnah[16] which lists some of the eligible persons who can evaluate certain tort damages, states that the witnesses are to be freemen and of the Jewish faith. The Talmud answers that the term "freeman" excludes a slave, who may not testify. The term "of the Jewish faith" excludes Gentiles. And both exclusions are necessary. For if the Mishnah would have stated only "freemen," which would have excluded slaves, it might have been thought that the reason for the exclusion is that the slave has no pedigree, but a Gentile who has pedigree might have been able to testify regarding tort damages. And conversely if the Mishnah had stated that only a Jew could testify, which would have excluded Gentiles, it might have been thought that a slave could testify, since he is obligated to perform certain commandments of the Torah.

Therefore both terms, "freemen" and "Jews," are mentioned in the Mishnah to teach that slaves and Gentiles are both excluded from testifying in tort actions.

Maimonides,[17] (living in twelfth-century Sephardic Egypt), relying on this Talmudic passage, writes in his code:

One should not think that because only slaves, shepherds, or similarly ineligible persons are found in horse stables, animal stalls or sheep enclosures, that they may testify that one animal damaged another animal; or that women or children should be permitted to testify that one person has injured another person, or that they may testify about other types of injury. This is not

---

15. *Baba Kamma* 15a.
16. *Baba Kamma*, Chapter 1, Mishnah 3.
17. Maimonides, *Laws of Damages Caused by Chattels*, Chapter 8, para. 13.

so. No person will ever be required to pay compensation on the testimony of witnesses unless the witnesses are eligible to testify in other cases.

In Maimonides' opinion, the Talmud deems both clauses necessary to show that a person who is excluded cannot become eligible in tort cases just because there are no eligible slaves or Gentiles. It was necessary to exclude the latter since it might have been thought the law was made lenient in matters of torts. Most torts take place where slaves and Gentiles are present and only a few torts where the eligible witnesses are present. Most torts, whether committed by people or by animals, are usually in the presence of unlearned persons, slaves, and Gentiles, therefore, the necessity to teach us that witnesses must be only eligible witnesses, as in all other cases.

Maimonides contends that if an act takes place where there are usually only ineligible witnesses, such witnesses are nonetheless not permitted to testify. This would effectively preclude from testifying the woman who witnessed the automobile accident. Rashba,[18] living in the thirteenth century in Spain, also a Sephardic country, was approached by the local rabbis, who wished to permit testimony of women regarding a transfer by a woman of her seats in the synagogue to a member of her family. Rashba in a responsum held that even if a thousand women testified to the same facts, their testimony is not admissible in monetary matters.[19] He told the local rabbis to reject the earlier authorities who permitted women to testify regarding seats in the women's section of the synagogue. The case before him was not like the case in the Talmud regarding the midwife, since in the case of the midwife it was inconceivable that a man would be present when the birth took place. But the transfer of the seats could have been witnessed by men. He also distinguishes situations where women may testify in certain matters, such as testifying that a woman's husband had died, since not permitting such testimony would leave the wife perpetually unable to remarry. In such a case even a slave or maidservant could testify. (In spite of the fact that the wife could remarry, the son would not be able to inherit his estate without regular proof.)

---

18. Rashba, R. Solomon b. Adret, lived in Barcelona, 1245–1310.
19. Volume 2, responsum 182.

Asheri, a contemporary of Rashba, although writing in Spain, generally followed the Ashkenazic/Germanic/northern French tradition.[20] In this case, however, he follows the Sephardic tradition. In commenting on the aforementioned Talmudic passage, he states there was a necessity to disqualify slaves and Gentiles.[21] In a Gentile court, the plaintiff could be successful on the basis of their testimony, in the event that there was a lawsuit between a Jew and a Gentile. It might have been thought that in cases of torts they could also testify in beth din; therefore it is taught that they may *not* testify. The same would apply to all ineligible witnesses.

His son, R. Jacob Tur, also writing in Spain, in discussing the same law, quotes the language of Maimonides.[22] *Sefer haHinuch*, generally attributed to R. Aaron ben Yosef haLevy of Barcelona, also a thirteenth century contemporary of Rashba and Asheri, asserts that women may not testify because of *kalath datan*. *Kalath datan* may be translated, in its most generous sense, to mean that they are not interested in learning the facts of the case.[23]

R. Karo[24], following the Sephardic tradition during the sixteenth century, is more concise in discussing the testimony necessary in damage cases and states "Tortfeasors are adjudicated liable to pay for the damages on clear proof and on the testimony of eligible witnesses." R. Ramo,[25] a younger contemporary of R. Karo, writing in Poland, generally follows the Ashkenazic/Germanic/northern French tradition. He does not offer any glosses to the law as stated by R. Karo, but, as will be seen, this does not indicate his acceptance of R. Karo's views.

Thus it seems that Rashba, Asheri, Tur, and R. Karo follow the lead of Maimonides in asserting that the unavailability of *eligible* witnesses in a situation will not permit *ineligible* witnesses to testify. But this is

---

20. R. Asher b. Yehiel lived in Germany and Spain, 1260–1327.

21. *Baba Kamma*, Chapter 1, para. 19.

22. R. Jacob b. Asher lived in Spain, 1270–1340. *Tur Hoshen haMishpat*, Chapter 408.

23. *Sefer haHinuch* generally attributed to R. Aaron ben Yosef haLevi, living in Barcelona during the end of the thirteenth century. See commandment 124 toward the end.

24. R. Karo, *Shulhan Aruch, Hoshen haMishpat*, Chapter 408.

25. Apparently R. Ramo, in Chapter 408, relies on his comments in Chapter 35 and thus does not deem it necessary to repeat them in Chapter 408. See discussion in text.

true not only where eligible witnesses happened not to be present, but even where eligible witnesses could not have been present.

At the same time there was another a school of thought on this position.

Another Talmudic[26] passage teaches that a midwife is believed when she states which of twins was born first. This can make a difference in inheritances, since a firstborn son inherits twice as much as any other son. If the twins were a boy and a girl, and if the firstborn was the son, the father would have to pay five silver coins to the Kohen for the redemption of the first born son.[27]

Maimonides,[28] Tur,[29] and Karo[30] state the law without any comment, although it states that a woman may testify in an important monetary matter. Ramo does not add any glosses. It seems to me that the difference is one of degree in that there is no possible way for the information to be obtained except through the midwife. By contrast, in the case of the shepherds, it is unlikely that an eligible person would be found among the stables, but it is certainly possible. Maimonides treats the midwife case as a *res gestae* exception. It is a spontaneous, contemporaneous utterance of a present-sense impression. The Talmud itself shows that this is so when it brings two opinions to show the span of time during which the midwife is believed when she declares one or the other child to be the firstborn. One opinion maintains that she is believed as long as she did not leave the room where the children were born. The other opinion holds that the moment she turns her face from the children she is no longer believed.

Asheri[31] cites the language of the Talmud.

Tur in Chapter 35 of *Hoshen haMishpat*, dealing with ineligible witnesses, states the various laws of ineligible witnesses, including the statement that women are not eligible to testify. R. Karo, in his Beth Yosef commentary on Tur, first cites the aforequoted responsum of Rashba, rejecting the authorities who permitted women to testify in

---

26. *Kiddushin* 73b.

27. Maimonides, *Laws Concerning First Fruits and Other Gifts to the Priesthood*, Chapter 11.

28. Maimonides, *Laws of Inheritance*, Chapter 2, law 14.

29. Tur, *Hoshen haMishpat*, Chapter 277, para. 15.

30. R. Karo, *Shulhan Aruch, Hoshen haMishpat*, Chapter 277, para. 12.

31. See note 2. See Asheri's compendium on *Kiddushin*, Chapter 4, para. 11.

places where men would not be present. R. Karo continues, that the aforequoted conclusion of Maimonides in *Laws of Damages* also necessitates that women cannot be permitted to testify in such cases. R. Karo then cites R. Yosef Kolon in a responsum and R. Israel Isserlein in his *Trumath haDeshen*, both of whom permitted women to testify in such matters. R. Karo rejected their holdings.

R. Ramo, however, in his Darkai Moshe commentary on Tur, takes a different approach. He states:

And this is the language of Mordechai [b. Hillel] at the conclusion of the laws of bans, "Although a person may be put under a ban without prior warning, the ban is not pronounced until there is competent testimony by eligible witnesses and clear proof. It appears to me that, although according to legal principles women may not testify even in those places where men are usually not present, according to the words of Rambam and Rashba, nevertheless it is an ancient decree from Rabbeinu [Yakov] Tam that a woman, herself, or a kinsman or a minor may testify in matters dealing with assaults, or insults to scholars and in all other matters of strife in which there are not always persons prepared in advance to witness the occurrence, and there is no opportunity to prepare witnesses. The same applies to cases of informers." All this appears in Kolon in chapter 180 in the name of Rabbeinu Tam. So also writes Kolbo in chapter 116 as a decree of Rabbeinu Gershon Meir haGolah and this also appears in the novella of Agudah on the last chapter of *Kiddushin* when he writes that, in all places where men are usually not found, women may testify. This is explained at length by Trumath haDeshen in chapter 353. He writes that this is true exclusively in the situation where this is a chance happening as where a woman testifies that another woman's husband was still alive [to establish ownership of the garment, whether in the deceased husband's estate or belonging to the widow] since in such matters men are not wont to notice, and similarly regarding seats belonging to women in the women's section of the synagogue. In cases of assaults and injuries women are eligible as stated by Rabbeinu Tam, since these too are not usual, as seen below in chapter 403. Therefore it seems to me that they may not be disregarded unless on convincing proof. See also Mordechai's comments on chapter six

authorities against him, but proved damages only partly by eligible witnesses and partly by ineligible witnesses, then only the part provable by eligible witnesses was admissible, and the part proved by ineligible witnesses was not admissible. Appraisement was not a method to be employed. Luria states further that this is also the view of R. Meir of Rottenberg, the teacher of both R. Mordechai b. Hillel and Asheri. R. Luria then cites a "Rabbi Pinhas,[46]" Me'il Zedek, who wrote that ineligible witnesses, such as women, minors, or relatives, may testify if there was no opportunity to prepare eligible witnesses in advance.

R. Luria rejects the proofs of R. Pinhas and other responsa to the same effect and again states that if there were such decrees, they were limited to their specific times. R. Luria preferred the view of Maimonides, but confronted a growing array of authorities who were expanding the admissibility of ineligible witnesses. To counter them, R. Luria devised a novel approach. He concluded that the ineligible witnesses could testify when both sides to a dispute agreed that a question existed before the beth din as to the amount of damages or the amount of inheritance. Thus the Mishnah concerning the midwife dealt with the question of who would inherit more, but did not deal with the question of whether the child was an heir which was being denied by other parties to the dispute.

Similarly in all disputes, as, for example, Reuven and Shimon each claiming that the other had started a dispute, ineligible witnesses could testify. Both sides admitted that there was a dispute. If, however, one side claimed that there was no dispute, ineligible witnesses could not testify. Similarly in the case of the clothing that belonged to a widow, there was no doubt that she had some clothing, for she was certainly not going around naked. The sole question was whether certain clothing was part of her wardrobe and thus belonged to her, instead of to the estate of her husband. Perhaps in the case of informers, the case most often cited by the new line of cases, admissibility was only in the manner of an appraisement that might be permissible in such cases. Thus, if the defendant admitted that he had informed on the plaintiff, only the question of damages remained. For the defendant

---

46. Rabbi Pinhas. See *Shem haGedolim* of Rav Chaim Yosef David Azulai, who writes that the correct name of the author of *Me'il Zedek* was Rav Menahem b. Pinhas, who was either a contemporary or student of R. Isserlein.

might argue that the secular ruler would have in any event taxed the plaintiff in the same amount that resulted from the informing. But if the defendant denied that he had informed on plaintiff, ineligible witnesses could not testify. Ineligible witnesses included only women and minors who had the understanding to testify. It did not include relatives. This last statement of R. Luria puts him into conflict with R. Kolon, who held that relatives, although in general ineligible, could testify in such cases.

Another contemporary of both R. Luria and R. Ramo, R. Mordechai Jaffe[47], in his code Lebush, cites the conclusion of R. Karo and of R. Ramo that women can testify in the instances cited by R. Ramo.

Thus, at the conclusion of the *Shulhan Aruch* in the middle of the sixteenth century, there were two distinct schools of thought regarding the eligibility of women to testify in situations where there were no men to testify: the Sephardic authorities who denied eligibility in such cases, and the Ashkenazic/French/German/Polish authorities who were permitting eligibility.

I shall now examine some of the post-*Shulhan Aruch* authorities to see how they based themselves upon these two schools of thought.

The classical commentaries on *Shulhan Aruch* that appear in most editions on the printed page do not add much to the discussion. R. Joshua Falk[48], living in Eastern Europe in the late sixteenth to early seventeenth century, in his *Meiroth Ainayim* commentary, notes that in chapter 408, neither Tur nor R. Karo nor R. Ramo cite the discussion permitting ineligible witnesses to testify. He concludes that this shows that they do not consider torts to be so unusual that eligible witnesses could not be found. He also refers the reader to *Shulhan Aruch, Yoreh De'ah* Chapter 127, for an instance where women are eligible to testify.

In *Yoreh De'ah*, Chapter 127 R. Ramo[49] states that a woman may testify that she rectified ritually prohibited things which required correction to make them permitted. R. Shabtai Cohen,[50] writing in

---

47. R. Mordechai Jaffe. Polish Rabbinic authority (1530–1612).

48. R. Joshua Falk lived in Poland, 1555–1614. His work on *Shulhan Aruch, Hoshen haMishpat* is called *Sefer Meiroth Ainayim (Sma)*. The cited comment comes from Chapter 35, para. 30.

49. R. Ramo, glosses on *Shulhan Aruch Yoreh De'ah*, Chapter 127, para. 14.

50. R. Shabtai Cohen lived in Vilna and Germany, 1622–1663. His commentary on the *Shulhan Aruch* is known as *Siftat Cohen or Shach*. The cited comment comes

mid–seventeenth-century eastern Europe, adds the provision that the woman must have the ability to rectify the items, or that they belonged to her before she rectified them.

R. Yakov Castro,[51] who lived in Sephardic Egypt at the end of the sixteenth century, in his commentary on *Hoshen haMishpat*, Chapter 35 cites Isserlein and R. Kolon. He concludes, however, that Sephardic countries follow Maimonides and that there are no exceptions to the rule that a woman may not testify.

The same Sephardic tradition was again seen in a decision rendered in Tunis at the beginning of the nineteenth century.

R. Uzziel Alhayk[52] was asked to decide the following case. A woman alleged that her husband beat her and sued for monetary damages. Her only witnesses were women who alleged that they saw the husband beat the wife. The husband denied the allegations. After citing authorities on both sides of the issue of whether women may testify, he held that even R. Ramo's statement that they *may* testify was not his prime opinion, but only an opinion rendered in the name of "those who say." This indicates that even R. Ramo does not hold this to be a decree for all times. But most importantly, R. Karo, whose opinion the Sephardic community must follow, does not agree that women may testify in such cases.

Another Sephardic authority, R. Yonah Navon,[53] writing in the middle of the eighteenth century, decided the following case. A woman had taken an oath not to curse her husband's parents. Her husband alleged that she had violated the oath. The only witnesses were women. R. Navon acknowledges the opinion of R. Ramo that in certain instances, especially like the one in question, where women are the only witnesses, women should be able to testify. He cites R. Castro, however, that the Sephardic tradition follows the holding of R. Karo that they are not eligible. Furthermore, even R. Luria, who follows the Germanic/French/eastern European school, would not permit them to testify if the defendant denied the entire claim, as was

---

from *Yoreh De'ah*, Chapter 127, para. 29.

51. R. Yakov Castro lived in Egypt from 1525 to 1610. His comments are from his *Erech Lehem*, Chapter 35.

52. R. Uzziel Alhayk lived in Tunis, 1740–1820. See his *Mishkenot haRoim*, letter *ayin'* para. 65.

53. R. Yonah Navon lived in Jerusalem, 1713–1760. His comments are from his *Nechpa baKessef*, part 2, on *Shulhan Aruch, Even haEzer*, Chapter 12.

the case before him where the woman denied ever having cursed her husband's parents.

R. Hayim Palache,[54] living in Sephardic Izmir, Turkey, in the nineteenth century, was asked to decide a case in which a school board wished to remove a teacher on the alleged grounds of his molesting some children. The children and some mothers were the only witnesses. This was a classic case of the unavailability of eligible witnesses. Could the teacher be dismissed on the testimony of minors and their mothers? He concluded that the teacher could not be dismissed on the basis of ineligible witnesses. The decree permitting ineligible witnesses to testify where eligible witnesses were not available was not part of the halachah of Sephardic countries.

In 1843, in Leghorn, Italy, R. Isaac Teib[55] wrote that some authorities permitted ineligible witnesses to testify in matters other than torts, if it was unusual for eligible witnesses to be found in such places. However, since Maimonides holds that, even in torts, which he considers unusual, ineligible witnesses may not testify, the prohibition applies equally to all cases, whether usual or not. Thus the tradition of the school of Maimonides was again followed in a Sephardic country.

It is thus seen that the two traditions were simultaneously being applied.

In eighteenth century Poland R. Yonathan Eybeschuetz,[56] in his double commentary on *Hoshen haMishpat*, follows the Ashkenazic tradition. He cites R. Yakov Popper,[57] an older contemporary, who stated that if Maimonides had not stated that the Talmudic rejection of Gentiles and slaves certainly applied to all other ineligible witnesses, it might have been thought that the ineligibility was limited only to Gentiles and slaves, and that all other ineligible persons would be eligible to testify in tort cases. R. Eybeschuetz rejects this by stating

---

54. R. Hayim Palache lived in Turkey, 1788–1869. The decision is from his *Hikkekai Lev*, on *Shulhan Aruch, Yoreh De'ah*, Chapter 46.

55. R. Isaac Teib lived in Leghorn (Livorno) Italy in the nineteenth century. The holding comes from his *Erech haShulhan*, supplement to Chapter 35 of *Hoshen haMishpat*.

56. R. Yonathan Eybeschuetz lived in Poland and Prague, 1690–1764. His comments appear in Tummim on *Hoshen haMishpat*, Chapter 35, para. 9.

57. R. Yakov haKohen Popper lived in Germany during the end of the seventeenth and early eighteenth century and died in 1740. His comments are found in Shev Yakov, on *Shulhan Aruch, Even haEzer*, Chapter 3.

that women would certainly not be found in the places that slaves and Gentile women frequent. Thus he seeks to limit the application of the decree. Again in the Ashkenazic tradition, R. Ezekiel Landau,[58] living in Poland in the eighteenth century, was asked to decide the following case. Reuven had a reputation in the community as a thief. Something was stolen from Shimon's home. Two young women saw Reuven with the stolen item. Could Reuven be sued by Shimon on the basis of the testimony of the two women? R. Landau writes that even under the decree permitting ineligible persons to testify in certain matters, ineligible witnesses could not testify in tort cases, because it was suspected that they would be more prone to be persuaded to give false testimony and many persons would be found liable on the basis of perjured testimony. The present case was a classic example of such a situation. Also, the exceptions applied only to those situations in which they were the only witnesses to a spontaneous occurrence. In this case they did not see the actual theft, which might be construed to be a spontaneous occurrence. But seeing the stolen object in Reuven's possession was not such a spontaneous occurrence that eligible witnesses could not duplicate. R. Landau concludes with a caveat that even if they had witnessed the actual theft, he is not sure how he would have decided the case. His decision indicates that the doctrine would be narrowly construed, especially in cases of criminal conduct.

A work which reviews many of the views discussed in *Petach Beth David*, written by R. Yosef David[59] and published in Salonika, Greece, in the middle of the eighteenth century. He states that there are two opinions amongst the authorities. The view of Rabbeinu Tam as cited in R. Kolon and Kolbo, that there is a decree permitting ineligible witnesses to testify, because it is not possible to prepare eligible witnesses to witness a spontaneous event. Thus in cases of fights, or informers when the words were uttered and there might not be eligible witnesses, the ineligible witnesses become eligible for this limited purpose. But R. Isserlein, Mordechai and Agudah hold that it is

---

58. R. Ezekiel Landau lived in Prague and Poland, 1713–1793. The responsum is from *Noda B'Yehuda* (tnina), responsum 58.

59. R. Yosef David is named in the *Ozar haSefarim* as having lived in Salonika. The edition I examined in the library of Yad haRav Herzog was the original edition printed in 1750 in Salonika.

not merely an ancient decree, but the actual law, that asserts they may testify in such events. This is based on the Talmudic statement that a midwife may testify in such a situation. *Beth David* goes on to state that Maimonides and Rashba, who are cited by R. Karo, do not dispute Rabbeinu Tam, but only dispute R. Isserlein. Thus Maimonides and his school would agree with Rabbeinu Tam. I find this statement difficult in view of the fact that so many of the codes, commentators and respondents seem convinced that Maimonides and his school maintain otherwise. In addition, the wording of Maimonides and Rashba would have to be stretched to read such agreement with the view of Rabbeinu Tam into their words. Also the wording of R. Ramo seems to be that R. Isserlein and Mordechai held the eligibility of women to testify in spontaneous events to be a decree.

In a case decided on appeal by the Rabbinic High Court in Jerusalem less than thirty years ago, the question of ineligible witnesses was discussed, including the ineligibility of women, although that last point was not in issue.[60] The burial society of Raanana sued the defendant for the cost of the plot in which they had buried the defendant's father. The defense was that a lesser sum than was being sued for had been agreed upon between the burial society and the defendant prior to the burial. (This was one of many defenses, including duress, because the decedent's body was awaiting burial, and thus the defendant was not able to conclude the transaction properly.) The major witness called by the burial society was the uncle of the defendant, the decedent's brother. The defendant raised an objection to permitting him to testify, since a relative is not eligible to testify. In passing on this question, the appeals court stated that they most likely would have followed the school of ancient tradition that ineligible witnesses could testify if there were no eligible witnesses.

In the case before it, even if the ineligible person testified, only one witness would exist and the case required two witnesses to impose the liability sought against the defendant.

About twenty-two years ago, Rav Menashe Klein, in Brooklyn, wrote a responsum in which this question was discussed.[61] He

---

60. Decisions of the Rabbinic Courts, vol. 3, p. 235. Chaim Bezzuza, Defendant, Appellant v. Burial Society of Raanana, Plaintiff, cross-appellant.
61. Responsa of Rav Menashe Klein, *Mishnah Halachah*, vol. 5, responsum 269.

differed with the reason of some of those who would deny women the right to testify, even in the limited cases where the Ramo permits them to testify. Some stated that women could not testify since they were not trustworthy witnesses. R. Klein utterly rejected this by showing that in many areas of ritual law, they were as trustworthy as men. The reasoning of the Maimonides school is based on the same Torah source that also prohibited Moses and his brother Aaron from acting as witnesses in the same matter.

As already stated, there are many personal matters in which women may testify; for example, that her husband had died, or that a husband of another woman had died; and in either case the woman may remarry. In most ritual matters a woman is believed. There are still questions regarding the eligibility of a woman to testify in a beth din regarding monetary matters. There is of course the holding of Ramo and the entire Ashkenazic school that in the matters in which only a woman is apt to be present, or in a spontaneous event, where there is not time to prepare eligible witnesses, the woman may testify. Thus, in the case of an accident, she would be able to testify.

The foregoing shows that some communities have qualified the prohibition against women testifying before beth din in certain ways. In some communities, women testify under the status of their declarations in the beth din not being direct testimony but informed observations; they tell the beth din what they saw rather than what they witnessed.

Another possible approach is via stipulation. There is a general principle that all stipulations regarding monetary matters are effective. This principle appears in the Talmud at least five times[62] and in Maimonides in several places,[63] as well as in the *Shulhan Aruch* itself.[64] In Chapter 37 of *Hoshen haMishpat,* Karo states that there is another exception. Ineligible witnesses may testify in matters affecting the community at large, since this is the accepted practice.[65] R. Ramo there adds that all these things depend upon the practice of the

---

62. See *Baba Mezia* 51a; *Baba Mezia* 94a; *Kiddushin* 19b; *Kethuboth* 56a; *Baba Bathra* 126b.

63. See Maimonides, *Laws of Sales,* Chapter 19, para. 8; *Laws of Marriage,* Chapter 12, para. 9.

64. See Ramo, Chapter 16, para. 2; R. Karo, Chapter 102, para. 5; R. Karo, Chapter 206, para. 1; R. Karo, Chapter 225, para. 5; R. Karo, Chapter 296, para. 5.

65. *Shulhan Aruch, Hoshen haMishpat,* Chapter 37, para. 22.

community.[66] Moreover the entire Chapter 22 in *Hoshen haMishpat* deals with individual litigants accepting ineligible witnesses as eligible witnesses. It may be possible that the litigants who come before the beth din accept by *kinyan* women as witnesses in the case before them. Consider a responsum of a leading respondent, R. Shimon ben Zemach Duran who lived in Majorca and Algiers from 1361 until he died in 1444. He was asked to pass upon the validity of a decree made by a small community.[67] Most of the citizens of the community were related and thus it would often be difficult to find eligible witnesses, since related persons may not testify in a lawsuit, whether they are related to a litigant, to the judges or to one another. They agreed and legislated that henceforth the ineligibility of relatives would not be raised as an issue in beth din. In a lengthy responsum in which he cites many of the sources already cited, he concludes that the decree is valid and binding: "And although an individual who has accepted an ineligible witness to testify may change his mind before the beth din renders its decision, R. Solomon ben Adret [Rashba] stated that the interests of the community override this right." The majority may compel the minority to agree to the procedure. Also, R. Meir of Rotenburg was asked to decide a similar question and decided the same way, and he concluded his responsum by stating that the practice of the community has the force of Torah. In a similar way, it is said that the practice may vitiate the law, and this has also been the response of other respondents. R. Shimon Duran's son, R. Solomon, also was asked to decide two similar cases.[68] He concluded that the decree to accept otherwise ineligible witnesses was valid if it had the consent of the sage of the community, or if there was no such sage, if it was done with the consent of all of the inhabitants of the community.

The last topic of this appendex deals with the eligibility of a woman to be a judge on the beth din. In respect of this matter, no division exists any longer between the Sephardic and the Ashkenazic traditions. Indeed, some of the authorities of the twelfth and thirteenth

---

66. See R. Ramo, *Shulhan Aruch, Hoshen haMishpat,* Chapter 37, para. 22.

67. Responsum of R. Shimon b. Zemach Duran, who lived in Majorca and Algiers 1361–1444. See responsum in vol. 2, part 4, section 1, responsum 15.

68. Responsa of R. Solomon b. Shimon Duran, who lived in North Africa, 1400–1467. See responsa 211 and 612.

centuries were more lenient in the question of women judging than are the later authorities.

R. Karo[69] in the *Shulchan Aruch* makes rather short shrift of this topic. He devotes just three words to it. *Isha p'sulah ladon* (women cannot judge). They are not eligible to judge. R. Ramo does not add any emendations or additions to this concise statement of R. Karo.

The basis of the law is a Mishnah[70] that states that whoever may be a judge may be a witness, but not everyone who may be a witness may be a judge. The inference from this Mishnah is that the class of witnesses is larger than the class of judges, and that all judges are included in the class of witnesses. Thus a person who may not be a witness may surely not be a judge. Since as has been stated, in general a woman could not be a witness in monetary matters, she could therefore not be a judge.

Maimonides does not have a separate law dealing with women judges. He apparently relies on his statement in another context that women are not eligible for appointive positions.[71] The commentaries on Maimonides cite the *Sifri* as the source of his statement, but the current editions of the *Sifri* state only that a woman may not be appointed the queen of the people, since the Torah verse states: "One from among thy brethren shalt thou appoint king."[72]

Tosafoth, in five different places, discusses the question of a woman judging.[73] Tosafoth was disturbed by a basic question raised by the biblical verse: "Devorah, a prophetess, the wife of Lapidoth, judged Israel at that time."[74] Equally disturbing to Tosafoth is the aforementioned Talmudic passage which discusses the verse: "Now these are the ordinances which thou shalt set before them."[75] The Talmud interprets this verse to show that men and women are equal before the law as parties before the beth din.[76] Thus both the verse regarding

---

69. R. Karo, *Shulhan Aruch, Hoshen haMishpat,* Chapter 7, para. 4.

70. Mishnah, *Niddah* 49b.

71. See Maimonides, *Laws of Kings and Their Wars,* Chapter 1, para. 5.

72. Deuteronomy 17:15.

73. Tosafoth *Niddah* 50, introductory words *kol hakasher;* Tosafoth *Yebamoth* 45b, introductory words, *mi lo tavla;* Tosafoth *Baba Kamma* 15a, introductory words, *asher tasim lifnahem;* Tosafoth *Gittin* 88b, introductory words, *v'lo lifnai hedyototh;* Tosafoth *Shebu'oth* 29b, introductory words, *shevooth ha'aodoth.*

74. Judges 4:4.

75. Exodus 21:1.

76. *Baba Kamma* 15a.

Devorah and the Talmudic passage just cited seem to indicate that women may indeed judge. Yet the inference from the other Talmudic passage cited, that one who may not testify may not judge, seems to justify a contrary conclusion.

Tosafoth gives several answers. It asserts first that the inference in question applies only to men; that if a man is ineligible to testify, he may not be a judge. This exclusion does not apply to women. In other answers, Tosafoth asserts that Devorah merely advised the judges as to the law, but that the men actually judged. Thus the verse regarding equating women with men enables women only to be parties before the beth din, and to be judged, but not to judge. Or else the case of Devorah is sui generis, or unique. She did judge, but no lessons may be derived from that incident, since she was appointed as a judge by Divine command. Another answer suggested by Tosafoth is that the people accepted her as a judge. The first answer of Tosafoth, however, infers that women may indeed act as judges. Even if that answer is not definitive, one of the other answers, that the people may *accept* a woman as a judge, is an interesting qualification.

It has also been suggested[77] that the authority of Devorah derived from an emergency situation, and once again it does not serve as an example unless another emergency comes about.

About a hundred years after the Tosafists, Asheri, living in the late thirteenth early fourteenth centuries, wrote that women may not judge since they may not testify. This would seem to place him again directly in the Maimonides Sephardic grouping. He does, however, make some concession to the answers of the Tosafists, namely that either Devorah taught the judges how to judge, or else she was accepted as a judge because of a prophecy. R. Yerucham, a younger French contemporary, cites Asheri with approval. Thus as was already noted, no sharp sectional division exists regarding women judges.

In *Sefer haHinuch*, which has been attributed to R. Aaron ben Yosef haLevi, living in Barcelona in the thirteenth century, we read:

[the laws of appointing judges] is applicable for males, but not for women, since they may not judge as appears in many sources. One should not raise the question from the incident involving

---

77. See *Be'ir haGolah* of Rav Moshe Ravkash who lived in Lithuania and Poland in the seventeenth century. *Hoshen haMishpat*, Chapter 7.

Devorah the prophetess, where it is stated that she judged Israel, for it is possible to explain that the actual judgment of the cases was not delivered by her, but since she was a wise woman and a prophetess, the judges discussed the cases with her—even cases involving matters of ritual prohibitions and monetary cases. That is why it is written that she judged Israel. Or it may be said that the leaders of the people accepted her as a judge, and thereafter all of the people accepted her to judge them. This is valid since all stipulations made between persons regarding monetary matters are binding upon them. Nevertheless, all that which I have just written regarding the ineligibility of a woman to judge follows a few of the commentators and the opinion of the Jerusalem Talmud, which states the foregoing explicitly. But according to a few of the commentaries, women may judge and they base this on the verse that she [Devorah] judged. And as for that which was said in Tractate *Sanhedrin* that whoever is not eligible to testify may not judge, and women may certainly not testify, as is shown there, perhaps this law may not be derived from the general principle.

This almost evenhanded view allows for the opinion that women *may* judge.

A Spanish contemporary, R. Solomon ben Adret (Rashba) also cites both opinions.[78] R. Jacob Tur states that women are ineligible to judge and that Devorah did not judge but rather taught the judges how to judge.[79] R. Karo, in his *Beth Yosef* commentary on Tur, cites the passages from the Jerusalem Talmud that women may not judge.[80] He also cites Tosafoth to the same effect, and allows that Tosafoth showed that Devorah did judge, but only because she was accepted because of Divine intervention. R. Karo thus does not even mention that Tosafoth did at one point answer that perhaps women are indeed eligible to judge. This is, of course, the basis for R. Karo's later statement in *Shulhan Aruch*[81] that women cannot judge.

Three Polish contemporaries of the late sixteenth and early seven-

78. Rashba, *Baba Kamma* 15a.
79. R. Tur, *Hoshen haMishpat*, Chapter 7, para. 5.
80. Rav Joseph Karo, Beth Yosef commentary on Tur *Hoshen haMishpat*, Chapter 7.
81. R. Karo, *Shulhan Aruch, Hoshen haMishpat*, Chapter 7, para. 4.

teenth centuries, R. Joshua Falk,[82] and R. Yoel Sirkis,[83] in their commentaries on Tur, and R. Mordechai Jaffe[84] in his own code, all state that women may not judge. R. Yonathan Eybeschuetz[85] in his Urim commentary on R. Karo, states that there is no reason why women may not judge except that it is so stated in the Torah. R. Hayim Yosef David Azulai,[86] living in Israel at the end of the eighteenth century, cites sources on both sides, including the opinions that a woman may indeed judge. He also concludes that in all events a wise woman may teach the judges how to judge. R. Yehiel Epstein,[87] at the beginning of this century, does not limit himself to the ineligibility of women judging but cites the statement of Maimonides that women cannot be eligible for any appointive posts. He also asserts that Devorah did not judge, but merely advised the judges how to judge. Or else she judged because of a Divine command. And furthermore all of the people accepted her as a judge. As can be seen from the foregoing, some authorities in the twelfth and thirteenth centuries cited the view that women can indeed judge. Almost all of the subsequent authorities limited women to judging cases when the litigants accepted her as a judge, or else stated that she could participate only by advising the judge or judges of the beth din. In an analogous situation, that of women ritually slaughtering cattle and fowl for eating purposes, Tosafoth[88] asserts that women may slaughter. R.

---

82. R. Joshua Falk lived in Poland end of the sixteenth and beginning of the seventeenth centuries. See his Prisha commentary on Tur, Chapter 7.

83. R. Yoel Sirkis lived in Poland end of the sixteenth and beginning of the seventeenth centuries. See his *Bayit Chodosh* commentary on Tur, Chapter 7.

84. R. Mordechai Jaffe lived in Poland end of the sixteenth and beginning of the seventeenth centuries. See his Lebush code, volume *Eer Shushan*, Chapter 7, para. 5.

85. R. Jonathan Eybeschuetz lived in Poland end of the sixteenth and beginning of the seventeenth centuries. See his Urim commentary on *Shulhan Aruch, Hoshen haMishpat*, Chapter 7, para. 9.

86. R. Hayim Yosef David Azulai lived in Palestine in the eighteenth century into the beginning of the nineteenth century. See his Birkai Yosef commentary on *Shulhan Aruch, Hoshen haMishpat*, Chapter 7, para. 4.

87. R. Yehiel Epstein lived in Russia during the nineteenth century and into the beginning of the twentieth century. See his *Aruch haShulhan, Hoshen haMishpat*, Chapter 7, para. 4.

88. Tosafoth, a school of scholars living in France and Germany during the twelfth and thirteenth centuries, whose commentaries on the Talmud are included in all printed editions as part of the Talmud page. The cited comment comes from *Chullin* 2a.

Karo follows this view in *Shulhan Aruch Yoreh De'ah*.[89] But as is pointed out by R. Shabtai Cohen[90], the fact that they have not slaughtered for so many generations vitiates this law, and they should no longer be allowed to slaughter. This may very well be the situation regarding judging by women.

---

89. *Yoreh De'ah*, Chapter 1, para. 1.

90. R. Shabtai Cohen lived in Vilna and Germany, 1622–1663. His commentary on the *Shulhan Aruch* is known as Siftai Cohen or Shach. The cited comment comes from *Yoreh De'ah*, Chapter 1, para. 1.

GLOSSARY

arrur: A person who is *arrur* is cursed. It may apply to the curses that the Torah sets forth in several places (Leviticus 26 and Deuteronomy 27). It may apply to persons whom the sages have cursed because of unbecoming conduct. For example, a person agreeing to buy or sell something, money changing hands, but legal title not having been transferred as required by Chapter 189. The person who reneges on the deal is cursed by the rabbis.

avairah: A transgression. There are 613 commandments in the Torah, 248 positive commandments and 365 negative commandments. If one does not fulfill a positive commandment or violates a negative commandment, he has committed an *avairah*.

bedikah: An examination. In laws of evidence it means that the witness was examined as to the matters that do not deal directly with the guilt or innocence of a defendant in a criminal matter, or to the proving of a case by a party to a litigation. It concerns itself with collateral matters. For example, if the witness to a homicide had testified to all of the facts of the homicide, he would be questioned as to the color of the clothes worn by the slayer or the victim. The examination regarding the facts of the event are known as *drisha* and *hakiran*.

beth din: A *beth din* is a duly constituted court that has jurisdiction over certain cases. Nowadays, the jurisdiction of the *beth din* is almost exclusively limited to the judging of commercial cases.

dina d'malchutah dina: The literal translation of the term means "the law of the land is the law." A Jew is required to follow the laws of the land in which he resides, for example, in matters of criminal law, in matters of taxes and real estate. This is discussed in Chapter 369.

drisha and **hakirah:** These are examinations of witnesses that go to the essence of the act to which they are testifying. In a criminal case it may mean questioning the witness as to time and place of the crime, the facts that constituted the crime, and any other details the judges deem significant. In civil cases it would consist of the facts of the transaction. For example, in a case of a loan, it would consist of identifying the lender, the borrower, the time and place of the loan, the amount of the loan, the terms of repayment agreed upon, and if there was a note of indebtedness executed, the facts of that note.

gabbai: A functionary, usually of a synagogue. He coordinates the services to see that certain persons will lead the services, who will read from the Torah, and who will receive the honor of opening the Holy Ark and so on. The *gabbai* may function outside of the synagogue, as for example a *gabbai zedakah*. He is the person who distributes moneys, food, and clothing to the needy. There may also be a *gabbai* in charge of collecting funds for a community or a synagogue.

hakhchashah: Witnesses may be contradicted by other witnesses in one of two ways. One is by *hazamah* and the other is by *hakhchashah*. In the case of *hakhchashah*, the witness contradicts the testimony of another witness bearing on the facts of the lawsuit. Thus, if witness A says there was a loan made by Rueven to Shimon in a certain amount on a certain date and time, and witness B testifies that the transaction was not a loan, but that the money was in payment for an item that Shimon sold to Ruven, this is *hakhchashah*. Such witnesses may be called contradicted witnesses.

halachah: The status of the law at a given time. What may have been the *halachah* at a certain point in time may change because of the Sages' decrees. *Halachah* may vary in different Jewish communities. A Jewish community in Spain is more apt to follow the holdings of Rabbi Joseph Karo, whereas a Jewish community in Russia is more apt to be following the holdings of Rabbi Moshe Isserles.

halizah: If a husband dies without any children or issue of children surviving, then his wife, according to Torah law, is to be married to the deceased husband's brother (Deuteronomy 25:5–10.) This is known as *yibbum.* If the widow or the brother does not want to conclude the ceremony of *yibbum,* then they perform the ceremony of *halizah,* also described in Deuteronomy 25. After this, the widow is free to marry whomever she wishes.

hazamah: A method whereby a witness is refuted. (I have called such a witness a *refuted witness* as opposed to the witness who has been contradicted by *hakhchashah,* therefore a contradicted witness.) In *hazamah,* the second pair of witnesses do not testify as to the event at all. The testify that the earlier pair of witnesses could not have witnessed the event since they were with the second pair of witnesses in a place where it was not possible to witness the event. For example, the first pair of witnesses testify that they saw a car driven by the defendant strike a pedestrian, who is the plaintiff in the action, on January 10, 1990, at 10 A.M. at the corner of Broadway and 42nd Street in New York City. The second pair of witnesses testify that on January 10, 1990, at 10 A.M. the first pair of witnesses were together with the second pair of witnesses at a meeting in London. The second pair of witnesses do not testify as to the occurrence on January 10, 1990. For all they know, the defendant's car could very well have struck the plaintiff at that time and place. They testify only to the trustworthiness of the first pair of witnesses. The *halachah* is that the latest pair of witnesses are always believed in the case of *hazamah.*

herem: A state of excommunication. In a religious sense a person is in *herem* for conduct unbecoming a Jew. In a civil law sense, it means the ban proclaimed against a person for not coming forth to

testify *as to certain conduct of which he is suspected, or a general
herem* to seek out persons who may be familiar with certain
information. A plaintiff may ask *beth din* to proclaim a *herem* against
anyone who has knowledge about a certain occurrence but does not
come forth to testify. The plaintiff knows that there were witnesses
when he was struck by defendant's automobile, but does not know
who they are.

heresh: A person who cannot speak and hear is designated as a
heresh. In *halachah* it is assumed that such a person is usually not
educable and thus generally does not have the status of a person who
has reached majority regarding legal actions taken by him, or being
able to witness occurrences and then to act as a witness.

Holy Day: In the Jewish calendar there are differences among
Holy Days. Certain Holy Days prohibit all work, whereas other Holy
Days permit some work. All the Holy Days have certain rituals
attached to them, some applying to all or most of the Holy Days and
some unique to certain Holy Days. The Holy Days are described in
Chapter 5, notes 3 and 4.

ir hanadachas: A city whose majority of inhabitants have been
accused of idiolatry, and have been judged by the Great Sanhedrin and
convicted of idolatry. The procedure to be followed with such a city
is described in Deuteronomy 13:13–19.

katan: A person who has not attained his or her majority is a *katan*
(female, *kattanah*). In the case of girls the age is 12 and one day, and
in the case of boys, the age is 13 and one day.

kethubah: A document in which the groom undertakes certain
obligations to his bride. Besides general obligations of support, he
undertakes to pay her the sum stipulated in the *kethubah* in the event
that he divorces her. In the event of his death, his estate will pay the
widow the same sum. The Rabbis have fixed the minimum sum. The
wife cannot waive the *kethubah*. The *kethubah* places a lien on all of
the real estate of the husband that remains, even if the real estate is
sold, or until the death of the wife if she predeceases the husband.

kinyan: An act of acquisition. Thus there must be a formal act of

acquiring personal property or real estate. Every acquisition has a different type of *kinyan*. These are discussed in Chapters 189–226. The most common type of *kinyan*, for example, is where the seller gives his handkerchief to the purchaser and the purchaser takes hold of the handkerchief. Title has then passed. The seller has delivered the goods and the purchaser is obligated to pay. There may be a *kinyan* in which a person obligates himself to perform an act or to refrain from performing an act. The person who seeks the performance will give his handkerchief to the person who will perform and as soon as the latter has taken hold of the handkerchief, he is obligated to perform. See Chapters 189, 195, 201, and 203, as well as note to Chapter 12.

lifnim mishurath hadin: When a person acts over and above what the *halachah* demands of him, he is acting *lifnim mishurath hadin*. Thus, if the law allows a person to renege on a certain contract, but he insists on honoring his commitment, he may be acting *lifnim mishurath hadin*. See *Lifnim Mishurath Hadin* by the author in *Annual Volume of the Council of Young Israel Rabbis in Israel*, Volume 2, Jerusalem: 1988.

maneh: A weight of gold or silver. In U.S. equivalent, if a *perutah*, the smallest coin, is equivalent to a penny, a *maneh* is worth $192.

mi'un: According to Torah law the father of a minor daughter had the right to betrothe her to a husband. The Sages added certain situations where the mother or adult brothers of a minor girl whose father had died might betrothe her to a husband. In the cases enacted by the Sages, the enactment provided that the girl upon reaching her majority could disaffirm that contract. Such a disaffirmation is known as *mi'un*.

minyan: A quorum consisting of ten adult Jewish males. There are certain religious acts or rituals that require a *minyan*.

Mishnah: From the time of Moses until the end of the second century c.e., the Oral Law that Moses received on Mount Sinai from God was handed down orally from generation to generation. Due to the Roman persecutions in Israel beginning 66 c.e. it became increasingly difficult to orally transmit the Oral Law. Rabbi Judah the Prince

and his academy organized the Oral Law into sixty-three books. Each book contains many chapters and each chapter contains paragraphs of law relating to the subject matter of that particular book. Each paragraph is called a *Mishnah* and the entire body of these books is called The *Mishnah*. (The plural of *Mishnah* is *Mishnayoth*.)

moches: A tax collector. Very often he would collect taxes beyond the amount authorized by legitimate government authorities.

niddui: A light form of *herem* (excommunication). The person under a *niddui* was given the opportunity to clear himself, usually within a period of thirty days, and failing that he might be given another thirty days. If he failed to cease the conduct that had placed him under the *niddui*, he would be placed in *herem*.

Nissan: A month in the Jewish calendar corresponding to March/April. The festival of Passover occurs in this month.

perutah: The smallest copper coin mentioned in Rabbinic literature. If a thing was not worth at least a *perutah*, it was for many legal purposed deemed to be worthless.

rasha: A wicked person. He may be called wicked because of his conduct to his fellow men and/or his conduct in violating laws of the Torah that relate to man's relationship to God. The person becomes a *rasha* if he persists after being warned to cease such conduct. Generally there must be at least two witnesses who have testified before a *beth din* as to his conduct.

semichah: The laying on of hands. *Semichah* was the act whereby a person was ordained by an already ordained person. *Semichah* traces its origins to Moses laying his hands upon Joshua and Joshua thereby becoming ordained. Thereafter the *semichah* was given by the person who had *semichah*, in the presence of at least two other persons authorizing the person to be ordained to judge matters of ritual and/or matters of civil law. All the members of the Great Sanhedrin and the Lesser Sanhedrin had to be ordained. The members of the *beth din* did not ordinarily have to be ordained to judge most monetary cases. The giving of *semichah* lapsed in the middle of the fourth century C.E.

shemitah: The years in the Jewish calendar are divided into groups of seven. The number of the year determines which tithes and other agricultural dues would be given to the priests, the Levites, and the poor. The seventh year of each cycle marked a period when the fields would lie fallow and the poor could take whatever aftergrowth there was in the fields. At the termination of the *shemitah* year, debts were usually forgiven unless there was a procedure followed to keep the debt alive. See Chapter 67.

shikul hadath: This concept permits the judge on a case to weigh the precedents. There may be a dispute among rabbis on the *Mishnah* or the Talmud, and the *halachah* is not specifically decided. The authorities have thereafter accepted one view, and the judge or the *beth din* decides in accordance with the view not generally accepted. This would be a violation of the *shikul hadath*.

shoodah dedaini: This concept gives the judge or *beth din* who is judging the case wide discretion to decide in the direction that the evidence and testimony is inclined, although there is no fully competent testimony or proof.

shotah: An imbecile. The *halachah* views him as a person who is not responsible for his acts, nor can he take care of himself.

sinar: Either a belt or other garment that women wore to protect their modesty.

takkanah: A decree made by the Sages.

Tishrei: A month in the Jewish calendar corresponding to September/October. Many of the Jewish Holy Days occur in this month.

zedek: Justice or righteousness.

zommemim: When witnesses have been refuted by *hazamah*, they become *zommemim*, refuted witnesses.

Index

contemporary of R. Suslein, R. Menahem of Merseburg, Germany,[37] was asked to decide the following case.[38] A woman had been accused by her husband and father-in-law of sexually prohibited conduct. She produced women witnesses who heard her husband and father-in-law accuse her of such conduct. The women were permitted to testify.

R. Israel Isserlein,[39] living in Germany in the first half of the fifteenth century, in his *Trumoth haDeshen*[40] discusses the following case, which he was asked to decide. Leah and Rachel both claimed the same seats in the women's section of the synagogue. Leah produced two women to testify that the seats were hers and Rachel produced one man to testify that the seats were hers. In passing, he states that in those matters in which women have unique knowledge since men are not apt to know the facts, such as if a woman had worn certain garments, other women may testify. This is based on the fact that a midwife may testify as to who is the firstborn. Similarly, a woman may testify as to seats in the women's section, since men are not knowledgeable about what goes on there. Then he supports his contention with the very Talmudic case which Maimonides had used to prove the limitations placed on ineligible witnesses. Isserlein cites the passage where Maimonides cited the Mishnah passage that only freemen and Jews could testify. The exclusions mentioned in the Talmud which flow from the inclusions of only these persons in the Mishnah prompted Maimonides to state that they are excluded even if there are no other persons present. Otherwise, it is known that they may not testify. Why exclude them again? This reiteration of the exclusion prompted Maimonides to state that the exclusion is present even if there are usually no men present there. It might have been thought that the ineligibility is limited to slaves and Gentiles, but not to women who are both Jewish and have pedigree. It might have been thought that women may testify in those instances where men are usually not found, in the very situation which the Talmud discusses, namely, injuries. This, Maimonides teaches, is not so. In cases dealing

---

37. R. Menahem of Merseburg, German rabbinic authority (first half of the fourteenth century).

38. The case is reported together with other fragments of his decisions in a section in the back of the printed editions of the responsa of Rav Yakov Weil, who died in 1456.

39. R. Israel Isserlein, German rabbinic authority (1390–1460).

40. *Trumoth haDeshen*, Responsa 353.

contemporary of R. Suslein, R. Menahem of Merseburg, Germany,[37] was asked to decide the following case.[38] A woman had been accused by her husband and father-in-law of sexually prohibited conduct. She produced women witnesses who heard her husband and father-in-law accuse her of such conduct. The women were permitted to testify.

R. Israel Isserlein,[39] living in Germany in the first half of the fifteenth century, in his *Trumoth haDeshen*[40] discusses the following case, which he was asked to decide. Leah and Rachel both claimed the same seats in the women's section of the synagogue. Leah produced two women to testify that the seats were hers and Rachel produced one man to testify that the seats were hers. In passing, he states that in those matters in which women have unique knowledge since men are not apt to know the facts, such as if a woman had worn certain garments, other women may testify. This is based on the fact that a midwife may testify as to who is the firstborn. Similarly, a woman may testify as to seats in the women's section, since men are not knowledgeable about what goes on there. Then he supports his contention with the very Talmudic case which Maimonides had used to prove the limitations placed on ineligible witnesses. Isserlein cites the passage where Maimonides cited the Mishnah passage that only freemen and Jews could testify. The exclusions mentioned in the Talmud which flow from the inclusions of only these persons in the Mishnah prompted Maimonides to state that they are excluded even if there are no other persons present. Otherwise, it is known that they may not testify. Why exclude them again? This reiteration of the exclusion prompted Maimonides to state that the exclusion is present even if there are usually no men present there. It might have been thought that the ineligibility is limited to slaves and Gentiles, but not to women who are both Jewish and have pedigree. It might have been thought that women may testify in those instances where men are usually not found, in the very situation which the Talmud discusses, namely, injuries. This, Maimonides teaches, is not so. In cases dealing

---

37. R. Menahem of Merseburg, German rabbinic authority (first half of the fourteenth century).

38. The case is reported together with other fragments of his decisions in a section in the back of the printed editions of the responsa of Rav Yakov Weil, who died in 1456.

39. R. Israel Isserlein, German rabbinic authority (1390–1460).

40. *Trumoth haDeshen*, Responsa 353.

with injuries, ineligible witnesses may not testify even in situations where men are usually not found.

Isserlein continues that the implication of the Talmud, however, is that only in cases of torts is the exclusion of ineligible witnesses applicable also to places where eligible witnesses are not to be found. But in other matters if no eligible witnesses be found, ineligible witnesses may testify. The special reason for the broad rule in tort cases is that a person would look for ineligible persons who presumably would be more apt to be persuaded to testify that they saw a tort being committed and people would be sued continuously without justification.

These exclusions do not apply to occasional happenings such as to whether a woman had worn certain garments or to seats in the women's section of the synagogue.

A view was thus becoming known amongst the authorities living in Germany, that women could testify in these exceptional cases. (Usually the Germanic and northern French authorities followed the same precedents.) This view differed from the view of the authorities living in the Sephardic communities of Spain and the Mediterranean region.

The Germanic (and northern French) authorities seemed to be following the view of earlier great Ashkenazic/Germanic/northern French authorities such as Rabbeinu Gershom[41] and Rabbeinu Tam.[42] Kolbo,[43] in Chapter 116 enumerates various decrees promulgated by Rabbeinu Gershom and his beth din in the eleventh century and by Rabbeinu Tam and his beth din in the twelfth century. Since they are both included in the same enumeration, it may be that the decree is sometimes attributed to one and sometimes to the other authority. A younger contemporary of Isserlein, living in Italy, was the respondent R. Yosef Kolon.[44] In a case that was presented to him for decision, he

---

41. Rabbeinu Gershom ben Yehuda (meor haGolah) lived in Germany, 960–1028.

42. Rabbeinu Tam, Rav Yakov b. Meir, lived in France, 1096–1171.

43. Kolbo. An anonymous halachic work written in the late thirteenth or early fourteenth century. Probably written in southern France.

44. R. Yosef Kolon. Respondent lived in Italy 1410–1480. His responsa were very popular and often reprinted. Very often the printers of newer editions would revise the numerical sequence of the responsa. Thus it is sometimes difficult to parallel the number of a responsum with some of the printed editions. Although Ramo speaks of

passed on the question of women as witnesses. The Jewish community assessed a tax on Reuven that he refused to pay. Shimon, a member of the Jewish tax commission, went to the local secular judge to compel Reuven to pay. Reuven then went to the secular authorities, and in the presence of Levi and Leah, falsely informed the authorities that Shimon was guilty of secular tax evasion. After it was found that Reuven's allegations against Shimon were groundless, Shimon sued Reuven in beth din and one of the questions dealt with Leah's eligibility to testify. R. Kolon writes: "I have found written in the name of Rabbeinu Tam that a woman or a relative are eligible to testify in such situations, and in all matters regarding discord in which [eligible] witnesses are not apt to be there. Similarly in cases of slander, since [eligible] witnesses are not present 'there'. This shows conclusively that in all matters of discord, a woman or a relative is eligible to testify. Also Mordechai [b. Hillel] writes that in monetary matters of disputes and quarrels and blasphemies, women are eligible to testify."

The movement of halachic scholarship from the French/Germanic centers to Polish/Lithuanian centers expanded the former's teachings, since the latter scholars generally adhered closely to the views of the former.

An older contemporary of R. Ramo, R. Shlomo Luria, cites the various authorities and analyzes them before coming to his conclusions. In his code,[45] R. Luria commences by quoting from Maimonides. He then cites Isserlein and says that apparently R. Isserlein did not see Maimonides' commentary on the Mishnah. He states that Isserlein maintained that both Maimonides and Asheri rejected ineligible witnesses from testifying. He cites R. Kolon who cited Rabbeinu Tam. Luria reasons that since Rabbeinu Tam is not followed by Asheri and Tur or others, the decree of Rabbeinu Tam must have been intended only for his generation and not for the future.

Moreover, Tur cites his father Asheri's ruling that if a person was able with eligible evidence to prove that another informed the

---

R. Kolon's responsum 180, I have quoted from a copy of the Venice edition of 1651 edition where it appears as responsum number 179.

45. R. Solomon Luria, Yam Shel Shlomo, on Baba Kamma, Chapter 1, para. 41. Luria lived in Poland, 1510–1574.

authorities against him, but proved damages only partly by eligible witnesses and partly by ineligible witnesses, then only the part provable by eligible witnesses was admissible, and the part proved by ineligible witnesses was not admissible. Appraisement was not a method to be employed. Luria states further that this is also the view of R. Meir of Rottenberg, the teacher of both R. Mordechai b. Hillel and Asheri. R. Luria then cites a "Rabbi Pinhas,[46]" Me'il Zedek, who wrote that ineligible witnesses, such as women, minors, or relatives, may testify if there was no opportunity to prepare eligible witnesses in advance.

R. Luria rejects the proofs of R. Pinhas and other responsa to the same effect and again states that if there were such decrees, they were limited to their specific times. R. Luria preferred the view of Maimonides, but confronted a growing array of authorities who were expanding the admissibility of ineligible witnesses. To counter them, R. Luria devised a novel approach. He concluded that the ineligible witnesses could testify when both sides to a dispute agreed that a question existed before the beth din as to the amount of damages or the amount of inheritance. Thus the Mishnah concerning the midwife dealt with the question of who would inherit more, but did not deal with the question of whether the child was an heir which was being denied by other parties to the dispute.

Similarly in all disputes, as, for example, Reuven and Shimon each claiming that the other had started a dispute, ineligible witnesses could testify. Both sides admitted that there was a dispute. If, however, one side claimed that there was no dispute, ineligible witnesses could not testify. Similarly in the case of the clothing that belonged to a widow, there was no doubt that she had some clothing, for she was certainly not going around naked. The sole question was whether certain clothing was part of her wardrobe and thus belonged to her, instead of to the estate of her husband. Perhaps in the case of informers, the case most often cited by the new line of cases, admissibility was only in the manner of an appraisement that might be permissible in such cases. Thus, if the defendant admitted that he had informed on the plaintiff, only the question of damages remained. For the defendant

---

46. Rabbi Pinhas. See *Shem haGedolim* of Rav Chaim Yosef David Azulai, who writes that the correct name of the author of *Me'il Zedek* was Rav Menahem b. Pinhas, who was either a contemporary or student of R. Isserlein.

there were no men present when the event occurred. Several citations are given. There is one citation which I have not been able to locate since it refers to a responsum appended to his code on the eighth chapter *Baba Kamma*. The current editions do not seem to contain this appended responsum. In his code on *Yebamoth*[34], Mordechai includes eight cases where the testimony of a woman is admissible.

(1) A midwife may testify which child is a Kohen, which a Levite, which a Gibeonite, which a bastard, in cases in which there is no contest. (2) A midwife may testify which child is the firstborn. (3) A woman may testify (in the absence of witnesses) that she was once married and is now unmarried. (4) A woman may testify (in the absence of witnesses) that she was kidnapped but was not raped. (5) A woman who had previously stated that she was married, may, if she has a good reason why she made the previous statement, now testify that she was really unmarried. (This is not the same as case 3. There she states that the marriage was followed by a state of being unmarried. In this case she first testified that she was married on a certain date, and then she testified that she was not married on that date.) (6) With certain limited exceptions, a woman may say that her husband or the husband of some other woman died. (7) A woman may as part of a *res gestae* state that a swarm of bees came from a certain beehive while two men, each claiming that the bees are from his beehive, are running to catch them. (8) A woman may inform the beth din that a person who died is the brother of another person, since this is only information.

R. Alexander Suslein,[35] who died in 1349 in Germany, in his Agudah[36] commenting on the passage in *Kiddushin*, writes "I have heard that there are decisions based on this passage that a person is believed in the matter in which he is engrossed, just as the midwife is believed. This makes a difference regarding revilers. It appears to me that regarding revilers, and those matters which take place in the women's portion of the synagogue, we rely on women to testify." A

---

34. See glosses of Mordechai to *Yebamoth*, Chapter 6, para. 117, page 7 of the current printed editions of the Talmud.

35. R. Alexander Suslein lived in Frankfort, Germany, where he died in 1349.

36. Abbreviated version on *Kiddushin*, found in the printed version of responsa of Rav Yakov Wiel.

of *Yebamoth* page 464, that a woman may testify in eight different situations.

R. Ramo thus seems to take an approach opposite to that of R. Karo, who follows the school of Maimonides. R. Ramo cites a most impressive array of authorities who differ from the school of Maimonides: Rabbeinu Gershom, Rabbeinu Tam, Mordechai, Kolbo, R. Kolon, R. Isserlein and Agudah. R. Ramo aligns himself with this latter school.

The differences between R. Karo and R. Ramo in their respective commentaries on Tur manifest themselves in the *Shulhan Aruch.*

R. Karo in para. 14 of Chapter 35 states: "Women are ineligible. A person of unknown sex and a hermaphrodite may not testify. All those as to whom there is a doubt whether they are eligible ... are ineligible."

In his glosses, R. Ramo adds: "And all those who are ineligible are so even in those situations where there are no eligible men to testify. This is according to the law. But there are those who say that there is an ancient decree that in a place where there are usually no eligible men present, such as the women's section of the synagogue, or in any other spontaneous happening where women are present and not men, such as to testify that a woman had worn certain clothing and thus they belong to her, and men are not apt to notice such things, the woman is believed in her testimony. And there are those who write that even a woman herself or a kinsman or a minor is eligible in matters of assault, or insult to a scholar, or other strife, or matters pertaining to informers, since it is not possible to prepare in advance eligible witnesses in these matters."

I shall now discuss some of the authorities cited by R. Ramo and later authorities to show how the law developed in those schools which follow R. Ramo, and also those later authorities who follow the school of Maimonides.

R. Mordechai b. Hillel[32], like Asheri, was a student of R. Meir of Rotenberg.[33] He is cited by R. Kolon and R. Ramo for his views on the admissibility of permitting women to testify in situations where

---

32. R. Mordechai b. Hillel lived in Germany, 1240–1298.
33. R. Meir of Rotenberg lived in Germany, 1215–1293. Because of his responsa, and because many students were prolific writers, his influence is seen in almost every phase of halachah.